# The Principles and Practice of Export Marketing

**The Institute of Marketing**

*Marketing means Business*

The Institute of Marketing was founded in 1911. It is now the largest and most successful marketing management organisation in Europe with over 20,000 members and 16,000 students throughout the world. The Institute is a democratic organisation and is run for the members by the members with the assistance of a permanent staff headed by the Director General. The Headquarters of the Institute are at Moor Hall, Cookham, near Maidenhead, in Berkshire.

**Objectives:** The objectives of the Institute are to develop knowledge about marketing, to provide services for members and registered students and to make the principles and practices of marketing more widely known and used throughout industry and commerce.

**Range of activities:** The Institute's activities are divided into four main areas:
    Membership and membership activities
    Corporate activities
    Marketing education
    Marketing training

# The Principles and Practice of Export Marketing

### E. P. HIBBERT

MA (Cantab), PhD, FInst M, MIEx

Published on behalf of the Institute of Marketing

HEINEMANN : LONDON

Heinemann Professional Publishing Ltd
22 Bedford Square, London WC1B 3HH

LONDON    MELBOURNE
JOHANNESBURG    AUCKLAND

To Heather, Dudley and Hayden

First published 1985
Reprinted 1986, 1987
© E. P. Hibbert 1985

ISBN 0 434 90746 4


**British Library Cataloguing in Publication Data**

Hibbert, E. P.
   The principles and practice of export marketing.
   1. Export marketing—Great Britain
   I. Title    II. Institute of Marketing
   658.8'48'0941    HF1009

Phototypeset by Wilmaset, Birkenhead, Merseyside
Printed in Great Britain by
Redwood Burn Ltd., Trowbridge, Wiltshire

# FOREWORD

Economic forecasting is an uncertain business. It is, however, difficult to imagine any development of the world economy in the foreseeable future which could make the United Kingdom less dependent than it now is on international trade. The steady increase we have seen in the proportion of the gross domestic product which derives from overseas trade is likely to continue. A larger proportion of the working population are also likely to earn their living from activities which are wholly or partially related to exporting, importing and overseas trade.

In the same context, the chances are that the present trend whereby the U.K. earns an increasing proportion of its foreign income from selling highly specialized goods and services will also continue. Nor is there any reason to suppose that competition in world markets will abate. Every element in the marketing mix will need to be well fashioned and blended if overseas buyers are to be persuaded to buy British.

Against this background Edgar Hibbert's *The Principles and Practice of Export Marketing* is a welcome addition to the literature in this field. In one volume Dr Hibbert has brought together a wealth of information which will be useful both to the student of export marketing and to those involved in its practice and its management. The Institute of Export share the marketing philosophy of the Institute of Marketing. Our common aim is to set and raise the standard of marketing practice and management throughout business so that everyone works in the knowledge that it is the satisfied customer who pays the wages. Those who read and then apply what Dr Hibbert has so ably presented will undoubtedly increase their ability to satisfy customers and thus to add to earnings and the well-being of this country.

D. N. Royce,
Director General
The Institute of Export
London

# CONTENTS

# ACKNOWLEDGEMENTS

The author has made use of a large amount of primary and secondary data as source materials. He wishes to acknowledge fully the following published material from which he has quoted in full or in part. Permission to use this material has been obtained as follows:

Chapter 1, Section 1 on International Treaty Organizations (pages 2 and 3) quoted from *Handbook of International Trade*, Volume 2 (Issue 3, Sections 7.1 and 7.2) published by Kluwer Publishing Ltd, 1 Harlequin Avenue, Brentford, Middlesex TW8 9EW, U.K. 1983.

Chapter 1, Section 1 on Multi-Lateral Trade Negotiations (pages 12, 13, 14) quoted from *World Trade Strategies in a Decade of Change* published by Business International Corporation, New York, NY 1007, U.S.A. 1983.

Chapter 3, Section 4 on Price and Non-Price Competition, (pages 94, 95, 97) quoted from *Factors for International Success: Industrial and Export Performances of France, UK and West Germany* by ITI Research published by Barclays Bank International, London, EC4M 8EH, U.K. in 1979.

Chapter 2, Section 4 on Analysing International Trade Data, (pages 51, 52, 53) quoted from *Introduction to Export Market Research* published by the International Trade Centre UNCTAD/GATT, Geneva, Switzerland, 1981.

Chapter 6, Section 1 on British Overseas Trade Board; Crown Copyright Reserved; quoted from *Handbook of BOTB Services*, Department of Trade and Industry, 1 Victoria Street, London SW1H 0ET, U.K. 1984.

Chapter 6, Sections 3 and 5 on Documentary Credits, (pages 200, 201, 202) and Coping with International Trade Regulations (pages 212, 213) quoted from the journal *Export*, December 1977 and June 1980, of the Institute of Export, World Trade Centre, London E1 9AA, U.K.

The author gladly acknowledges advice on technical aspects of export finance in section 4.3, given by Mr D. Edwards of Export Finance Consultants Ltd.; 50 Carter Lane, London EC4V 5EA. The author also wishes to express his thanks to Mr David Royce, Director General, Institute of Export for his valued comments and advice.

# 1. INTERNATIONAL TRADE: POLICIES AND ORGANIZATIONS

## 1.1 International Treaty Organizations

The terms and conditions of international trade have been increasingly influenced by treaties designed to improve economic relationships, and with them, the prosperity of the signatories. These treaties originate from a series of inter-linked agreements made at the end of the Second World War. The principal objectives of these treaties are referred to in Article 2 of the United Nations Charter. Effectively, the General Agreement on Tarrifs and Trade (GATT) and the Articles of Association of the International Bank for Reconstruction and Development (IBRD) and of the International Monetary Fund (IMF) were set up to give effect to the benevolent intentions implicit in the economic objectives of Article 2 of the UN Charter. This was significant as a collective endeavour to prevent any recurrence of what had amounted to, in the 1930s, a virtual trading war as national Governments endeavoured to repair the damage done by the slump of 1929; in particular, the U.S. Government at that time sought to limit, and no doubt remove, the system of 'imperial preference' (by which the U.K. granted preferential tariffs to imports from the Colonies and Dominions).

Within the terms of these treaties, provisions were made for derogations in favour of Customs Unions and Free Trade Areas on grounds set out in Article 24 of GATT. The treaties themselves vary from major international agreements, which have brought GATT and other organizations into existence, to more modest arrangements between individual governments (who may be members of several at the same time). Many of these treaty organizations are changing and becoming more influential; indeed some of the large ones form substantial markets in their own right, with, like other bureaucracies, demand for supplies and services. In addition to the promotion of trade, most also have political and cultural objectives.

Thus, those treaty organizations concerned with world membership consist of the United Nations and its derivative bodies such as GATT, IMF and the World Bank. Indeed, the UN makes its principal impact on trading decisions precisely through those bodies which influence the world market in a number of ways. There are market opportunities opened up by IBRD funding of capital projects which require servicing, licensing or direct supply; on the other hand, calls on the IMF to assist a country with balance of payments problems will damage that market as a result of restrictions likely to accompany any loan. A new round of GATT can open up new markets (such as the Tokyo Round, referred to in Section 1.2), although

1

the agreement is often slow to take effect. The work of the various aid and advice agencies can also develop new markets and influence the means of servicing existing ones. Some specialized agencies are also influential. For instance, the United Nations Centre for Transnational Corporations has published a number of proposals for corporate behaviour and is preparing a code of conduct; even more important in its influence on trade patterns is likely to be the Centre's advisory role to governments. The advice on a number of issues, including knowledge agreements and the transfer of technology as well as direct investment, strengthens the bargaining position of governments as against companies.

The divisions of the United Nations, therefore, cover a wide range of trade and aid, including the Food and Agriculture Organization, General Agreement on Tariffs and Trade (GATT), the International Development Association (IDA), the International Finance Corporation (IFC), the International Fund for Agricultural Development (IFAD), the International Monetary Fund (IMF), the United Nations Conference on Trade and Development (UNCTAD), the United Nations Development Programme (UNDP), the United Nations Industrial Development Organization (UNIDO), the World Bank, the World Health Organization (WHO), the World Intellectual Property Organization and the World Food Programme, as well as the regional economic commissions and many other bodies of less interest to the trader.

The United Nations Conference on Trade and Development (UNCTAD) has been convened (five times since 1964) to improve the access of Developing Countries' exports into industrial countries (and to raise these countries' shares of trade in manufactures). Special agreements have also been made by commodity producers in attempts to allocate markets and production to raise export earnings. Note should also be made of international Agencies such as the Asian Development Bank and World Bank which make finance available for Government-guaranteed capital projects, particularly in communications, port installations, dams, irrigation schemes, welfare and housing projects etc. This is particularly so where such loans would not be forthcoming from the private banking sector and where equipment, plant and technology etc. have to be imported because they are not available locally.

The Organization for Economic Co-operation and Development (OECD) has a membership of 24 of the industrialized countries. The OECD, as a voluntary organization, has achieved authority through its expertise. It developed via a predecessor founded to channel American aid to the belligerent countries after 1945, and was originally concerned with moves to liberate trade. It now concentrates on the provision of services to assist trade development. It provides a statistical and information service which influences government policies, and it provides advice which affects the development of trade. In addition, its code of conduct for multinational companies has influenced policies.

The code provides that member countries should treat foreign and national firms in the same way, that foreign enterprises should not use their power against the social or economic policies of host countries, and that they should contribute to the country's scientific and technical progress at a reasonable price. The code was tested soon after it was signed in 1976 when the Badger Corporation (a United States-based engineering consultancy, itself a subsidiary of the Raytheon Corporation) refused to make redundancy payments to its Belgian employees on the grounds that Badger Belgium was bankrupt. Although the code of conduct specifically excluded action against individual firms, the pressure built up through OECD resulted in the payment of the moneys owed in spite of repeated refusals before the Belgian government appealed to that organization.

Bi-lateral trade treaties, though less publicized than multi-lateral agreements, can have a more direct effect on the opening and closing of markets. Bi-lateral trade treaties are constantly under negotiation, and usually have the effect of enabling a country to export goods of a sort which it is particularly well equipped to produce in exchange for a similar benefit to its trading partner. In the case of the European Community, the Community as a whole has made arrangements with individual countries like Japan and Canada which are similar to bilateral treaties. On the whole, the emergence of the regional organizations has meant a decline in the importance of bilateral arrangements but there are still some countries, like the two named, which belong to a number of them. Even though their number grows less, the effects of these treaties, both by increasing competition and by stimulating new ideas need watching by all traders. The 1981 treaty between Japan and East Germany, for instance, shows that the Japanese market is open to the import of photographic equipment.

A major part of the work of the United Nations (UN) is economic and therefore impinges directly and indirectly on international business. Development assistance through various UN agencies creates demand for consultancy services, technical assistance and many goods involved in the construction and operation of development projects in the developing countries. Less directly, debates, recommendations and resolutions in UN bodies such as the Economic and Social Council (ECOSOC), the United Nations Conference on Trade and Development (UNCTAD) and the International Labour Organization (ILO) can influence the general climate of opinion affecting trade and investment relationships between companies and the governments of developing countries. Research documents from these agencies and others such as the secretariats of the General Agreement on Tariffs and Trade (GATT), the International Trade Centre UNCTAD/ GATT (ITC) set up in 1964 to promote exports of developing countries, the International Bank for Reconstruction and Development (or World Bank) (IBRD) and the International Monetary Fund (IMF) are widely used sources of economic information on a vast range of topics, from the state of the world economy down to the prospects of an individual market for specific types of goods. The basic framework of rules governing trade relations between most nations are set by GATT, and its activities condition a great many international business transactions.

IBRD, and its affiliates, the International Development Association, (IDA) and the International Finance Corporation (IFC) have as their major task the financing of economic development. As suppliers of capital goods, materials and expertise needed in development projects and planning, both manufacturers and consultancy firms must see the Bank group as an important target area. The Bank and IDA lend amounts to over $10,000 million per annum, which is clearly a great deal of business opportunity. But this actually underestimates the Bank's influence. Through consortial arrangements with bi-lateral donors the Bank does have some indirect influence over far greater flows of finance.

It has also encouraged private investment in developing countries by providing infrastructure, by encouraging collaboration of private capital with IFC funds, and by reducing investment risks through its Convention on the Settlement of Investment Disputes between States and Nationals of Other States (ICSID). Many contracts and treaties now include clauses providing for settlement of disputes through the agencies of the ICSID.

As it emerged from the 1944 Bretton Woods negotiations, the International Monetary Fund (IMF) had two basic aims: the provision of sufficient international liquidity to enable nations to overcome temporary balance of payments difficulties without recourse to restrictions on trade, and the maintenance of stable exchange rates. The widespread adoption of floating exchange rates in the early 1970s might seem to have rendered both these aims obsolete. In theory, if exchange rates are left free to be determined by supply and demand, balance of payments deficits or surpluses should be automatically corrected by the depreciation or appreciation of the exchange rate. Nations should then have little or no need for reserves or other sources of official financing of deficits. Equally, stable exchange rates would seem to have been abandoned as an objective of policy. In practice, this is not so. Few, if any, governments are willing to leave such an important issue as the rate of exchange entirely to market forces. Its impact upon the domestic price level and on employment makes the exchange rate an important instrument of government policy. As a result, nations remain concerned about movements in the relative value of their and other nations' currencies and still have a need for access to international reserves to intervene in foreign exchange markets.

Finally, it is interesting to note the original objectives of national and international action when GATT itself was first established. The Geneva Draft Charter contains these objectives:

(a) To assure a large and steadily growing volume of real income and effective demand; to increase the production, consumption, and exchange of goods; and thus to contribute to a balanced and expanding world economy.
(b) To foster and assist industrial and general economic development particularly of those countries which are still in the early stages of industrial development, and to encourage the international flow of capital for productive investment.
(c) To further the enjoyment by all countries, on equal terms, of access to the markets, products, and productive facilities which are needed for their economic prosperity and development.

(d) To reduce tariffs and other barriers to trade and to eliminate discriminatory treatment in international commerce.

(e) To enable countries, by increasing the opportunites for their trade and economic development on a mutually advantageous basis, to abstain from measures which would disrupt world commerce, reduce productive employment, economic development, commercial policy, business practices, and commodity policy.

And the section on Commercial Policy lays down several important principles. It stipulates unconditional most-favoured nation treatment among members, ruling out any new preferential arrangements or any increase in existing preferential margins. It demands the general elimination of quantitative import restrictions such as quotas and licences and in the special cases where such restrictions are continued, they are to be applied indiscriminately to all countries. Tariffs and preferential margins are to be reduced. Export subsidies are to be discontinued. In short, international trade is to revert to the pre-1914 pattern, conducted on a strictly multi-lateral basis, free from all restrictions except tariffs.

## 1.2 Multi-Lateral Trade Negotiations

The General Agreement on Tariffs and Trade (GATT), set up in 1948, has thus provided a forum for substantial trade liberalization measures through a series of multi-lateral trade 'Rounds', beginning in the early 1960s with the Kennedy Round and culminating (so far) with the 1979 Tokyo Round; an analysis of the salient aspects of the Tokyo Round is given later in this section. At this stage it is important to grasp that GATT (now ratified by most of the Free World's trading countries) has provided a set of rules for these multi-lateral tariff and non-tariff conferences, and more importantly, some mechanism for monitoring the implementation of these rules. Signatories to GATT must, for example, conform to the principle: Most Favoured Nation (MFN). This requires a country to extend any concession on tariffs, licences or quotas granted to one trading partner, to all others; there are some exceptions to MFN which require mention:

(a) Manufactured products from developing countries may be given preferential treatment compared to those from other countries.

(b) It does not apply to those commodities covered by the Generalized System of Preferences (GSP) under which industrialized countries offer special tariff concessions to imports from developing countries on a bi-lateral basis.

(c) Concessions granted to other members of a trading bloc do not have to be extended to other countries.

(d) Countries whose products are arbitrarily discriminated against by another country are not obliged to give MFN treatment to that country's products.

The importance of MFN is clearly that all signatories have undertaken to apply the same trade regulations to nearly all the world's trading countries (outside U.S.S.R. and COMECON), thus further increasing the process of liberalization. It also has the effect of simplifying the process of negotiations by allowing exporters from most nations to have the same access, in terms of regulations to the market of any participating country.

The long-term effect of the MFN principle is to encourage the location of production of each traded good in those countries which have the greatest advantages. It makes a country more willing to grant concessions to trading partners in return for reciprocal concession from them, in the knowledge that they cannot go behind its back and erode the benefit by giving greater concessions on the same goods to other countries. The MFN clause also means that within GATT any concession made to a trading partner is automatically extended to all members of GATT. This is of particular benefit to smaller or less developed countries with little to offer by way of concessions in the bargaining process.

The main exception to the MFN clause in GATT is that countries are permitted to form customs unions or free trade areas provided that:

(a) These do not increase tariffs or other barriers to trade to GATT members who are outside the union; and

(b) The union or agreement results in the elimination of tariffs on most trade between the parties to the union or free trade area (Article 24).

This exception was intended to permit the integration of Europe in the European Community, largely for political reasons.

GATT provides a system of rules to govern trade. This is important because it reduces the risk of arbitrary changes in trading opportunities through sudden impositions of quotas, tariffs or subsidies. As uncertainty is an important obstacle to trade and investment this is a boon to international business. Because GATT generally works to promote and sustain free trade in manufactures, all businesses with a substantial interest in exports or in imports of manufactured inputs such as machinery, steel or aluminium have an interest in preserving GATT and urging their governments to adhere to it. Businesses whose activities are largely in their domestic market may take a more ambivalent attitude. In the long run their welfare is likely to be promoted by the general gains which free trade brings, but in the short run they may see themselves threatened by competition from foreign firms with increasing access to their markets. It is then that accusations of unfair competition or dumping arise and the need for safeguards against sudden surges of imports comes to the fore.

GATT does make provision for the investigation of such complaints and for procedures to be taken to protect industries against dumping or to slow down imports while countries are given time to make structural adjustments in industries which have become uncompetitive. If firms in industry feel that they are suffering unfair competition from imports which are being 'dumped' in their markets – that is, being sold at prices within their country which are below the prices at which they are sold in the country of origin, after allowing for taxes and transport costs – they can complain to their government. If satisfied that they have a case, the government can take the issue up with the government of the offending country. If it fails to get satisfaction it can impose an anti-dumping duty equal to the difference between the two prices. It is then up to the other country to take the dispute to GATT if it feels injured: should it do so a panel of experts, drawn from the contracting parties to GATT, will consider the issue on the basis of whether dumping has been proved and serious injury to the domestic industry has been established. This is governed by Article 6 of GATT and a subsequent code. A similar procedure is followed where there is evidence of government subsidies to exports which cause injury to the domestic industries of another GATT member. The latter can as a last resort impose countervailing duties (Articles 26, 6, (3)).

Safeguards procedures under the GATT deal with a different issue. Article 19 permits countries temporarily to replace barriers against an unexpected rise in specific imports which threatens serious injury to a domestic industry. But it requires that the country which wishes to invoke Article 19 should give advance notice of its intention, should consult with all exporters of the product and should compensate them for any injury due to the withdrawal of the concession. Moreover, it cannot discriminate between exporters but must impose its barrier on all exporters equally.

In practice, many industrial nations including the United States, the United Kingdom individually, and the European Community as a group, have chosen to limit imports from dynamic newcomers such as Japan and the newly industrialized countries of Hong Kong, Korea, Singapore, Taiwan, Mexico, Brazil and some East European countries by the use of so-called voluntary export restraints (VER) or orderly marketing arrangements (OMA). These methods are outside the rules of GATT and represent a growing threat to the maintenance of free international trade. They are often arrived at in secret, are not subject to multilateral surveillance, and can be maintained indefinitely. They are often an abuse of power by strong nations against weak ones. They sap faith in the rule of law and create uncertainty which deters manufacturers in the weaker countries from expanding their industries. Consumers have to pay higher prices, as do those firms which utilize such goods as imports, and the prospects for development of some less developed countries are impaired.

It is important for international business that the rules of the game should be clear and adhered to. Failure in this would lead to an arbitrariness in the conditions under which goods and services can be traded.

The GATT Tokyo Round has achieved a substantial cut in tariffs, overall by about 33%, starting in 1980 for an eight-year period; for example, tariffs between the E.E.C and U.S.A. were reduced by 35% each way and U.S. imports into Japan by 45%. The comparable overall cut in the Kennedy Round was 35%; all tariff reductions are on MFN basis. To take two products as an example, the present E.E.C. tariff of 13% on photographic equipment and cameras and 6% on office machinery will be cut to 7.2% and 4.4% respectively by 1987. The reductions will occur so slowly that they will be hardly noticeable to consumers, but they will have beneficial effect on company's pricing policies.

Although tariff cuts may be beneficial, currency fluctuations are likely to be much more important. The major currencies' exchange movements over the past few years have greatly offset or compounded the effect of differential tariff rates. And although tariffs will no longer be significant for most industries, a few products such as textiles, clothing, footwear and some chemicals will continue to have substantial protection. Even after the cuts, U.S. tariffs on clothing will go as high as 35%, and outer garments in E.E.C. will still carry tariffs of 14%. While some tariffs will remain high, other industries will experience a significant drop, those products benefiting most will include, for instance, forest product imports into U.S.A, office computing equipment into the E.E.C. and Japan and certain types of machinery imports into Canada. Some tariffs on industrial goods were cut by as much as 60% and the number of industrial products subject to tariffs of under 5% increased substantially. It has to be recognized, however, that average tariff reduction figures are practically meaningless for most companies, which face a specific rate for each product that can vary considerably from the average tariff rate in that industry. Companies should obtain comparable tariff reductions for their products in key markets.

The Tokyo Round was, however, particularly concerned to deal with a number of non-tariff measures (NTMs), and as these are analysed specifically from the exporter's viewpoint later, it is essential to this stage to grasp something of their complexities and the Codes of Conduct agreed by all signatories of GATT. For the reality of international trade today is that, as tariffs have been progressively reduced worldwide since the Kennedy Round, so NTM's have become even more complex and intractible as governments seek to protect domestic industries, and the jobs that go with them, from foreign competition, and to cut inflation by reducing imports from high-cost countries.

The Codes of Conduct establish rules and procedures designed to prevent government policies from becoming barriers to trade. The Codes cover five basic trade policies and came into effect in 1980 and 1981. Not all countries have ratified these Codes; and some have signed only parts (see Table 1.3). The Codes are based on acceptance by signatories of the requirement for 'transparency' and complaints registration and dispute settlement. These will be decisive in determining what companies will actually gain or lose from the Codes, and it is vital that managements understand them. 'Transparency' means open and public regulation and investigation of any restrictions; it is intended to limit uncertainty and should enable a company to know exactly what regulations and restrictions it faces. Whether the issue is a dumping investigation, a new product standard, an import licence, or bids on government procurement, a company should be able to identify the criteria being used in government decision-making. If a company believes that a country's regulations, restrictions or policies do not meet the Codes' guidelines, it can complain to its own government. The dispute settlement mechanism has provisions on signatories' rights to bring complaints, time limits on issue investigation and procedural guidelines for resolving disputes.

These Codes, then, cover five policy aspects, all of which are of vital concern to management in setting up export policy and planning; they are as follows:

(a) Code on Subsidies and Counterveiling Measures

Governments have developed many ingenious ways to stimulate export sales. Visible export subsidies are relatively few but practices that effectively benefit exports are numerous. This Code, the most important of the five, reflects the complexity of government grants, tax credits and incentives; it prohibits export subsidies on products except certain agricultural, metal and mineral products. This includes direct subsidies contingent upon export performance, currency retention schemes that involve a bonus for exports, and exemption from any indirect taxes on exported products in excess of the taxes on similar items for domestic consumption. It also deals with domestic subsidies that are held to distort trade. Of course, the impact of this Code will vary from sector to sector: manufacturers of import-sensitive products such as steel, textiles, footwear, consumer electronics and an array of labour- and capital-intensive goods will be most affected. High-technology companies should be relatively untouched by the changes, since their products are rarely subject to subsidy investigations. In fact, export subsidy practices are expected to change little, as a direct result of this Code; most subsidies stipulated in it play a minor part in the export-incentive schemes of industrialized countries, though many developing countries have export incentives in direct violation of the Code and so far few of these have ratified it (see Table 1.1). Nevertheless, the Code does not tackle one or two of the more controversial schemes: rebate of the value-added tax upon export is not defined as a subsidy under the Code, and the U.S. tax deferral of export income under Domestic International Sales Corporation (DISC) is also exempt from the Code. The essence of the Code is not so much the prohibited subsidy practices themselves, but the opportunity it presents for companies and their governments to contest such practices.

(b) Customs Valuation Code

This Code deals with the uncertainty exporters face on Customs levies and with delays in Customs determinations, by setting an equitable and 'transparent' system to be applied uniformly. Exporters should see more regular and neutral customs valuation procedures overseas now that the Code is in force. It will make it more difficult for signatories to manipulate customs valuation procedures, by requiring customs value to be based almost entirely on transaction value. The Code spells out how costs are to be computed; and import duties must be based on the transaction value – the price actually paid or payable for the goods – plus any additional import costs incurred. The Code specifies that brokerage fees, container and packing costs, selling commissions, royalties and licence fees and tangible assets (including engineering development, design and art work, plans and sketches undertaken abroad,

*Table 1.1*

### TOKYO ROUND TRADE AGREEMENT
*Acceptance of GATT Codes by Country (1982)*

| Country | Tariff Protocol | Standards | Government Procurement | Subsidies/ Countervailing Duties |
|---|---|---|---|---|
| Argentina | * | 1 | | |
| Australia | | | | |
| Austria | * | 1 | 1 | 1 |
| Brazil | | * | | * |
| Bulgaria | | | | |
| Canada | 1 | * | | * |
| Chile | | 1 | | 1 |
| E.E.C. | * | * | 2 | * |
| Finland | * | 1 | 1 | 1 |
| Hungary | * | | | |
| Iceland | | | | |
| India | | | | |
| Israel | 1 | | | |
| Jamaica | * | | | |
| Japan | * | 1 | 1 | 1 |
| New Zealand | * | * | | |
| Norway | * | * | * | * |
| South Africa | * | | | |
| Sweden | * | 1 | | * |
| Switzerland | * | * | * | * |
| U.S.A. | * | * | 1 | * |
| Uruguay | | | | * |

\* Accepted; 1 Subject to ratification; 2 Accepted with reservations or conditions.

Source: Business International Corporation

| Customs Valuation | Licensing | Aircraft | Anti-Dumping | Beef | Dairy |
|---|---|---|---|---|---|
|  | 1 |  |  | 1 | 1 |
|  |  |  |  | * | * |
| 1 | * |  | 1 | 1 |  |
|  |  |  | 2 | * |  |
|  |  |  |  | 1 | 1 |
| 2 | * | 2 | * | * |  |
|  | 1 |  |  |  |  |
| * | * | * | * | * | * |
| 1 | 1 |  | 1 |  | 1 |
|  | * |  |  | * | * |
|  | 1 |  |  |  |  |
| * | 1 | * | 1 | * | * |
|  | * |  |  | * | * |
| 1 | * | * | * | * | * |
|  | * |  |  | * | * |
| * | * | * | * | * | * |
| * | * | 1 | * | * | * |
| 1 | * | * | * | * | * |

dies, tools, materials and components) are all dutiable and must be added to the price of the imports if not already included. There are certain exemptions to the transaction value requirement (if the seller places restrictions on the buyer as to the use of the goods, or if the value of a factor on which the sale price depends cannot be ascertained). Thus, in signatory countries, imported products should no longer face arbitrary uplift practices (whereby Customs officials raise the value of imports above invoice prices and levy higher duties on the assumption that these do not reflect the product's true value) in some cases as part of a deliberate policy to create a Non Tariff Barrier. So, it is clearly up to exporting companies themselves, if they are to benefit fully from this Code, to monitor foreign customs laws and procedures to ensure that they are consistent with it.

(c)   Technical and Trade Standards Code

Exporting companies have for many years had to cope with complex and discriminatory standards and certification systems, against which they have had little recourse. Coping with technical and trade standards takes up management time and is costly, particularly in certain sectors: Section 5.6 deals with further practical aspects including Rules of Origin. Here they are dealt with in the context of the relevant Code, which deals specifically with three types of technical barriers – product standards, tests to determine conformity with Government regulations (e.g. on safety and health) and certification systems. Standards drawn up by all governing authorities (states, provinces, localities etc.) are subject to the Code; it is binding only on central Governments which are obligated to ensure that local and non-government agencies (e.g. U.S. Underwriters' Laboratories) comply with its provisions. This Code requires that standards be applied without discrimination and that technical regulations do not create unnecessary obstacles to trade; there is also a key clause providing for 'transparency' in drawing up newer revised standards when international standards are not used or do not exist. All standard-making bodies are thus required to publish a notice of a proposed standard (through a central standards information centre) and allow adequate time both for comment, and for producers in exporting countries to adapt their goods and production methods to the new criteria. The lack of transparency in the standards area has undoubtedly been a significant barrier to trade; for example, French authorities recently imposed a unique standard for forklifts: it reportedly differed appreciably from those used in E.E.C. and was instituted without any warning. Exporters of highly standards-sensitive products should be the most favourably affected if this Code is properly enforced. Manufacturers of power-generating machinery, scientific and medical instruments, transportation equipment, office machines and other high-technology products have most to gain; and the Code provides numerous opportunities for these and other companies to protect their interests.

(d) Government Procurement Code

This Code, effective from 1981, should open up new markets for many exporting companies. Manufacturers of a wide range of machinery products, including construction equipment and other non-electric machinery, medical, hospital and scientific instruments, computers and other electrical equipment are now in a position to benefit. For others (e.g. transportation equipment, telecommunications products and power-generating machinery) the Code will offer few new opportunities. Whilst not eliminating 'buy national' policies, the Code does now open up a large part of the government market worldwide to fair and competitive international bidding. The Code also sets out detailed criteria to ensure that procurement procedures are non-discrimatory, under the supervision of the GATT Committee on Government procurement; and if a company believes that it has lost a sale because of discrimatory procurement practices, it can apply to its Government for an investigation. The Code's most important element is the extent of its coverage; it will not apply to all Government purchases uniformly (being binding only on federal or national entities), and in addition, all signatories have reserved certain items for domestic supplies. To begin with, no purchase of less than SDR 150,000 (SDR 1=US \$1.28) will be subject to the Code, nor will procurement for national defence purposes. In the U.S.A. for example, the Code will not cover procurement by Amtrak, Comsat, U.S. Postal Service, Department of Energy and Transportation and Tennessee Valley Authority; in the E.E.C., railways, aircraft, telecommunications, switchgear and power-generating equipment will not be covered.

(e) Import Licensing Procedures Code

This will reform the licensing systems of the industrialized countries and reduce discriminatory treatment, with a dispute settlement procedure. Companies should obtain speedier licence approvals, wider licence allocations and more regular licensing rules. This Code also requires disclosure of information on administration of restrictions, import licences granted over a recent period, distribution of licences among supplying countries, and import statistics about products subject to licensing.

Of course, these Codes provide only an agreed basis for policy and action: how effective they prove to be will depend entirely on how rigorously each signatory implements the Codes within its national borders. The entire Agreement's effectiveness depends on method and extent of national implementation. Further, these achievements of the Tokyo Round, impressive though they are, are partially offset by the failure to reach an accord on safeguards and continued delay in the agreement regarding Commercial Counterfeiting Codes. Safeguards to protect domestic industries will continue to be used as the most common and visible form of trade restriction. Commercial Counterfeiting Code is designed to protect against trademark and trade name piracy (the Code's main element is the required forfeiture of pirated goods). Trade Officials have yet to determine whether this Code should be extended to cover designs, models and copyrights.

An understanding of these Codes, and their methods of interpretation and implementation is therefore essential to management since exporting companies have much to gain from their provisions. The difficulty is undoubtedly going to be the effectiveness and fairness with which they will be implemented by national governments over the next decade.

## 1.3 Regional Economic Communities

Regional trading and economic blocs represent a significant development in international trade in the era since 1945. Basically these blocs have been set up:

(a)  To foster intra-regional trade;
(b)  To expand export trade with other trading blocs.

An important feature of regional economic communities is that by operating a common external tariff e.g. (Common Customs Tariff of the E.E.C.) and progressively abolishing internal tariffs, member countries undertake not to discriminate against each others' products in favour of domestic goods. In practice, it does not always work out like this, as there are often political problems raised in the sharing of resources, equalizing interstate freight revenues, overproduction as a result of high guaranteed producer prices, and in agreeing to proportions of investment for new industries and regional development (the establishment of an integrated, regionally-based steel mill for OCAM, the Central African Common Market, nearly foundered on the question of sovereignty). But regional economic groupings can bring tangible benefits: regional markets can be exploited large enough to justify higher levels of investment in industries with export potential to the point where economies of scale can make domestic sales more profitable, thus stimulating further investment, particularly in processing, assembling and finishing factories whose products can earn higher export revenues than primary products or raw materials.

The growing significance of these regional trading blocs in world trade is underlined by a number of factors.

First, the availability of internal resources which because of their use in manufacturing and tertiary industries of the consuming nations have an increasing external value; there is also the point that worldwide allocation of high-value resources can become related to the financial credibility and strength of the using or importing country's currency – those countries with very hard currencies are clearly better placed to command preferential supplies of commodities and raw materials. Third, a major change in the price levels of finished manufactured goods and commodities has taken place, and this has directly affected the bargaining strengths in import and export transactions. Until the mid-1970s the delivered or purchase price

## Table 1.2
### Regional Economic Communities

| Name | Membership | Date of Origin |
|---|---|---|
| ANCOM: Andean Common Market | Bolivia, Columbia, Ecuador, Peru, Venezuela | 1967 |
| ASEAN: Association of Southeast Asian Nations | Indonesia, Malaysia, Philippines, Singapore, Thailand | 1967 |
| CACM: Central American Common Market | Costa Rica, El Salvador, Guatemala, Honduras, Nicaragua | 1960 |
| CARICOM: Caribbean Common Market | Antigua, Barbados, Dominica, Grenada, Guyana, Jamaica, Montserrat, St. Christopher, St. Lucia, St. Vincent, Trinidad and Tobago | 1973 |
| CMEA: Council for Mutual Economic Assistance | Bulgarian, Czechoslovakia, German Democratic Rep., Hungary, Mongolia, Poland, Romania, USSR, Cuba, Vietnam | 1949 |
| EEC: European Economic Community | Belgium, France, West Germany, Italy, Luxembourg, The Netherlands, Denmark, Ireland, United Kingdom, Greece | 1958 |
| EFTA: European Free Trade Area | Austria, Norway, Portugal, Sweden, Switzerland, Iceland, Finland (associate) | 1960 |
| LAIA: Latin American Integration Association (Replaced LAFTA) | Argentina, Bolivia, Brazil, Chile, Columbia, Ecuador, Mexico, Paraguay, Peru, Uruguay, Venezuela | 1980 |
| The Nordic Council | Denmark, Finland, Iceland, Norway, Sweden | 1953 |
| OCAM: Organisation Commune Africaine et Malgache | Central African Republic, Dahomey, Gabon, Ivory Coast, Mauritius, Niger, Rwanda, Senegal, Togo, Upper Volta. | 1965 |

fluctuations moved together, with no substantial divergences. Since then, with the impetus of the five-fold oil price increase, prices of manufactured and consumer goods have diverged sharply, the commodity prices being now on a strong upward trend, while prices of manufactured goods have not increased at the same rate, and this divergence of price levels is providing the impetus for western industrial countries to develop new technologies for industry which use few imports, particularly energy. Furthermore, the reduction of trade barriers can directly bring about increased competition, productivity and innovation in the industries of the member countries. Furthermore, regional blocs are better placed to resource and finance new large-scale capital projects beyond the capability of any one member, and indeed to provide a regional market with sufficient volume demand to absorb the output.

All these regional blocs, therefore, have economic and trading objectives. They differ in their organization. In a Free Trade Area two special features apply:

(a)  There is no common external tariff.
(b)  There is free movement of goods among member countries.

In South America six of the original members of LAFTA formed a new group, LAIA (see Table 1.2). LAFTA was beset by difficulties among members as to how the benefits of integration would be shared out, and the effects of tariff competition from neighbouring states. It was difficulties of this sort that led to the break-up of the East African Community. A Customs Union goes beyond a Free Trade Area in requiring its members to give up their national sovereignty in matters of trade policy and in operating a Common External Tariff.

The current designations and membership of Regional Economic communities are contained in Table 1.2.

These regional trading blocs form significant 'market aggregates' and require study and assessment by management of all export companies. A detailed analysis of 'market aggregates' is contained in Chapter 3. It is of interest to note even at this stage, though, that these trading blocs have for some years provided opportunities for 'complementation agreements'. Although, for instance, in LAIA, as has been pointed out, integration has been slow, complementation agreements have been one way to accelerate integration in certain product areas. Such an agreement involves two or more LAIA countries who grant each other tariff concessions on a few products in the same industry; its operation is illustrated by the IBM Agreement in which Argentina, Brazil, Chile and Uruguay formed a free trade area for data processing equipment and punch cards; so for these products and countries, the benefits of rationalization of production and distribution are already realized.

E.E.C. implements trading policies among its member countries through Articles and Directives; the former are incorporated in the original 1953 Treaty of Rome, but it is the Directives emanating from the Commission of the European Communites in Brussels which give legislative effect to the provisions of these Articles. Once a Directive has been issued, member

**EEC Trade Structure by Region: 1980**

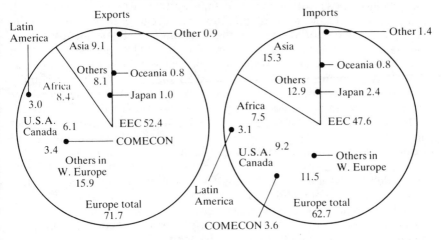

OECD *Trade by Commodities, 1980.*

Figure 1.1 The breakdown of regional trade worldwide among the major groups both for imports and exports. What clearly emerges is the dominance enjoyed by European Economic Community (EEC) in terms of its shares of both total imports and exports.

governments are set a time limit within which they are required to pass appropriate enabling legislation through their governing institutions (parliaments, assemblies, councils, etc.). The hierarchy of E.E.C. external relationships and the status of Members and Associated Members are contained in Appendix 5 and should be consulted for reference.

By far the most significant Articles for those companies trading internationally are Articles 85 and 86 (which apply equally to companies of Member countries and to companies of non-Member countries operating within E.E.C.). Whilst there are other Articles dealing with, for example, 'refusal to supply' (Article 67) and 'harmonization of technical standards' (Article 100), 85 and 86, in principle, prohibit any trading practice which 'restricts, distorts or prevents free movement of goods or fair competition'.

Article 85 bars agreements between enterprises that either directly or indirectly fix prices or limit control of production. Article 86 deals with abuses by one or more companies of a dominant position within the Common Market or a substantial part of it, and include the imposition of unfair purchase or selling prices, the limiting of production, to the prejudice of consumers. Only companies with combined turnover of up to £25 million a year and market shares of less than 5 per cent are exempted. These Articles are, therefore, principally concerned to protect and extend free movement of goods within E.E.C. and therefore any practice, whether refusal to supply, operating exclusive dealership, discriminatory pricing, which restricts such free movement is actionable by the Commission under the terms of these Articles. And as they have for some time been given legislative force by Directives and Regulations (Regulation 67 for instance deals with distributorships and licensing agreements), all companies in Britain, for example, must have registered all their Trading Agreements and contracts with the Commission. Subsequently, many companies have been required to modify their Agreements to conform with Articles 85 and 86, and some examples will shortly be given. Failure to register Agreements is an offence against 85 and 86, as is failure to comply with an Order to modify an Agreement within a specified time. Fines for such offences can be levied by the Commission at up to 10% of turnover.

The Regulation relating to pricing policies in E.E.C. is particularly strict and repays attention: it forbids two or more parties from combining and fixing prices for products or services; it also forbids them from sharing markets, charging discriminatory prices (including the use of cumulative and 'fidelity' discounts), or making it a condition of buying one product or service that the purchaser takes an unrelated one at the same time (e.g. a flight booking linked with hotel accommodation or car rental). This particular Regulation has so far been rigorously applied in recent years against European manufacturers of dyestuffs, fertilizers, whisky, pharmaceuticals and synthetic yarn. In principle, companies are required to charge the same price for each unit of the same product throughout E.E.C.; in practice, Articles 85 and 86 recognize that some 'defences' of differential pricing across national boundaries which derive from actual cost differences beyond the exporter's control must be (and are) permitted. These defences can be based on:

(a) Actual differences in direct costs of getting to the product outlets (e.g. a consumer product is likely to incur more handling costs in Italy than in West Germany because of the larger number of intermediaries typically involved there);
(b) Offers by competitors;
(c) Demand (levels of income and demand elasticity).

Some illustrations of recent cases where companies have contravened Articles 85 and 86 and have been required to modify or annul their Trading Agreements on pricing practices can be given:

(a) Omega Company was required to permit its General Agent based in one E.E.C. country to export to other E.E.C. countries as well as outside E.E.C.
(b) Distillers Company was required to end discriminatory pricing of its brand 'Red Label' and to raise the price level in U.K. to that charged in other member countries (brand was withdrawn from U.K. by company).
(c) Kawasaki Company Dealer in UK refused to supply customer from Belgium with lower priced stock and Kawasaki were heavily fined.
(d) Kodak Company had to modify substantially its trading practices so that its subsidiaries in one E.E.C. country were allowed to export elsewhere in the E.E.C. and its subsidiaries could not be held to a fixed selling price.

(e) Grundig Company had a Distributor Agreement in France confer-
ring sole right of import into the E.E.C. and exclusive use of
Grundig trade mark; this Agreement had to be completely revised
to comply with 85 and 86.

Reference has already been made to the severe impact of competition on
industry in the E.E.C. not only from Japan, but from newly industrializing
countries where unit labour costs are substantially lower. This has
undoubtedly given rise to some protectionist tendencies in Europe as
imports in sensitive industries have risen, and has led to some export-
restricting Cartels in steel and fibres. At the same time, the E.E.C. has
imposed bilateral restraints on foreign textile supplies, and some voluntary
limits have at last been accepted by Japanese exporters in a wide range of
industries. Such agreements, whether they are negotiated at Government
level or made between industry associations, inevitably involve some
cartelization of E.E.C. trade, by:

(a) limiting the overall foreign share of the protected European
markets;
(b) dividing up this share among various supplier countries;
(c) forcing each supplier country to create some kind of export cartel so
that market shares can be divided out among competing firms.

These protectionist trends reflect slow economic growth rates, high
unemployment, high inflation and interest rates in some Member
countries, structural problems in some industry sectors and a decline in
some demographic trends. The question, therefore, as to whether this kind
of protectionist policy in Europe will spread or intensify throughout 1980s
is clearly critical for industries that depend on open international trade
channels, as well as those companies, British included, whose prospects
throughout Europe are threatened by increasing competition, particularly
price-competition, from non-Eureopean suppliers. Moreover, uncertainty
about trade rules and the effectiveness of the Codes agreed at the Tokyo
Round (see Section 1.2) tends to discourage investment in industries that
depend on access to foreign markets for their economies of scale. And
lower import competition diminishes the pressure on E.E.C. countries to
hold down wages and reduce industry's incentive for technological
improvement. Even selective protection, when granted to an intermediate
industry like steel, means higher costs for end-users, which in turn become
more vulnerable to import competition.

Indeed, increased competition from outside the E.E.C. has also brought
about a profusion of government incentives to support local industry
especially if these can improve its export competitiveness. Many of these
have been provided under the European Development Fund (EDF) to
upgrade the economies for developed regions and to eliminate disparities
in regional economies, for example in Italy and Belgium. Regional
investment grants, employment aids, creation of enterprise zones, R and D
and direct financial support operations have proliferated in the E.E.C. in
recent years. Other common forms of indirect export incentives to

European manufacturers include export insurance, concessionary export financing and rebate of Value Added Tax (VAT) on exported goods. Whilst these type of incentives are not specifically prohibited by the Tokyo Trade Agreement, in the long-term they could jeopardize the intrinsic strength of the E.E.C. by making domestic manufacturers in already declining industries increasingly uncompetitive, forcing up user prices, and inviting retaliation from the E.E.C.'s principal suppliers, most notably the U.S.A.

In the E.E.C.'s external trade relations, there has been some reference to curbs on Japanese exports. In fact, the long-term rise in the value of the yen is expected to blunt some of the competitiveness of the Japanese exports to Europe in the rest of this decade; Japanese may well also become more susceptible to some of the problems currently facing industry in the E.E.C., including rising raw material and environmental protection costs, high wages and diminishing labour mobility. Indeed, one or two of the Newly Industrializing Countries (NICs) notably South Korea, are already displacing Japan in many sensitive product areas, such as shipbuilding and consumer electronics.

As far as Developing Countries as a whole are concerned, the E.E.C. currently has a surplus of over $50 billion annually in its exchange of manufactured goods with the Third World, which takes 20% of Europe's manufactured exports while supplying only 5% of manufactured imports.

The position is radically different in E.E.C. trading relations with the U.S.A: here E.E.C. exports to U.S.A. account for 7% of Community's total exports, and the E.E.C. records a sizeable trade deficit with the U.S.A. year after year. A substantial proportion of imports from the U.S.A. are, however, agricultural goods. E.E.C.'s Common Agricultural Policy (CAP) imposes a series of import levies and subsidies on a wide range of agricultural products, and the U.S.A. intends to use the Tokyo Round Subsidies Code to minimize 'description of Trade' to U.S. producers that has resulted from CAP. Despite the protectionist nature of CAP, the E.E.C. is actually the world's largest importer of agricultural goods, with a deficit with the rest of the world of more than $20 billion (imbalance with the U.S.A. is $5 billion). Nevertheless, companies in the E.E.C. exporting food products and agricultural produce can expect increasing counterveiling duties to be imposed by the U.S.A. in trade with the E.E.C. in these sectors, (U.S. producers arguing that E.E.C. agricultural subsidies are displacing U.S. sales).

However, E.E.C. ties with the U.S.A. will probably strengthen at other levels; as European firms increase their investment in the U.S.A. they will circumvent protectionist measures, while maintaining the current level of exports to the U.S.A.

**1.4 Private Sector Organizations**

The International Chamber of Commerce (ICC) associates, producers, manufacturers, traders, bankers and consumers from 70 countries, in order to 'pool experience and forge a common policy adapted to both national

Table 1.3
European Community's Trade Pattern 1965–78 ($ Millions)

| | 1965 | 1970 | 1975 | 1976 | 1977 | 1978 |
|---|---|---|---|---|---|---|
| WORLD | 100.0% | 100.0% | 100.0% | 100.0% | 100.0% | 100.0% |
| Exports to | 44,940 | 112,622 | 298,319 | 328,442 | 382,212 | 462,145 |
| Imports from | 49,041 | 116,530 | 301,810 | 345,110 | 390,039 | 463,196 |
| Balance | (4,101) | (3,908) | (3,491) | (16,668) | (7,827) | (1,051) |
| Intra-E.E.C. | 41.3% | 49.4% | 49.0% | 50.1% | 49.9% | 51.2% |
| U.S.A. | 9.7% | 9.4% | 6.9% | 6.8% | 6.7% | 7.0% |
| Exports to | 3,425 | 9,269 | 16,399 | 18,162 | 22,826 | 29,539 |
| Imports from | 5,691 | 12,303 | 24,766 | 27,409 | 29,004 | 35,496 |
| Balance | (2,266) | (3,034) | (8,367) | (9,247) | (6,178) | (5,957) |
| Japan | 0.8% | 1.3% | 1.4% | 1.5% | 1.6% | 1.7% |
| Exports to | 341 | 1,378 | 2,765 | 3,041 | 3,541 | 4,769 |
| Imports from | 454 | 1,649 | 5,901 | 7,040 | 8,774 | 11,075 |
| Balance | (113) | (271) | (3,136) | (3,999) | (5,233) | (6,306) |
| OPEC | na | 5.8% | 10.5% | 10.7% | 10.5% | 9.4% |
| Exports to | na | 3,917 | 22,667 | 25,901 | 33,489 | 39,285 |
| Imports from | na | 9,288 | 40,506 | 46,168 | 47,835 | 47,746 |
| Balance | na | (5,371) | (17,839) | (20,267) | (14,346) | (8,461) |
| Saudia Arabia | 0.6% | 0.7% | 2.2% | 2.5% | 2.6% | 2.1% |
| Exports to | 104 | 267 | 1,816 | 3,422 | 5,214 | 7,224 |
| Imports from | 423 | 1,286 | 11,229 | 13,285 | 14,606 | 12,632 |
| Balance | (319) | (1,109) | (9,413) | (9,863) | (9,392) | (5,408) |

Source: *Direction of Trade Yearbook*, International Monetary Fund 1980.

and international requirements'. ICC has an International Court of Arbitration, and runs a programme of work in conjunction with various international technical commissions and organizations. This programme can be divided into four main areas.

(a) Economic and financial policy;
(b) Production, distribution and advertising;
(c) Transport and communications;
(d) Law and commercial practice.

The International Chamber of Commerce has National Committees in 50 countries and is represented in 30 others; officially ICC acts:

(a) To promote business interests at international level;
(b) To foster the greater freedom of international trade;
(c) To harmonize and facilitate business and trade practices.

ICC's most tangible contribution towards achieving these aims has undoubtedly been 'INCOTERMS' which became operative in 1953, and has, since then, provided 'a set of international rules for the interpretation of the chief terms used in foreign trade contracts'. These include familiar designations such as FOB (Free on Board), FOT (Free on Truck – it is often the buyer's truck which is used in an FOT contract), CIF (Cost Insurance Freight) and FAS (Free Alongside – a numbered wharf is often specified). FAS for example, provides a service to exporters who, by arrangement with the port authorities, can consign their goods by tender to ships at an inclusive rate. By specifying that the export transaction will be negotiated and implemented on the basis of 'INCOTERMS' the buyer and seller in an export trade transaction can work out precisely the terms of payments, the transit, tariff and other costs the goods will be subjected to and at which point in transit, the proportion of costs which each party contracts to bear and the services provided. 'INCOTERMS' apply in most countries though applications can differ, and these should be ascertained beforehand (some countries, for example, stipulate that all freight insurance must be provided by the national insurance agency).

ICC operates an extensive research and publication service: subjects of topical interest to exporters have been published in booklet form on *The Problem of Clean Bills of Lading, International Codes of Marketing Practice, Uniform Customs and Practice for Documentary Credits*, and *Guidelines for Applications of the International Code of Sales Promotion Practice, Uniform Rules for Collection*. An explanation of these and other trade terms is contained in Sections 6.2 and 6.3.

At the national level, chambers of commerce sponsor Trade Missions, and provide research and other services. In the U.K. chambers of commerce in a number of cities provide information, help and advice to their members on various aspects of exporting, arbitration, consular regulations, customs duties and regulations, documentation, exchange control regulations, fairs and exhibitions, foreign competition and import regulations, introductions to trading houses and other contacts, marking of goods, missions, packing, patents, shipping regulations, standards, tariffs, taxation and transport, and, in some cases, translation services. Particularly useful is advice and guidance on dealing with foreign governments and purchasing agencies which insist on a certificated inspection of the exporter's goods, prior to shipment, by inspectorates such as General Superintendence, and the submission of a Clean Report of Findings (CRF).

The London Chamber of Commerce and Industry (LCCI) and the Association of British Chambers of Commerce (ABCC) provide focal points for guidance and effective use of these services for the benefit of exporters. There are also, mainly in London, offices of overseas Chambers such as Anglo-American Chamber, and similar joint Chambers operating in foreign capitals. Some chambers of commerce are authorized to issue Certificates of Origin for exporters, who should note that certificates issued by other than authorized Chambers may be rejected by overseas Customs authorities. Mention should also be made of the two U.K. professional bodies which, in addition to their membership of practising managers, provide educational programmes leading to Diplomas which are internationally recognized to be of a high standard. These bodies are:

(a) Institute of Marketing, Moor Hall, Cookham, Maidenhead, Berkshire SL6 9QH – Diploma in Marketing (Dip. M.).
(b) Institute of Export, World Trade Centre, London E1 9AA.

Exporter's Associations form another significant private-sector organization and are typically industry- or trade-based: that is, they are organized effectively to represent the national interest of a trade or industry, both in negotiating terms and sales with foreign customers, and in dealing with the national government on all matters affecting its conditions and prospects. Moreover, an independent association of exporters is listened to and can influence policy in places where the sole exporter would find it difficult to get a hearing and, from the viewpoint of national export strategy, exporters' associations can be an important instrument in developing the export trade. Any such organization also has a continuing duty: to put across to Government and to the national press the importance of the marketing concept as it applies to exporting. An association of exporters can achieve much that an exporter on his own cannot; for instance, selection of agents or business partners for overseas trading is better undertaken under the auspices of such an association, as it creates confidence in overseas customers, and in others who are interested in trading with or representing the exporter in an overseas market.

Such an association can also operate a joint selling organization in export markets, appointing buying or selling agents resident abroad who will represent it and negotiate sales on behalf of member firms. Overseas advertising, too, can be mounted and financed by a national exporters' association to promote the products or services of a particular trade or industry. Also, such associations sometimes sponsor research/consultancy on an industry basis, making available only to subscribing member firms the findings and recommendations of the reports; many of these are often submitted on contract assignments to management consultants or research agencies. Sponsored research can also qualify for financial support under the Overseas Marketing Research Scheme of the British Overseas Trade Board. The Export Marketing Research Scheme exists to encourage and assist UK firms and trade associations to mount research in export markets, and in certain cases a financial contribution towards its cost is made. Through this Scheme the Board has helped to pay for over 400 overseas marketing research projects and expert advice is provided to about 800 firms annually.

Exporters' Associations have a further important representational role: an apt illustration of this is the British Machine Tool Exporters' Association: this has not only sponsored research into investment in the industry and the applications of computerized control systems, it has recently made representations:

(a) To the government about the need for higher investment levels in those industries buying machine tools; and

(b) To the major industrial buyers of machine tools themselves.

(c) To customers in the manufacturing/engineering sectors who buy machine tools, pointing out that the Association members, having achieved a high volume of export orders, do not expect to be able to meet a surge of domestic orders unless these are placed in the very near future. The seriousness of this for the nation's balance of payments is that unless domestic manufacturers re-equip, their requirements cannot be met later from local output capacity, but will have to be satisfied by imports of new foreign machine tools.

The main functions of national exporters' associations can be summarized as follows:

(a) Planning and implementing export promotion activities by trade fairs, trade missions, etc.

(b) Liaison with trade and industry associations and chambers of commerce seeking to develop export interests/contacts on behalf of members, and sometimes negotiating terms with foreign buyers on behalf of trade associations.

(c) Making representations to government to help exporters in particular industries by, for example, new investment incentives or improved export incentives.

(d) Sponsoring or undertaking overseas market research on an industry-wide basis.

(e) Encouraging member suppliers to improve quality, delivery and specifications to gain export markets, and to comply with overseas standards inspectorates.

(f) Streamlining export documentation for members and providing information on foreign technical and commercial legislation, (e.g. health and foreign exchange regulations, packaging laws and any price controls).

(g) Negotiating the appointment of buying and selling agents resident overseas on an industry basis.

(h) Liaison with importers' associations overseas.

(i) Representing members' trade negotiations with foreign governments, particularly in removing or lowering tariffs and other barriers to trade; negotiating improved terms of trade (export values as % of import values) with a particular export country, by remedying a trade imbalance or in achieving more profitable export prices (terms of trade improve if export prices rise faster than import prices).

There are two other services provided by exporters' associations which require more detailed discussion. First, liaison with official commercial representation services of the government (e.g. trade commissioners and commercial attaches resident at missions overseas). These officials can help exporters' associations to organize outgoing selling missions to the overseas market and to receive incoming selling missions to the home country, and particularly in sales and promotional 'follow-up' to such missions. Commercial attaches can also provide these associations with advice on agency evaluation and selection for member companies, can arrange introductions to foreign buyers or agents, provide information overseas about British products available for export and provide technical and commercial data about British industry.

In the U.K., there are a number of non-governmental organizations which represent exporters' interests and provide a forum for discussion of problems and prospects:

(a)  Export Clubs (usually regionally based),
(b)  Scottish Export Committee.

Further, there are a number of exporters' associations in the U.K. representing particular sectors of U.K. manufacturing and trade such as the British Food Export Manufacturers' Association.

## 1.5 State and Para-statal Organizations

An increasingly significant trend in export is the growth and power of state trading organizations which, in many countries in the Third World, and in most countries of the Soviet and East European bloc, control import and export operations across the whole spectrum of trade and industry. Indeed, not only do central banks directly control payments for foreign trade, but often central bank authority is required in many countries before other ministries, such as Commerce or Planning, can issue import, export or trading licences or permits to set up warehouses or sales offices. Sometimes, an exporter has to obtain permission from no less than the State President's Office before he conducts any negotiations with, or has any contacts with trade officials in that overseas country; this is particularly so if the President himself is a military officer. Guidance on the correct approaches to dealing or trading with such state corporations is available to the exporter usually from the chamber of commerce or the commercial officer in the overseas post (see Section 1.2 and 7.1).

Most of these organizations are set up by statute or decree and include the following:

(a)  Industrial development corporations;
(b)  Utility undertakings;
(c)  Central purchasing boards;
(d)  Regulatory trade commissions;
(e)  Agricultural marketing boards;
(f)  Central banks;
(g)  State trading and import-export corporations;
(h)  State insurance and credit finance corporations;
(i)  Co-operative unions;
(j)  Military supply organizations.

The scope of these organizations' power is considerable, and they are to be found most commonly in Third World and COMECON countries, where no exporting company does business without dealing with them. Often the general nature of their objectives as set out in statutes has impelled Governments to circumscribe their activities in enabling legislation, thus facilitating continuing political interference, and the exporter should be aware of this aspect. In many of these countries they enjoy a monopeony position in key sectors (i.e. monopoly of purchasing).

In COMECON countries, particularly the U.S.S.R., all import and export trade is handled exclusively by state agencies; in the U.S.S.R., these include Sudimport (which handles imports) and other agencies responsible for industry sectors, GOSPLAN (the state planning commission for distribution) and NIKI (Institute of Research) and the all important Soviet Ministry of Foreign Trade. And, in third world countries, many state trading corporations have been set up to achieve social and economic goals which, operationally, are:

(a)  To generate funds for new industrial enterprises (particularly those using local materials) import substitution processing, and small industries in rural localities;
(b)  To develop management skills among local businessmen;
(c)  To provide low-cost housing welfare and other services;
(d)  To deliver low-cost goods to the local population;
(e)  To control expenditures on imports and investment in exports to accord with national economic planning.

The exporter in Western Europe must, therefore, study the organization and policies of these organizations; examples of such bodies include the State Trading Corporation of India, Panta Niaga in Indonesia, Zambia Industrial Development Corporation, Kenya National Trading Corporation, Philippines International Trading Company.

Agricultural marketing boards have a special role in many countries' export trade and their functions are diverse. Some are merely advisory or regulatory, and do not actively engage in trade at all, but regulate or control distributive channels[1]. These functions depend upon the board's methods of participation in the market; and second, their position in the market. And these two factors differ from one marketing board to another in the following ways:

(a)  A self-trading board enjoys a two-sided monopoly both for the domestic and export markets;
(b)  A non self-trading board appoints an agent or agents upon whom a domestic or export market monopoly is conferred.
(c)  A board which has nothing to do with the physical handling of the produce either directly or through agents, but has the power to direct a specific commodity through a single distributive channel.
(d)  Finally, a board undertaking no trading activities, but which can license producers, fix production quotas and guarantee minimum producer prices.

Marketing boards are becoming more involved in the physical handling, storage, transport and processing, as well as in the financing of the commodities which they control or sell.

As far as export commodities are concerned, continued use of large commercial firms in any sector of the marketing system is not favoured by many governments in developing countries. Their place is being taken by local traders, as in Nigeria; cooperatives in Tanzania; or by the boards themselves in Ghana. Boards can implement administrative measures such as selective licensing of agents and the provision of buying points at an economic cost when products pass through controllable channels as, for example, export commodities. Even in this case, the supervision for buying operations often remains loose, as non-trading boards are unable to exercise a sufficiently strong hold over produce traders or registered agents. Control of buying operations by these boards can be facilitated when the bulk of the crop is channelled through co-operatives. The licensing policy of some Boards discriminate against private agencies in order to eliminate them in favour of co-operatives. However, the use of inexperienced co-operatives as agents can hamper a board's programmes.

In Europe, the functions and organization of these marketing boards have mostly been taken over by the E.E.C. Directorate General for Agriculture (among Member countries), though co-operatives still play an important part in export promotion, particularly of produce. In the U.K. there are still a few marketing boards such as Milk Marketing Board in operation, which were set up in 1930s to stabilize prices and make distribution more efficient. There is, of course, now in UK also a Board covering all agricultural produce, operating as part of the E.E.C. Common Agricultural Policy (CAP); this is the Agricultural Products Intervention Board (APIB) which buys up surplus production at the minimum price guaranteed to farmers under CAP.

There is also the long-established policy in Europe of associating co-operatives with marketing boards, and in some countries the boards are almost entirely controlled by growers' co-operatives. For example, the fish marketing organizations of Norway and Sweden, Currant Board of Greece, wheat organizations in France. In Switzerland, the export of the finest cheese is in the hands of producers' co-operatives, and so is the marketing of Danish bacon and butter and, outside Europe, Citrus and Dried Fruit Boards of South Africa, New Zealand Dairy Board and Milk Marketing Orders of the U.S.A.

**References**

1. Abbott, J. C. and Creupland, H. C. *Agricultural Marketing Boards: their Establishment and Operation* F.A.O. Marketing Guide No. 5. (FAO: Rome, 1974).

# 2. RESEARCH AND ANALYSIS OF EXPORT MARKETS

## 2.1 Understanding and Assessment of Market Ecology

Market ecology encompasses not only the total environment within which a company promotes its products overseas but the interactions between the overseas business community and its environment. The term 'market ecology' is not, therefore, simply the study of the cultural, political, economic and social environment of one overseas country, but the analysis of what impact these parts of the environment have on business methods and export policy.

An understanding of market ecology is important to the management of any company setting up or managing the operation described in Chapter 3; without it, a company's longer-term market position cannot be assured. Export marketing research, therefore, should focus initially on market ecology, before any formal research is undertaken, and certainly before market entry is considered, or changes in marketing plans made.

So market selection overseas demands and indeed repays some study of cultural as well as geographical distances; it is these distances which give rise to what can be termed 'communications risks' encountered by exporting companies. Illustrations of the total environment as explained above and 'cultural distance' are given in Figures 2.2 and 2.3. Distance and risk can, of course, be caused by differences in language, culture, political systems, level of education; cultural may or may not be synonymous with geographical distance. The U.K. and Australia for example, are geographically far apart but culturally still close enough to facilitate trading. The U.S.A. and Cuba are geographically close, but are far apart in cultural and socio-economic terms. (Figure 2.1).

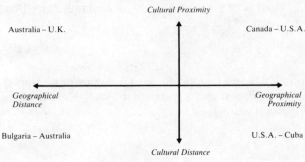

Figure 2.1

But what exactly is culture? A. Hoebel in *Man, Culture and Society* defines it as 'the integrated sum total of learned behavioural traits that are manifest and shared by members of a society'. Some awareness of the cultural aspects of the market ecology is essential to the export marketing manager. Combined with socio-economic and political factors, the key elements of market ecology can now be isolated. They are:

1.  Political and demographic
    (a)  Power structure in the society;
    (b)  Density and distribution of population;
    (c)  Legal system;
    (d)  Government fiscal policy;
    (e)  Role of ethnic minorities;
    (f)  Military aspects.

2.  Socio-economic
    (a)  Levels of disposable and per capita incomes;
    (b)  Centres of purchasing influence;
    (c)  New industrial development zoning;
    (d)  Availability and mobility of labour;
    (e)  Distribution of incomes;
    (f)  Structure of social classes;
    (g)  Government fiscal policies.

3.  Cultural
    (a)  Educational levels;
    (b)  Levels of technical and managerial training;
    (c)  Language;
    (d)  Status of women, status of the family and status of ancestors;
    (e)  Material culture such as tools, artifacts and technology of society;
    (f)  Aesthetics;
    (g)  Religious beliefs and attitudes;
    (h)  Reference groups of buyers;
    (j)  Consumption system;
    (k)  Concepts of time and manners.

4.  Geographical/environmental
    (a)  Communication systems;
    (b)  Climatic and topography;
    (c)  Proximity of sources of supply;
    (d)  Logistics systems.

This list summarizes the scope and significance of 'market ecology', but it is necessary to discuss some of the practical applications affecting as they do the way companies should do business overseas if they are to retain a long-term and profitable export presence.

Consider the question of time; when an exporter goes overseas, it is within a framework of time and his reference points are fixed in time, i.e. he usually has a set itinerary and plans to arrive and depart on certain days. However, a businessman may find that the time frame that applies to a business trip to Australia or the United States, for example, may not be applicable to the business environment in other countries. In some Asian countries, for instance, time is viewed differently, but no less meaningfully in terms of cultural values, than in some industrialized countries where the 'time is money' philosophy prevails. As a result of this different attitude towards time, a businessman visiting an Asian market may need to allow himself a longer period of time to transact business than he would, for instance, in the United States. He may find that, in the Asian market, although he has a firm appointment, he is kept waiting. When he is finally ushered in to see the business executive or official, his annoyance because of the delay may be reflected in his face – if he is not familiar with the customs of that country – and the business discussion will begin in a strained atmosphere. The person he has been waiting to see, on the other hand, considers that to tell his previous business visitor that his time is up is far ruder than to keep his next visitor waiting an extra half an hour.

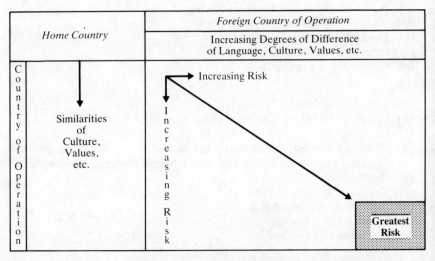

Figure 2.2 Communication Risk in Export Operations

The relationship of time and business decision-making also varies from culture to culture. In some, the time required to make a decision is directly proportional to the importance of the decision. To try to hurry the decision-making process is likely to be counter-productive, as it can in the eyes of the other party diminish the importance you attach to your own proposal. There are also different attitudes from one culture to another towards 'future time'. Whereas in Europe, managers plan for the future, in some cultures the future is considered to be too far away and too difficult to contemplate. This is evidenced in the lack of willingness to plan forward and the disinclination to establish what we consider to be realistic lead times.

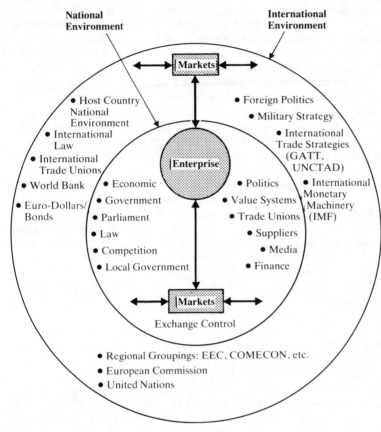

National Environment

International Environment

Markets

- Host Country National Environment
- International Law
- International Trade Unions
- World Bank
- Euro-Dollars/ Bonds

- Foreign Politics
  - Military Strategy
    - International Trade Strategies (GATT, UNCTAD)

Enterprise

- Economic
- Government
- Parliament
- Law
- Competition
- Local Government

- Politics
- Value Systems
- Trade Unions
- Suppliers
- Media
- Finance

- International Monetary Machinery (IMF)

Markets

Exchange Control

- Regional Groupings: EEC, COMECON, etc.
- European Commission
- United Nations

Figure 2.3

Cultural differences are also reflected in the attitudes towards space. In the Western business environment, space usually indicates status as reflected in the size of a person's office and its location. This is often not the case in other cultures. To evaluate a person's importance by your own norms for office space and location can therefore lead to serious misinterpretation of the status of the individual.

Differences in attitudes to space can be seen in matters of personal proximity. Distances between people when they speak, and the degree of loudness of the voice vary between cultures. British businessmen may 'freeze' and cause offence when people in other countries insist on holding them by the arm when speaking to them, but this is a common practice in many other countries.

Languages themselves also differ in how precisely they differentiate experience and the way in which they convey meaning. The way meaning is conveyed varies in matters such as the way things are said, the tone of the voice, the pitch of the voice, what is left unsaid, gestures when speaking and the degree of loquaciousness compared to brevity. Languages convey differences between cultures as far as formality and informality are concerned. In some languages there are a number of different words for "you" which vary according to the status of the person speaking and the person spoken to, while the others – English, for example – there is only one. Therefore, a businessman visiting a different culture should enquire regarding the style and basics of the language, because it is likely that those with whom he deals, although able to speak his language, will apply the thought patterns of their own language when interpreting what he says. Conversely, the meaning of what his foreign business associates say is liable to misinterpretation by him because their use of his language will be based on the thought patterns of their own language.

The degree to which the individual is a private being varies as does the way in which this privacy manifests itself. The easy assumption of familiarity and the use of first names regardless of rank, which is accepted in certain Western cultures, is considered in parts of Asia, for instance, to be an intrusion on a person's private world. Allied to this is the expression of emotion. A sensitivity to the differences in this respect is important in business negotiations especially when gauging the reaction to an offer or statement. While a Westerner, for example might interpret a smile or laugh as an indication of happiness, in some cultures it may in fact indicate disappointment or annoyance.

Cultural differences are also reflected in ways of negotiating and conducting business. In some countries in Asia, for instance, the nominated price is often the starting point for negotiations, not a 'take it or leave it figure' as it is in many Western countries. What is important in such situations is to ascertain the normal relationship between the asking price and the expected price and, if you are the buyer, for instance, to offer a little below the expected price so that each party is seen to 'give a little' in the negotiations; to do otherwise is to force the seller into a position of losing face, which can damage sales prospects.

The basis for business negotiations may be in the form of technical or legal rules, mutually agreed practices or informal customs. These may cover matters such as the point at which negotiations cease – is the signing of the contract the conclusion of negotiations or the starting point for a second round of discussions? The customary nature of an agreement is another variable between cultures – how binding is a verbal agreement and will insisting on a written contract be regarded as offensive? A few enquiries along these lines by the businessman before proceeding to the overseas market will prevent much disenchantment.

In commercial negotiations of substance, a legal agreement provides many businessmen with a feeling of security. However, not only does the basis of the legal system vary between cultures (e.g. English Common Law compared with the Napoleonic Code compared with the Shari's Law of Islam), but the interpretation of the law will also differ. In some cultures the law is absolute and is modified in the interpretation after it has been broken. In other cultures, the law has some flexibility, but once broken its interpretation is rigid. Familiarity with the legal system and its operation is a prerequisite to doing business in a different culture.

In researching the approach to export markets it is wise to consider that culture can have an impact on the product and its promotion. The culture in which a person lives affects his consumption patterns and also the meaning that he attaches to specific products. When promoting the product in a new culture it is easier initially to appeal to existing cultural requirements or expectations than to try to change them. Product promotion must be sensitive to the basic values of the country and the differences in patterns of consumption. For example, promoting a 'do it yourself' time-saving device in a country having widespread unemployment may be not only pointless but also yield unfavourable criticism of the exporting company.

Other examples of market ecology which demonstrate its importance to the exporting company can be cited as follows:

(a) The use of manufacturing and promotional symbols such as the owl which means 'wisdom' in the U.K. but 'disaster' in Africa;
(b) Any colours used in national flags or host countries are often better avoided in promotion and packaging;
(c) Women as symbols cannot be used at all for promotion in many Moslem countries, nor can there be any mention of alcohol or tobacco;
(d) The position of ethnic minorities in many overseas markets has to be fully understood, and approached with sensitivity by the business-man: some ethnic groups comprise major sub-sectors of the mass market in the U.S.A. with specialized tastes and consumption styles; other ethnic groups dominate particular trade or distributive sectors of the economy, and governmental trade policies often take into account the position of these ethnic minorities and the exporter should, therefore, be fully conversant with them.

The extended family, reverence for ancestors, and the family's business traditions, are also a vital part of the ecology to be understood by the exporting company. For example, a Western-based communictions company some years ago peremptorily dropped its agent in Thailand, simply to pass the Agency to another group newly headed by a relative; the product lost its position and the company had to withdraw from that market. Differences in communicating must also be understood: a European instrument manufacturer sent its export manager to Brazil to dismiss their agent because not one letter from him was on file, only to find that the agent had, in fact, spent the previous year establishing a network of service depots as a step to market penetration. In Chinese societies, throughout Asia, any commercial event or situation must be planned or assigned on a day and at a time 'propitious' to Chinese religion and ancestry (e.g. the opening of a new sales office). To ignore 'propitious' signs can damage exporters' business reputations and sales.

Consumption styles too, differ because of socio-economic differences: Brylcreem traditionally used to sell particularly well in parts of Africa, when the manufacturer discovered it was bought mainly as a sandwich spread.

Heinz, however, had difficulty establishing their baby foods initially in Africa because consumers took the packaging to mean that they would be eating tinned babies. Of course, brand names (referred to in more detail in Chapter 3), can be hazardous to develop and sometimes difficult and costly to protect.

Finally, environmental factors should be considered carefully. A British printing machine manufacturer had to re-design parts of the machine to take account of the different qualities of paper produced locally in some of its major Middle East markets. In Scandinavia, recently, where there is a powerful environmental protection lobby, new washing detergents had to be promoted on the basis that it was "pollution-free" rather than on its whitening power, and powered hand tools had to be callibrated by the British manufacturer to reduce noise levels/vibrations. In Switzerland, a few years ago, a newly imported dishwasher soon had to have its promotional concept changed from 'making housework easy and convenient' to 'the superior hygiene of machine washing at hotter than hand temperatures'; this latter concept was more appealing to Swiss housewives. A European chain-saw manufacturer selling to the Far East had to develop a special clutch because extreme humidity was causing condensation and rusting in standard units. Similarly, a British manufacturer of portable electric heaters found markets in Venezuela to dry coffee beans and in Jordan for use during cold nights, following an environmental study for the product.

The impact, therefore, of environmental and other factors on products for export is summarized in Table 2.1[1] and, in their totality, provide an apt insight into 'market ecology'.

*Table 2.1*

| *Environmental & other factors* | *Manufacturing/marketing Change* |
| --- | --- |
| Level of technical skills | Product simplification |
| Level of labour | Automation or manualization of product |
| Level of literacy | Remaking and simplification of product |
| Safety, health and noise Pollution control | Use modifications |
| Level of interest rates | Credit, costs of inventories margins |
| Level of maintenance | Changes in tolerances |
| Isolation (heavy repairs difficult and costly) | Product simplification and reliability improvement. Recalibration of product and re-sizing of specifications. |
| Differences in standards | Changes in product structure and fuelling |
| Availability of materials | Re-sizing of engine/power and specifications |
| Power availability | Product re-design/innovation in specifications, packaging or other adaptions. |

Market ecology also has import applications in the aggregation and segmentation of markets, and these are explored in Chapter 3.

Further illustrations of the importance of market ecology can be appropriately given at this point, and in particular, concepts of time and the giving of gifts.

(a) Time: one U.S. company lost a major contract opportunity in Greece partly because its manager tried to impose time limits for the meetings and for the conclusion of the deal. The Greeks, however, consider limits insulting and felt they showed a lack of finesse. And to save time, the Americans wanted the Greeks to first agree to principles, and then leave subordinates to work out the details; the Greeks regarded this as a deceptive ploy, and preferred to work everything out themselves, regardless of time.

(b) The offer by a businessman from India to 'come any time' represents a serious invitation, and should not be construed as a casual or polite remark as in the U.K. or U.S.A. What it means is that the Indian is requesting a visit but is politely allowing his business acquaintance to arrange the time: if no time is set, the Indian assumes the invitation has been refused, and the consequences might be the loss of a large sales order.

(c) Gifts: sometimes gifts are expected in business transactions, and failure to supply can prove insulting. At other times, however, the mere offer of such a token is considered offensive. In the Middle East, for exmple, hosts are insulted if guests bring food and drink to their homes because it implies that the businessman is not a good host (alcoholic drinks are particularly dangerous in this region). In many parts of Latin America, cutlery and handkerchiefs should not be given because these gifts imply a cutting off of relationships or the likelihood of a sad event. Even the way a gift is presented is important. In most parts of Asia, gifts should be given privately to avoid embarrassing the recipients, but they need to be offered publicly in the Middle East to reduce the possible impression that bribery is being attempted.

The fact is that a businessman from Western Europe or North America, for instance, cannot expect to become fully conversant with the complex 'market ecologies' of all the overseas countries he operates in. Common sense is often, in the last resort, the best guide; perhaps also, a reminder to distinguish continually among the following:

(a) Cultural 'imperative': what must be done
(b) Cultural 'exclusive': what must not be done
(c) Cultural 'discretion': what may or may not be done.

## 2.2 Setting up an Export Marketing Research Project

There are two major aspects of export market research of which the company's management should at least have some outline, practical grasp, and knowledge of which research sources can be consulted. It is not necessary, or even appropriate, in all cases that the exporting company should undertake the research itself. The time and cost of data collection, the technicalities of sampling and questionnaire design, and shortage of in-company expertise, may well necessitate the use of a research agency. The importance of accurate and cost-effective briefing of an agency is reflected in Section 2.3 which contains practical guidance on this for the export marketing manager.

Nevertheless, it is appropriate for the company's management to understand how data sources can be used cost-effectively, and how data collection methods should be chosen with care to reflect the different conditions of overseas countries. Most of the research design and project work will be concerned with examining, assessing and up-dating:

(a)  Market ecology as decribed in the last section;
(b)  Company's market position and prospects overseas;

Detailed data sources and organizations providing information are contained on pp. 214–15. However, before a company spends time and money investigating sources or embarking on data collection, some clear objectives and action plan must be formulated by management, even if implementation will be by an agency. Research design and objectives can be based on the Audit set out in Section 2.6, but some research objectives might include:

(a)  Survey and assess changes in attitudes and behaviour among distributors and customers towards company's products/services;
(b)  Measure market penetration and prospects of major competitors in overseas markets;
(c)  Analyse short and long sales potential of products for export in selected markets;
(d)  Research impact of promotion and advertising plans on samples of key customers;
(e)  Implement project on buyer research, particularly where major purchasing decisions are taken by committees or groups such as central tender boards, purchasing and supply agencies: buyer research includes analysing power structures, decision-making process, status of each group member, factors influencing decisions to buy, impact of sellers' presentations; need for follow up consultancy, training and management advice; succession policy;
(f)  Study the movement of major economic indicators in relation to resources required to service the market in the future;
(g)  Quantify, or at least examine, major risk elements present in target overseas markets, political, economic, financial, etc;
(h)  Study, in depth, tastes, preferences, motivations, shopping habits, living styles of consumers on a sample basis;
(i)  Examine development of technical specifications, applications, tolerances among major industrial buyers;
(j)  Study changes in social class structure, reference groups, etc. as they affect market prospects for exporter's company;

(k) Measure the relative importance of price sensitivity among customers and non-price factors such as delivery, service, quality, design and follow-up training;

(l) End-use analysis: business sectors using the product; each sector's share of total consumption, the growth of each utilizing sector and plans and forecasts of future growth for each major sector and related sectors (secondary or derived demand).

The various data sources offer considerable scope for research, and are fully detailed in pp. 37 and 38. It is appropriate at this stage, therefore, to point out the difference between primary and secondary data. Primary data is collected first hand from respondents (customers, interviewees, distributors, etc.) for a specific research project designed to meet pre-set client-based objectives, often with the use of a research agency. Industry and trade associations, and international management consultancies and government departments and universities often commission surveys and reports which employ primary data collection; for example, customer attitude surveys, manufacturing outlook and prospects, and major industrial buyers' level of purchasing and supply, and other industrial trends.

Secondary data consists mainly of classified information published regularly and available on subscription to purchasers in trade and industry, and private researchers; such data would include (for example) Customs and Excise reports, trade summaries, statistical digests, annual financial/economic reports, produced by government offices and para-statal corporations.

Certain data sources, in general, can prove to be particularly valuable to exporters, and whilst the authoritative list can be found in the Appendices, the following should be particularly noted for the purposes of what is known as desk research:

(a) Central and commercial banks (status reports and trade intelligence);

(b) Chambers of commerce, particularly London Chamber of Commerce and Industry, trade associations;

(c) BOTB Export Intelligence Service, Central Office of Information;

(d) Home and overseas embassies and consulates;

(e) University and business schools (students and tutors can provide research and project reports on overseas operations);

(f) Media owners (Kompass, Dun & Bradstreet, Kluwer and Croner);

(g) Departments of Trade and overseas governments (e.g. National Technical Information Service of U.S. Department of Commerce);

(h) Market research and advertising agencies (Nielsen, European Market Research Bureau).

(i) Management consultants (Economist Intelligence Unit, Hudson Institute);

(j) Other information abstracting services (ANBAR, EXTEL);

(k) Export Credits Guarantee Department (ECGD);

(l) Confederation of British Industry, Institute of Marketing, Institute of Export, Market Research Society;

(m) Trade associations, department stores.

A survey undertaken by the Department of Trade recently shows the secondary data sources most commonly used by British exporters (Table 2.2).

*Table 2.2*
*Use of Sources of Export Information*

| Information Source | All Recorded Use No. | % | Frequent Use No. | % |
|---|---|---|---|---|
| Overseas Agent | 182 | 84 | 138 | 64 |
| Export Services & Promotions Division* | 165 | 76 | 72 | 33 |
| Bank(s) | 163 | 75 | 33 | 15 |
| Local Department of Industry Office* | 153 | 71 | 66 | 30 |
| Overseas Embassies | 139 | 64 | 38 | 18 |
| U.K. Embassies | 128 | 59 | 13 | 6 |
| Chambers of Commerce | 123 | 57 | 22 | 10 |
| Trade Fairs | 110 | 51 | 25 | 12 |
| Personal Contacts, U.K. | 103 | 47 | 36 | 17 |
| CBI | 88 | 41 | 25 | 12 |
| Specialist Trade Associations | 11 | 35 | 28 | 13 |
| Public Library | 76 | 35 | 11 | 5 |
| Professional Institutions | 69 | 32 | 5 | 2 |
| Overseas Subsidiary Company | 60 | 28 | 39 | 18 |
| Industrial Liaison Officer | 48 | 22 | 5 | 2 |
| Industry Export Council | 24 | 11 | 3 | 1 |
| University/Polytechnic | 20 | 9 | 2 | 1 |
| TOTAL | 1,876 | 46 | 643 | 16 |

*U.K. Government Export Promotion Services

Collection of primary data encompasses a number of methods, which are well documented in research manuals and texts, and are normally referred to collectively as field research (as opposed to desk research).

Data collection methods are normally employed on behalf of client companies by research agencies (and specialists such as statisticians and psychologists). They can be outlined as follows:

(a) Questionnaire surveys (face to face, postal, telephone).
(b) Group methods (where a range of opinion, reaction or preference is sought by the researcher);
(c) Observation
(d) Motivational research (where 'projective' techniques are used to ascertain why people hold preferences, feelings, opinions, attitudes, and behave in ways they may be unable or unwilling to express in answer to direct questions);
(e) Industrial survey work.

What most concerns the exporting company, though, is not so much the technical aspects of primary data collection as the special applications and adaptations that are commonly required in undertaking this sort of field research in overseas countries. Whilst certain specialist advice is available from agencies, for example the translation of a complex questionnaire into a foreign language, an understanding of attitudes towards and applications of the research is essential. For example, literacy levels make written questionnaires useless in many countries; heads of households may be difficult to contact, whilst in other markets, women cannot be spoken to directly by researchers; in some countries interviewers may be regarded with suspicion as government inspectors prying into anti-social behaviour or undeclared incomes with consequent distortion of responses. Observation techniques (pioneered by anthropological researchers) can be particularly useful to exporters visiting overseas markets to identify new industrial development zones, distribution efficiency, performance of agents' sales staff, work patterns, social behaviour in groups in major purchasing or negotiating situations. Motivational research, provided that linguistic and psychological difficulties can be resolved, can be important in determining precisely what priorities consumers have in the pattern of purchasing (these are often quite different to those in the exporter's country, or even in neighbouring countries); West German consumers, for example, typically spend a higher proportion of their disposable income on quality furniture than British consumers; Italians spend more per capita on overseas holidays than the Swiss, and Belgians spend more per household on large, high quality cars than the French.

There is, of course, one final but vital stage in setting up, operating and benefitting from an export market research project; that is analysis and interpretation. These comprise the most important role for the export marketing manager, since, however sophisticated the research methodology has been, analysis and interpretation essentially form the basis of planning and action.

Misinterpretation of research results overseas can lead to unfortunate and costly misallocations of resources and misdirections of promotional activities and sales efforts. Some practical examples can highlight these points.

Take for example economic or sales growth rates as indicators of market potential: if expressed in values (and they usually are) rather than in units or quantities, these can be grossly distorted by foreign inflation rates and wide fluctuations in the value or parity of the currency they are expressed in: to counter this, indexation would be essential. Interpretative problems of language need special attention: words such as 'frequently', 'often', 'usually' can have very different meanings across linguistic and cultural boundaries. Rising imports of a product may appear to indicate market potential, but not if, on further research, it is found that much of this is re-exported to third countries. Again, research into total supply can give the exporter total 'apparent' consumption in an overseas market, and thereby the calculation of import content of this consumption; it is 'apparent' consumption only because total supply statistics (total supply=(local production−exports)+imports) do not include stock movements. There is, in practice, little or no time to deal with problems like stocks, and importers are usually unwilling to give information to researchers about their stock levels (many claim to be overstocked). For exporters, it is vital to research accurately the share of imports in 'apparent' total consumption: if this percentage is growing, it shows that the market is opening up for imports.

Qualitative market research is, therefore particularly concerned not just conceptually with market potential, but with the actual demand likely to be realized by marketing programmes. This can apply equally to industrial as well as to consumer products, as is illustrated by an engineering company which, on the basis of market tests, decided to export a technical product in Africa which was far superior to anything then available on the market; soon afterwards the product gained a reputation for being unreliable. This was true, but the machine broke down because the new owners did not understand its maintenance requirements and failed to oil it; the result was the withdrawal of the machine from the market. Two other market research projects are worth mentioning here to illustrate further problems involved:

(a)  On the basis of research indicating an adequate market, a Swiss pharmaceutical company built a £5 million manufacturing plant in South-east Asia. The researchers, though, had overlooked an extremely important aspect of the market – the local black market controlled by government officials. Because of this added competition, the company experienced lower earnings than expected and found itself with excess production capacity (with high unit costs).

(b)  In a research study conducted some years ago of spaghetti consumption in Western Europe, it was concluded that more spaghetti was consumed by West Germans and French than by Italians. Further analysis indicated that this false finding arose from the type of questions asked, which dealt with purchases of branded and packaged spaghetti. Many Italians, however, buy spaghetti in bulk; by qualifying the way in which the product was purchased, the researchers arrived at the false conclusion about the amounts of spaghetti consumed.

Qualitative analysis of research, however important, is not enough, and some quantitative data is needed. The theory and applications of statistical sampling and analysis have been well documented in other texts, but the export marketing manager should at least be aware throughout the research project that it is essential to design and apply correct statistical procedures. Without this statistical control, particularly in the context of export research, interpretation can indeed be hazardous.

The purpose of quantitative research is to produce reliable numerical data which will give guidance in answering questions like: how big is the market? how much to produce? how many people prefer sample A to sample B? and so on. For statistical data such as this to be reliable, it is essential that the techniques for data collection are based on sound statistical theory and principles. In particular, it is necessary for the sample of respondents chosen in any research survey to be selected in a manner based on probability theory. This is called 'random' or 'probability' sampling, in which the sample is selected in such a way that no bias exists in the selection process. The advantage of using these statistically based procedures is that results collected from the sample can be statistically analysed to indicate numbers and percentages which would be true for the whole population being studied. The results for the population of interest can be predicted with a specified degree of certainty (known as the 'confidence level') within a specified range of number (known as the 'limits of accuracy'). So, for example, the results of a quantitative survey would be expressed as:

'At the 95% level of confidence, the number of car-owning households in the population is 3.7 million±2%'.

This kind of statistic is useful because the level of confidence indicates the chances of it being wrong (1 in 20 in this case) and also the limits within which it is right (3,626,000–3,774,000 in this case). The same statistical formula which allows these calculations to be made can also be used to determine the size of sample necessary for results to be produced within predetermined limits of accuracy and at a pre-stated level of confidence.

The essential point to note from this brief discussion of quantitative research is that for quantitative research to produce reliable numerical answers, the research design and analysis requires the application of a high level of statistical expertise. It is for this reason that research agencies undertaking quantitative research employ statisticians, and the exporter commissioning quantitative research should check that a statistician is available to ensure that correct procedures for sampling and statistical analysis are employed in the conduct of a survey.

For random or probability sampling to be carried out, it is necessary to construct a 'sampling frame' or complete listing of the population of interest, from which the sample will be selected. It is often impossible to do this, and in this case 'quota sampling' is applied. Quota sampling involves selecting predetermined quotas of respondents from classified groups of people or sectors of trade or industry. If quota sampling is used, then the statistical formulae which govern random sampling do not apply. In practice, a compromise is often made by using the formulae for guidance on, say, the size of sample and then increasing the number subjectively to allow for the fact that a less than ideal sampling procedure has been used.

Another aspect of statistical interpretation is the simple correlation of sets of data to establish if there are statistically significant relationships. This applies particularly to import and export data, and overseas production and consumption data. This aspect can be illustrated from data in the *Commodity Yearbook*, presented in the form of graphs (see Section 2.4).

## 2.3 Briefing and Controlling the Research Agency

It is often necessary to employ market research specialists to undertake in-depth research into attitude and behaviour, or for large-scale data collection and statistical analysis. The advantage to the client company is the expertise and objectivity which an agency can bring to the company's operations and market analysis and measurement. The Market Research Society (London) has published useful guidelines for briefing and controlling an agency[2]: these cover instructions to the agency, setting objectives, agreed methods of payment, format of presentation, responsibility for interpretation and analysis, action recommendations (as appropriate).

These guidelines begin with what a research agency can expect from the client company. They include:

(a) A statement of the research problems, preferably in the form of a written brief;

(b) A setting of the problem in its general background and context (in some cases, users may be able to define their overall problem within its generalized context but not have the experience to define it in research terms);

(c) Opportunity to meet and discuss the problem and its background;

(d) An indication of the sorts of decision that are likely to be influenced by the research results and the uses to which the results are to be put (e.g. whether publication is envisaged);

(e) A broad indication of the budget available for the research project.

A research agency cannot be expected to provide satisfactory and comprehensive research proposals in the absence of any of the above; it is therefore in the client's interests to supply them. There are three other things an agency can reasonably expect, though of themselves they will not necessarily affect the quality of research proposals:

(f) That the client company only approach agencies on a formal basis when there is reasonable probability that the project under consideration will actually be commissioned;

(g) If it is the type of project which should be the subject of tenders, that the client should restrict the agencies approached to a reasonable number (say 2–4), and inform them that they are in a competitive situation;

(h) If a project is submitted to tender in this way, the agencies can reasonably expect an opportunity to meet with the client to discuss their reaction to the approach suggested in their research proposals before the final choice of agency is made.

Agencies will often spend a considerable amount of time in the preparation of research proposals. It is desirable that this practice should continue but this will only be the case if agencies perceive their investment has some chance of pay-off. In general terms, therefore, what can the client or commissioning company expect from the agency? The first check list details the criteria which can be used to assess the agency's general level of competence and will help in the decision as to whether in principle, a particular agency will suit the client's requirements.

(a) Evidence of the background quality of its research executives;
(b) Details of any specialists (psychologists, statisticians) employed full-time or on a consultant basis;
(c) Evidence of the agency's experience that may be relevant to the client's particular situation; work on similar kinds of problems; work within the same market; experience of using relevant research techniques;
(d) Details of the field operations; selection and training of interviewers; levels of supervision; checks on quality and accuracy;
(e) For large quantitative surveys, details of data processing plant, procedure, staff limitations;
(f) Details of normal standard of reporting; the style and content of reports;
(g) Details of accounting and legal aspects; normal billing procedures.

Finally, in specific terms, what can the client or commissioning company expect from the agency in service and expertise; particularly specific points to be covered in the agency's proposals:

(a) Demonstration, in their statement of the research objectives and of the scope of the enquiry, that the agency understands the client's problem;
(b) Detailed description of the research design including:
A statement of the scope and nature of any preliminary desk research, qualitative work or pilot studies
For any quantitative study a statement of: the data collection technique (how the information is to be obtained): the universe to be sampled (who is to be interviewed); the size of the sample (how many are to be interviewed); the method of sample selection (how the individuals are to be selected);
(c) A statement of the cost of the project and a clear indication of the assumptions on which it is based and what is included, e.g. assumptions made about the length of the interview; assumptions made about degree of executive involvement; whether personal briefing of interviewers is included; number of copies of report envisaged; approximate number of tabulations; whether visual presentation of results is included;
(d) A reasonably detailed timetable for the project and a reasonably firm reporting date;
(e) A statement of the specific executive(s) responsible for the project.

A list of overseas market research organizations is given on pp. 214–15.

## 2.4 Analysing International Trade Data

It is essential to explain briefly how world trade classifications operate, as all export research must increasingly utilize these classifications which are, in effect, codes.

Until comparatively recently, specific duties were used widely, and the tariffs of many countries, particularly those in the Middle East and Latin America, were very complex. Since then, however, the trend has been towards the 'ad valorem' system. Tariff administration has been greatly simplified by the adoption of two main trade classifications; these are as follows:

(a) Standard International Trade Classification (SITC) Revised. This has ten divisions split up into 625 sub-groups, and these include all commodities of international trade numbering more than 40,000 separate products. These are further sub-divided into over 2,000 items, designated by 5 digit code numbers, thus enabling the exporting company to pinpoint data on a specific product.

Currently, some 120 countries, accounting for nearly 90% of world trade, report their trade statistics to the United Nations using the SITC Code; these statistics are published regularly and represent the most complete set of international statistics in existence. The statistical values of goods for all countries are reported in U.S. dollars, giving even greater comparability. SITC is fully compatible with major commodity nomenclature systems used in international trade.

(b) Customs Co-operation Council Nomenclature (CCCN). This came into force with the setting up of the E.E.C. and is a 4-digit customs tariff nomenclature in which all products entering international trade are grouped according to the nature of the material from which they are made, and easily indentifiable. This facilitates a comparison between the duties applied by different countries and simplifies international tariff negotiations. Over two-thirds of world trade is now conducted under tariffs that are based on CCCN, and this includes almost all signatories to the General Agreement on Tariffs and Trade (GATT). Over 90 countries use CCCN for customs tariff purposes, but they submit trade statistics to the U.N. using the SITC Code above. In the SITC Manual, the CCCN code number appears opposite each SITC number. Thus, by using this key, it is a simple matter to obtain the customs import duty for any product in any country.

A development of CCCN is used to classify external and internal trade of all member countries of the E.E.C. under a system called NIMEXE. Here are two examples of SITC and CCCN.

| Product | SITC | CCCN |
|---------|------|------|
| Commercial Vehicles | 783.10 | 87.02 |
| Electrical Machinery | 716.21 | 85.01 |

It is essential for exporting companies to understand these classifications, particularly CCCN, and the practical advantages they offer. They guarantee, for example, to both government and business, maxium uniformity in the classification of goods in the national customs tariffs of target markets overseas. Exporting companies, therefore, can know in advance how their goods will be classified for customs purposes, and the tariffs their goods will be subject to. This is essential for the purpose of marketing planning and, in particular, pricing policy. Further accurate measurement by volume and value is ensured not only for exports, but for imports and re-exports. The language problem is practically eliminated and the exporter can identify the movements of a highly specific sub-group of products in overseas markets. Also provided is a standard measure for comparing exports and import statistics of different countries and trading blocs.

Two further, but less important, classifications are worthy of mention:

(a)  International Standard Industrial Classification (ISIC). ISIC is often confused with SITC, but the two coding systems were designed for different purposes. The ISIC is a system for classifying commodities by the industries which produce them and is widely used in reporting employment statistics, labour rates and other economic data related to industry classifications. The U.N. has published a key showing the relationship of the ISIC code numbers to the corresponding SITC numbers.

Since many trade directories are published according to ISIC codes, this conversion key is particularly helpful for finding the names of importers or buyers for a particular commodity.

(b)  ETNVT (Edinaia Tovarnaia Nomenklatura Vneshney Torgovli). This classification is used by U.S.S.R. and countries of Eastern Europe (COMECON) in reporting international trade statistics. This group is the only major trading bloc which does not report trade statistics according to SITC. This failure does not represent any major problem, however, since the U.N. converts the data into SITC code in its published statistics. The U.N. has also developed a conversion key from the ETNVT to the SITC.

Whilst these trade classifications can be applied extensively (see Appendix 6), it is important at this point to explain how the relationships between sets of data can be used to determine long-term market trends.

International Trade Centre UNCTAD/GATT has researched the following interesting applications.[3] Finding relationships between different series of data is an important step towards understanding the forces at work in a market. A simple comparison of trends is often revealing.

In Figure 2.4 such comparison reveals a widening gap between consumption and production of honey in the U.S.A. between 1961 and 1976. It is based on data on imports, production and exports. Apparent consumption was found by adding production and imports and then subtracting exports. It is clear that in the earlier part of the period production generally was close to consumption or even exceeded it, but since 1971 there has been a tendency for consumption to exceed production by a widening margin. While consumption rose only slightly between 1961 and 1976, production followed a basically downward trend.

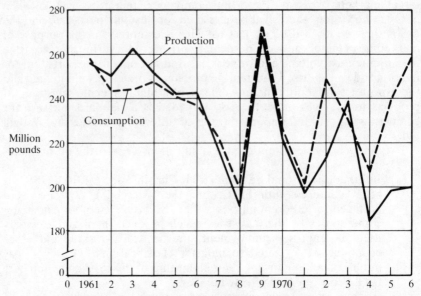

Figure 2.4 U.S. honey production and consumption 1961–1976 (production plus imports for consumption, minus domestic exports)
Source: *Commodity Yearbook*

Since the difference between production and consumption is made up by imports, it is clear that if these trends continue there will be an increasing market for imports even if consumption does not keep growing. Unless consumption begins to decline, or to grow more vigorously, the main factor in future import growth therefore will be what happens to production. What is not clear, however, is why production has been falling. Has production been falling because it could not compete with rising imports, or have imports been rising because production fell for other reasons, leaving the gap to be filled by imports? Another look at the data can give us more useful clues.

If we compare the changes in imports and production on a year-to-year basis as shown in Table 2.3 we see that:

(a) In six out of the 15 years imports rose and production fell, and in the other years production rose while imports fell;

(b) In the years when imports rose and production fell, the drop in production was almost always far larger than the rise in imports.

These figures suggest that while imports of honey may affect production over the long term, in a year-to-year basis the flow of imports is influenced by production levels, and not the other way around. (Note that for this comparison, it is more meaningful to compare changes in absolute volume terms than in percentages.) This is an example of how an analyst can develop information by comparing data in different ways.

Table 2.3
United States Production and Imports* of Honey

| YEAR | Production Quantity (million 1b) | Production Change (million 1b) | Imports Quantity (million 1b) | Imports Change (million 1b) |
|---|---|---|---|---|
| 1961 | 255.9 |  | 9.0 |  |
| 1962 | 249.6 | − 6.3 | 7.1 | − 1.9 |
| 1963 | 266.8 | +17.2 | 2.6 | − 4.5 |
| 1964 | 251.2 | −15.6 | 9.9 | + 2.3 |
| 1965 | 241.8 | − 9.4 | 13.3 | + 8.4 |
| 1966 | 241.6 | − 0.2 | 9.5 | − 3.8 |
| 1967 | 215.8 | −25.8 | 16.8 | + 7.3 |
| 1968 | 191.4 | −24.4 | 16.9 | + 0.1 |
| 1969 | 267.5 | +76.1 | 14.7 | − 2.2 |
| 1970 | 221.8 | −45.7 | 8.9 | − 5.8 |
| 1971 | 197.4 | −24.4 | 11.4 | + 2.5 |
| 1972 | 214.1 | +16.7 | 39.0 | +27.6 |
| 1973 | 237.7 | +23.6 | 10.7 | −28.3 |
| 1974 | 185.1 | −52.6 | 26.0 | +15.3 |
| 1975 | 197.9 | +12.8 | 46.4 | +20.4 |
| 1976 | 199.8 | + 1.9 | 65.0 | +18.2 |

* Imports for consumption
Source: *Commodity Yearbook*

One simple technique for checking the relationship between different 'variables' (series of data) is the scatter diagram. This uses the horizontal scale for the one series and the vertical scale for the other. The independent, or causual, variable is placed on the horizontal axis. There is no time scale. For each point in time, the values of each variable are plotted as a single point. For example, in Figure 2.5 the circled point was plotted for 1972: production, 214; imports, 39.

Figure 2.5 shows that there is a relationship between imports and production, because the points tend to form a path. The path slants downwards, indicating a negative relationship: when production rises, imports tend to fall, and vice versa. If there is a definite relationship between the variables, the points will form a definite path across the face of the diagram; if there is no relationship, there will be no path. If the relationship between the variables is perfect, the points form a perfect line. The greater the amount of 'scatter' of the points away from the main path, the less close is the relationship between the two variables.

If the path slants upwards from left to right, this shows that the relationship is positive – that is, both variables tend to rise and fall together. If the path slants downward, it shows a negative relationship – when one variable rises, the other tends to fall.

The first diagram shows a negative relationship between imports and production. There was considerable scatter, so the relationship was far from perfect; factors other than production were affecting imports.

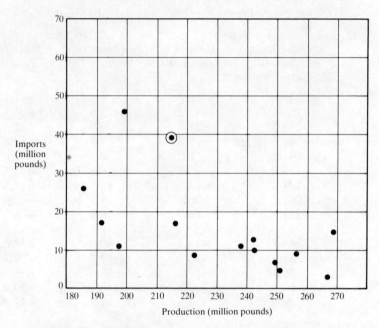

Figure 2.5 Relationship between U.S. Imports and Production of Honey
Source: *Commodity Yearbook*

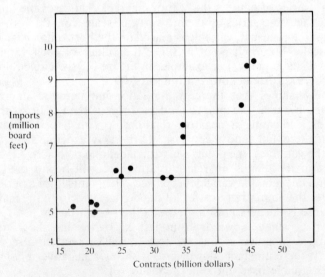

Figure 2.6 Relationship between Residential Construction Contracts awarded in U.S. and U.S. imports of sawmill products
Source: *Commodity Yearbook*

The scatter diagram (Figure 2.6) shows a closer relationship between two variables (there is less scatter). The relationship is positive (the path slants upwards). The diagram shows that U.S. imports of sawmill products are very sensitive to changes in construction activity: when construction increases, imports generally rise.

## 2.5 Export Market Research Audit

(A) *GENERAL INFORMATION*
(1) *The Target Country and its People*
    1.1   Economic Geography
       (i)  Area
      (ii)  Population (groups defined by race, religion, density, income, education, age and sex distribution, average annual rate of increase)
     (iii)  Languages (official, business, other indigenous languages)
     (iv)  Major commercial and industrial regions and centres (names and population concentration)
      (v)  Geography and climate (latitude and longitude, nature of terrain, daily mean maximum and minimum temperature, rainfall, humidity)

    1.2   Form and Nature of Government
       (i)  Type of constitution (monarchy, federation, republic)
      (ii)  Responsibilities of central and regional governments
     (iii)  Political climate
     (iv)  Economic and social policies

(2) *Basic Economic Data*
    2.1   Economic Indicators
       (i)  National currency, exchange rates and stability
      (ii)  Balance of payments, foreign currency reserves, debt situation
     (iii)  Gross national product
     (iv)  National and per capita income
      (v)  Consumer and wholesale price indices

    2.2   Present Structure of Economy
       (i)  Industrial origin of gross domestic products at current factor cost
      (ii)  Employment distribution
     (iii)  Output and nature of industrial sectors of commercial interest to your country, e.g. farm production, forestry, fisheries, livestock, mining, food processing industry, automotive industry, construction, public utilities

    2.3   Economic Development Plans
       (i)  Period involved and funds allocated
      (ii)  Target sectoral allocations and increases

    2.4   Foreign Investment Policy

    2.5   Budgetary Provisions

(3) *Transport and Communications Facilities*
   3.1  Sea
      (i) Main ports and port facilities
     (ii) Shipping services (from your country)

   3.2  Air
      (i) Airports for international traffic
     (ii) Airports for internal traffic
    (iii) Annual freight tonnages for each category
    (iv) Freight services (from your country)

   3.3  Road
      (i) Kilometres or miles of main transport routes
     (ii) Vehicles – cars, buses, trucks

   3.4  Rail
      (i) Kilometres or miles of track
     (ii) Freight tonnages carried
    (iii) Gauge

(4) *Foreign Trade Data (over a three-to-five-year period)*
   4.1  Total Foreign Trade
      (i) Total exports and imports
     (ii) Balance of trade
    (iii) Breakdown of imports by source of financing (exchange settlements, aid, other imports)

   4.2  Main Export Products
      (i) Products and values
     (ii) Countries of destination and values

   4.3  Main Import Products
      (i) Products and values
     (ii) Supplying countries and values

   4.4  Trade with Exporter's Country
      (i) Imports
     (ii) Exports

   4.5  Multi-lateral Trade Agreements

   4.6  Bilateral Trade Agreements between target country overseas and exporter's country
      (i) Products covered
     (ii) Services covered
    (iii) Duration and nature of Agreement
    (iv) Lines of Credit

   4.7  Long-term Loan Financing (IMF), IBRD, etc.
      (i) Capital projects involved
     (ii) Nature of financing
    (iii) Services (technology, consultancy, training)

(5) *Trading System*

| Nationalized | Semi-Nationalized | Private Sectors |
|---|---|---|
| (i) Controlling authority | (i) Controlling Ministry | (i) Concerned Ministry |
| (ii) Name of importing companies with their commodity/ territorial specialization | (ii) Government Monopolies | (ii) Government Monopolies |
| (iii) Payment Procedures | (iii) Public sector trading companies with their specialization | (iii) Federation of Associations and Chambers of Commerce, Major industry Associations, Major importers Associations |
| (iv) Agency requirements | (iv) Major private sector importing companies | (iv) Major importing companies |
| (v) Special points | (v) Payment procedures | (v) Major stockists/ Commission Agents Distributors |
| (vi) Special points | (vi) Agency requirements | (vi) Commodity produce exchanges |
| (vii) Special points | (vii) Special points | (vii) Department/ Chain Stores |

(B) *MARKET ACCESS*
(1) *General Import Policy*
    1.1   Membership in customs union or free trade area, GATT, etc.
    1.2   Special trade relationships

(2) *Import Licensing*
    2.1   Licence categories
    2.2   Basis of duty assessment
    2.3   Licensing procedures

(3) *Import Tariff System*
    3.1   Classification system (CCCN)
    3.2   Tariff rates
    3.3   Basis of duty assessment
    3.4   Basis of changes in tariff levels

(4) *Special Customs Provisions*
  4.1  Advance rulings on customs classifications
  4.2  Entry regulations and procedures
  4.3  Use of free ports and bonded warehouses
  4.4  Appeals and penalties
  4.5  Commercial samples, advertising matter and postal packages

(5) *Other Regulations and Factors Affecting Trade*
  5.1  Foreign exchange controls
     (i)  Licensing
     (ii)  Remittance of profits
     (iii)  Repatriation of capital
     (iv)  Convertibility of currency

  5.2  Import deposit and equalization schemes, etc.
  5.3  Anti-dumping and minimum-price regulations on imports
  5.4  Food, health, safety and quarantine regulations
  5.5  Marketing, packaging and labelling regulations
  5.6  Patents, trademarks and copyright
  5.7  Unfair competition and restrictive trade practices
  5.8  Taxation
  5.9  Official or unofficial boycotts
  5.10  Agency legislation
  5.11  Summary of shipping and other required documents

(C) *MARKET PROFILE*
(1) *Imports into Target Country*
  1.1  Statistics (table)
     (i)  Total imports, imports from your country, imports from individual major suppliers. For each of last five years, in quantitative and value terms
     (ii)  Percentage changes for each category over the five-year period
     (iii)  Average unit values (value divided by quantity) – if meaningful
     (iv)  Note any changes in system of recording; key for conversion to constant values; basis of values (CIF, etc.)

  1.2  Interpretation
     (i)  Indicate trends not related to above data
     (ii)  Relevance of statistics and trends to particular products of interest

(2) *Domestic Production in Target Country*
  2.1  Statistics (table)
     Annual production statistics for last five years, in quantitative and value terms

  2.2  Industry profile
     (i)  Principle production centres
     (ii)  Individual major producers, with market shares

(iii) Indicate any significant foreign control or affiliations
(iv) Significant trends in industrial structure, such as mergers, vertical integration

2.3 Production processes – Describe if significant to competitive situation

2.4 Production input factors
(i) Sources and availability of raw materials, parts and components, labour, transport
(ii) Costs of these factors relative to your own country's production costs (Note any direct or indirect subsidies)

2.5 Future production plans
(i) Production growth projections
(ii) Specific short- and long-term plans
(iii) Details of specific, important projects

(3) *Exports from Target Country*
3.1 Statistics (table)
(i) Annual export for last five years, total for each principal country of destination, in volume and value terms
(ii) Changes in system of recording; key for conversion to constant values; basis of values

3.2 Interpretation
(i) Trends not apparent from figures
(ii) Role of re-exports

3.3 Effect on market
(i) Relationship of exports to imports, including product differentiation between imports and exports and such factors as proximity to markets and special trading or business relationships
(ii) Outlook for exports and likely effect projected trends would have on domestic supply and demand picture

3.4 Incentives
Relevant export promotion incentives, export price subsidies, etc.

(4) *Consumption in Target Country*
4.1 Statistics (table)
(i) 'Consumption' (production plus imports minus exports), and if significant plus or minus changes in stock levels, for each of last five years. Express in both quantitative and value terms if possible
(ii) Average annual growth rate
(iii) Shares (%) of consumption accounted for by domestic production and by imports, latest year and five years ago
(iv) Future consumption growth trends (best available estimates)

    4.2   Forecast – Main factors that will affect consumption growth trend
      (i)  Size and growth of population and per capita income
     (ii)  Market penetration by substitute products
    (iii)  Growth rates of user industries (for industrial products)
    (iv)  Credit restrictions and other government policies
     (v)  Fashion and taste changes
    (vi)  Technological developments
   (vii)  Market saturation
  (viii)  Development plans

(5)  *Profiles of Major Competitors*
    5.1   Organization and trading policies
    5.2   Quality/availability of products/services
    5.3   Technical and financial resources
    5.4   Incentives, credit insurance and other assistance available from competitors' own government
    5.5   Overseas market position and prospects

**References**

1  Robinson, R. D. 'Challenge of the Underdeveloped National Market', *Proceedings of the American Marketing Association*, **25** (adapted) 1965.
2  Anon, *A Guide to the Commissioning of Survey Research* (Market Research Society: London) (adapted).
3  Weller, D. *Introduction to Export Market Research* (ITC/UNCTAD/GATT: Geneva, 1976) (adapted).

# 3. SETTING UP AND MANAGING EXPORT OPERATIONS

## 3.1 Export Markets in Aggregates and Segments

The basic classification of world markets in economic terms is traditionally broken down as shown in Table 3.1.

*Table 3.1*

|  | Industrialized Countries | Developing Countries | Less Developed Countries |
|---|---|---|---|
| Average annual GNP per capita | $6,980 | $1,140 | $300 |
| Annual Growth rate | 2.4 | 5.9 | 3.8 |
| % World's population | 32% | 53% | 15% |

Sources: World Bank Atlas and OECD, Paris. 1980

Some economists argue that in terms of long-term potential demand the prospects for some companies operating worldwide would seem to point to trade with developing and less developed countries. This is likely to apply particularly to the consumer goods sectors where the effects of price competition and economies of scale in production and distribution, will put goods such as household appliances, footwear, clothing and some leisure products within reach of more and more households. Worldwide potential for such products can be argued to be a function of the number of households, rather than income, and the less developed countries (LDCs) with 66% of world population should require special attention by companies in these sectors in their longer-term planning. What remains uncertain is the rate of economic growth of these countries, but there are certainly some, such as Nigeria, India, Indonesia, where, for example, there is already a growing penetration by manufacturers of portable but reliable TV sets.

Some precise account of the classification of countries by economic criteria is now required; for these are the aggregates of markets which should be known and studied by all companies selling overseas. LDC's and industrialized countries have been referred to, but further definition and elucidation are now given; these aggregates are classifications recognized by the OECD and ECE (U.N. Economic Commission for Europe):

(a) Industrialized Countries: U.S.A., U.K., Canada, West Germany, France, Italy, Belgium-Luxembourg, Netherlands, Switzerland, Sweden, Japan, Denmark, Norway, Finland, Austria;

(b) Semi-industrial: Australia, New Zealand, South Africa, U.S.S.R. and COMECON countries, Israel, India;
(c) Newly industrializing countries (NICs): Greece, Portugal, Spain, Turkey, Yugoslavia, Brazil, Mexico, Hong Kong, South Korea, Singapore, Taiwan;
(d) Developing countries other than NICs or LDCs (mostly primary producers);
(e) Less developed countries; landlocked and island countries recognized by U.N. economic commission as in need of special development aid, and having annual per capita GNP of less than $300.

Of course, these aggregates have not only economic significance: they require and repay some careful analysis by the management of exporting countries. The aggregates represent groups of countries at broadly similar and distinct stages of industrialization and market potential for consumer and industrial goods; these contain important implications for the exporter in market assessment and forward planning and these implications will shortly be made clear.

Meanwhile, certain inescapable anomalies in the make-up of these aggregates must at least be admitted and noted, even if they cannot be removed. The position of U.S.S.R. and Eastern Europe in this classification is unsatisfactory: it reflects the impossibility of finding accurate or realistic data about the size and value of their foreign trade; there are one or two COMECON countries fully industrialized such as Czechoslovakia (some reference to trading with COMECON countries is contained in Section 2.6). There is the highly affluent group of Middle East OPEC countries which are still funding massive programmes of industrialization, and these do not fit readily into the official classification; there are other countries officially classified Developing which have a well-developed industrial base selling in local markets, e.g. Pakistan, Thailand, India, Yugoslavia, Argentina, Chile and Cyprus. There are others, such as Indonesia, with vast resources and industrial potential but lacking capital and technology skills to develop these with their present organization. Again, the Republic of China is excluded from the classification which is absurd; this immense country is currently embarking on a massive programme of industrial modernization and the Chinese Government is looking to European suppliers to avoid any dependence on Russian or American technology (though there is again the problem of extracting accurate and realistic data).

Nevertheless, these aggregates of markets are sufficiently coherent in broad terms, to provide the management of the exporting company with sets of economic and business indicators which should be taken into account before and indeed, during, any process of market segmentation.

Aggregates (a) and (b), industrialized and semi-industrialized, are characterized by economic affluence, credit-based economy, mass application of technology but increasingly differentiated (even customized) products and services, a pervasive middle class, growing concern for quality of life, environment and conservation, accelerating rate of technical change and monopoly of high technology resources and skills. In the U.K. 40% of products available in 1980 were not even in the planning process in 1960. In the U.S.A., high technology involves interface with satellite industries where the technical skills are available already (e.g. California).

In the case of the NIC category (c), and a few others mentioned such as Pakistan and Yugoslavia, the principal characteristics are: a rapidly growing middle class, rising levels of consumption, limited applications of new technology, severe international debt problems (e.g. in South America), growing consumer orientation and limited product differentiation, self-sufficiency in cheap basic consumer goods, growing intra-regional trade; problem of transfer technology; market potential for financial and management services for technological products and processes, plant etc. needed in the industrialization process; also high-quality consumer goods.

The characteristics of developing countries and LDCs are broadly: shortage of skilled technicians and local managerial staff, dependence on production and exchange of commodities and produce, chronic shortage of foreign exchange (e.g. in Africa); market potential for capital projects, industrial goods and services in countries receiving development aid and financing from international agencies; some potential for mass-produced foods and household goods.

One further perspective on aggregates as markets is provided, of course, by the development and organization of regional economic communities. Whilst these common markets have been discussed at length in Section 1.3 because of their impact on international trading, it is appropriate at this point to view them purely from the standpoint of marketing. The salient points of common markets can be summarized in the following terms:

(a) Tariff-free movement of goods supplied within the market, facilitating competitive pricing;

(b) Market potential for industrial goods and services in sectors in receipt of regional development funds;

(c) Centralized purchasing (through economic or common secretariat) of agricultural machinery and industrial equipment essential to development of industrial base, particularly in South America;

(d) Funding of capital projects such as harbours, steel mills, oil exploration platforms and plant etc. which create substantial derived demand for a wide range of goods and services;

(e) Bilateral trade agreements between one common market and another trading bloc, with preferential entry for goods supplied from those countries, and often with the provision of lines of credit for exporters;

(f) Economies of scale in manufacturing, distribution and design. For example, a manufacturer of home care products closed down eight national production sources in Europe soon after the E.E.C. was formed. The company concentrated its European manufacturing in the Netherlands to gain economies of scale by standardizing its package designs, sizes and colours (with copy in different national languages).

Detailed statistical analyses of the volume and value of foreign trade are provided by the World Bank and U.S. Department of Commerce, and whilst these do not adhere in every respect to the classifications so far used here, they do provide some accurate measurements for aggregates and countries. These analyses are contained in Tables 3.2–3.7.

*Table 3.2*
**Differences in Consumption Behaviour on Major Consumer Expenditures:**
**Six Common Market Countries (Percentage Ownership)**

| Expenditure Item | Belgium | France | Germany | U.K. | Italy | Netherlands |
|---|---|---|---|---|---|---|
| Automatic washer | 39 | 46 | 59 | 25 | 67 | 53 |
| Freezer | 22 | 13 | 31 | 26 | 25 | 24 |
| Colour TV | 15 | 17 | 28 | 34 | 2 | 38 |
| Vacuum cleaner | 69 | 76 | 90 | 89 | 29 | 99 |
| Dishwasher | 7 | 6 | 6 | 4 | 10 | 7 |
| Food mixer | 70 | 66 | 66 | 36 | 37 | 70 |
| Central heating | 33 | 44 | 48 | 42 | 27 | 35 |
| Holiday abroad | 31 | 19 | 43 | 24 | 11 | 34 |

Source: *Consumer Europe* (Euromonitor Publications: London, 1976).

*Table 3.3*
**Free World Exports\*. Comparison of Market Share 1970 and 1979 –**
**Developed and Developing Countries**

| | | Developed Countries | | | Developing Countries | | |
|---|---|---|---|---|---|---|---|
| Year | Total | U.S.A. and Canada | W. Europe† | Other | Total | OPEC‡ | Other |
| 1970 | 81% | 21% | 50% | 10% | 19% | 6% | 13% |
| 1979 | 73% | 16% | 47% | 10% | 27% | 14% | 13% |

\* Free world includes all countries except Albania, Bulgaria, Czechoslovakia, German Democratic Republic, Hungary, Poland, Romania, U.S.S.R., People's Republic of China, North Korea, Vietnam, Outer Mongolia, and Cuba.
† Western Europe includes the E.E.C. countries – Belgium, Denmark, France, Germany, Ireland, Italy, Luxembourg, Netherlands, Greece and U.K. – plus Austria, Norway, Sweden, and Switzerland and Finland. Other includes all other developed countries, the most important being Japan, Australia and New Zealand.
‡ OPEC includes Algeria, Ecuador, Gabon, Indonesia, Iraq, Iran, Kuwait, Libya, Nigeria, Qatar, Saudi Arabia, United Arab Emirates, and Venezuela. Other includes all non-OPEC countries.

## Table 3.4
### Trends in Composition of World Trade

|  | 1963 | 1973 | 1979 |
|---|---|---|---|
| Exports (billion dollars) | 155 | 574 | 1,625 |
| *Percentage Share* |  |  |  |
| Agricultural products | 29 | 23 | 16 |
| Fuels | 10 | 11 | 20 |
| Minerals | 6 | 6 | 4 |
| Manufactured | 52 | 61 | 58 |

## Table 3.5
### World Exports by Aggregates 1963, 1979 (percentage of total)

| Exports from | | Industrial Areas | Exports to Developing Countries Oil Exporters | Developing Countries Others | Eastern Bloc | World |
|---|---|---|---|---|---|---|
| Industrial | 1963 | 45.1 | 2.5 | 11.7 | 2.3 | 64.0 |
| Areas | 1979 | 45.2 | 4.7 | 9.3 | 3.2 | 63.7 |
| Oil Exporters | 1963 | 4.3 | 0.0 | 1.3 | 0.1 | 5.9 |
|  | 1979 | 9.6 | 0.2 | 2.7 | 0.2 | 12.8 |
| Other Developing | 1963 | 10.2 | 0.3 | 2.8 | 1.0 | 14.6 |
| Countries | 1979 | 8.1 | 0.7 | 2.5 | 0.7 | 12.2 |
| Eastern Bloc | 1963 | 2.3 | 0.1 | 1.7 | 8.0 | 12.1 |
|  | 1979 | 2.8 | 0.4 | 1.2 | 4.8 | 9.2 |

Source: GATT

## Table 3.6
### Basic Socio-Economic Indicators[1]

|  | Population (millions) | Adult Literacy Rate | Life Expectancy at birth | Distribution of GNP Agriculture | Industry | Service |
|---|---|---|---|---|---|---|
| Industrialized Countries | 663.4 | 99% | 74 | 4% | 31% | 59% |
| Developing Countries | 901.2 | 69% | 60 | 15% | 36% | 49% |
| Less Developed Countries | 1,259.9 | 36% | 50 | 31% | 25% | 38% |

*Table 3.7*
*Per Capita GNP by Major Regions*[2]

| Region/Country | GNP Per Capita 1978 |
|---|---|
| North America | $9,660 |
| Japan | 7,700 |
| Oceania | 6,230 |
| Europe, excluding U.S.S.R. | 5,680 |
| U.S.S.R. | 3,700 |
| Middle East | 3,120 |
| South America | 1,470 |
| Central America | 1,260 |
| Africa | 560 |
| Asia, excluding Japan and Middle East | 280 |

A basic matrix showing a possible selection of market aggregates is given in Figure 3.1.

| Market Aggregates \ Product Configuration | Standard Product | More Sophisticated Product | More Basic Product |
|---|---|---|---|
| Industrial countres | | | |
| Semi industrialized countries | | | |
| New industrializing countries | | | |
| Developing countries | | | |
| Less developed countries | | | |

Figure 3.1

A more detailed matrix showing market characteristics is contained in the Figure 3.2. This analysis of aggregates leads, of course, directly to consideration of market assessment and a typology of markets which puts the focus on segments of the total market which are differentiated and within which demand is demonstrably homogeneous. It is not only the total market represented by a country or a group of countries, which the company should consider; it is the structure of sub-markets within this totality where promotion, selling and service should be targeted.

Particular reference should be made at this point to the segmentation of overseas markets by:

(a) Product life cycle (covered in Section 3.3);
(b) Socio-economic, cultural and other groups which have been identified and analysed in depth in Chapter 4, particularly in Section 4.1 on market ecology. These segments can be illustrated graphically as shown in Figure 3.3.

In consumer goods marketing, particularly, increasing use is made in market segmentation of 'psycho-graphic' characteristics of buyers. These include:

(a) Heavy, medium and light users. (It is known through research, for example, that heavy users of imported foreign products are much more defensive than users of similar domestic products);
(b) Types of shoppers (high search versus low search);
(c) Mobile and relatively immobile consumers;
(d) Perceived priorities of spending (e.g. holidays versus furniture);
(e) Motivations (e.g. status, security, esteem, belongingness);
(f) Attitudes (membership of reference groups);
(g) Persuasibility (word of mouth) recommendation, influence of peers, advertising effectiveness;
(h) Adoption process (innovators versus late adopters, the influence of opinion leaders such as international business executives on consumption patterns);
(i) Membership and reference groups;
(j) Other psychological factors ('inner and outer directed' consumers on which some important new research has been done in U.S.A.)

In the industrial goods, segmentation should be applied by:

(a) Industrial user segments (e.g. original equipment manufacturing (OEM) 'after markets')
(b) Institutional user segments (scientific laboratories, government departments, military)
(c) Technical applications in different segments of industry (e.g. fireproof, waterproof, dustproof and noiseless electrical machinery)
(d) Segments of purchasing influence (e.g. insurance companies for firefighting and security equipment, design companies for new furnishing and construction companies, political/military segments).

It is worth recalling too, that market segmentation is not just a theoretical concept: it has practical applications in many overseas markets which can be illustrated. The concept itself is shown in Figure 3.4.
One early but authoritative study[3] showed the applications of segmentation to the watch market in U.S.A. were three distinct segments emerged:

(a) Approximately 23% of the buyers bought the lowest-priced watch that would work
(b) Another 46% bought for durability and general product quality
(c) And 31% bought watches as presents and as a symbol of some important occasion.

| Characteristics | Market Aggregates | | | | |
|---|---|---|---|---|---|
| | Industrialized Countries | Semi Industrialized Countries | Newly Industrialized Countries | Developing Countries | Less Developed Countries |
| Currency Restrictions | | | | | |
| Political Status | | | | | |
| Legal Restrictions | | | | | |
| Different Competitive Practices | | | | | |
| Transportation Modes | | | | | |
| Cultural Problems | | | | | |
| Difficult Physical Environment | | | | | |
| Per Capita Incomes | | | | | |
| Levels of Technology | | | | | |
| Trade Structure | | | | | |
| Organization of Advertising Research Agencies | | | | | |
| Structure of Mass Media | | | | | |

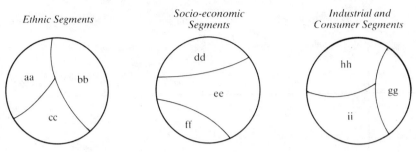

Figure 3.3  Structure of Segments of a Market

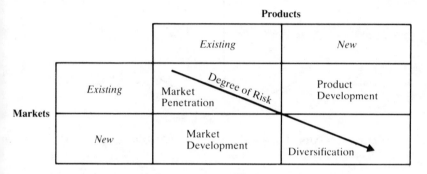

Figure 3.4  Product/Market Matrix
Source: H. Igor Anshott *Strategies for Diversification* Harvard University Press, 1963

What is often overlooked in this research is that the three principal income groups (high, medium and low) who bought the watches did not all match the expected segments i.e. research found that a higher proportion of the low-income groups bought the most expensive watches for special events than did the middle-income group, and so on.

The applications of market segmentation, therefore, are particularly crucial to overseas markets, where identifiable differences of income, culture, social status and attitudes, whilst sometimes presenting obstacles to selling, can, with correct forward planning and adaptation, be used as market opportunities. But understanding is not enough: it must be put into action, and in the complex conditions of overseas markets, this can most effectively be done by 'morphological analysis', i.e. putting markets into three dimensions in order to identify those 'cells' which offer the most sales potential. Accordingly, this morphological analysis is illustrated in Figures 3.5–3.8 (morphology is a scientific term meaning structure, and the analysis is concerned with the relationships among all the cells in multi-dimensional matrix). In each matrix there are $5 \times 3 \times 4 = 60$ cells each representing an actual or potential segment of the market. A particular cell is highlighted

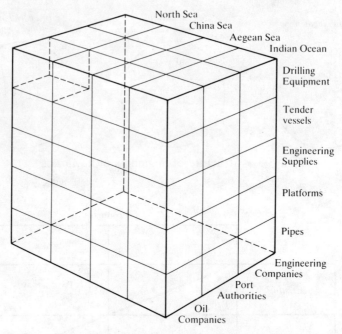

Figure 3.5 Morphological Analysis of off-shore oil industry

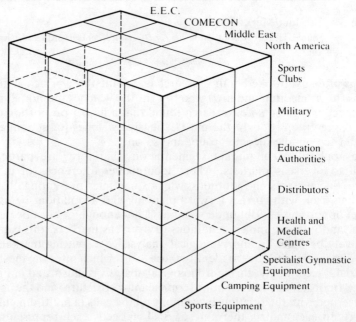

Figure 3.6 Morphological Analysis of Sports and Leisurewear

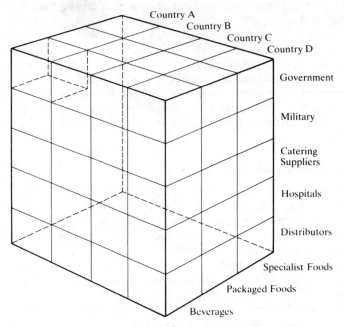

Figure 3.7 Morphological Analysis for Food and Beverages

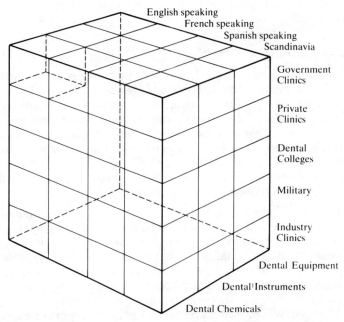

Figure 3.8 Morphological Analysis of Dental Supplies

in each figure to represent a segment of special interest (this is illustrative only) and figures are drawn from a selection of industries.

The significance of this morphology is that it focusses the attention of management on each segment of the market, actual and potential, throughout and after the planning process (see Section 3.4). In this way, the sales performance and potential of the market can be built up, segment by segment, in a logical, planned way. Without this, promotional methods cannot be targeted cost-effectively, nor the overseas sales force deployed productively, nor time and resources spent on and in the most lucrative segments.

## 3.2 Export Marketing Planning

Every manager must be aware of the applications and implications of the planning process; that the culmination of any plan must be action and control to develop export markets within clear guidelines and to specific objectives. To plan means to think ahead, to relate the known facts or problems of the present to the possibilities or probabilities of the future. Planning implies the ability to visualize future processes or situations or the ability to imagine what needs to be done to bring about a desired future situation.

Planning is the basis for a company's activities and determines how its resources – capital, equipment, manpower – are allocated in order to achieve certain aims or objectives. More specifically, planning involves four phases: situation analysis, both internal and external; setting objectives and goals; programming operations; export marketing evaluation and control.

### 3.21 Situation Analysis

Situation analysis is an investigation of the company's present situation, of its existing products, organization and markets and of its available resources (financial position, production capacity and technology, manpower and experience). In addition, the situation analysis covers external factors such as changes in existing markets, the appearance of new markets, changes in technology and in the use of the company's products. It is a very detailed answer to the question: 'Where do we stand now and what business are we in?'. Sometimes the situation analysis leads to a 'business definition' covering three main points:

  (a) Products: Which product or products does the company now manufacture and market, what technology and equipment is used in production, what is the production capacity – both in terms of quantity and of quality – what is the construction, design and composition of the product(s), are the products 'competitive' or do they have defects or deficiences not found in products of other companies serving the same markets?
  (b) Markets: Where – in domestic and possibly export markets – and how – through which distribution channels – are the company's

products now being sold? How strong is the company's market position (market share) in each market? Are there any changes now occurring or foreseeable which will influence the company's market position in the future?

(c) Company—Position and Resources: What is the company's sales volume (by products and by markets), how profitable are these sales and is their trend upwards, downwards or static? To what extent is its production capacity utilized? Does the company have capital reserves available for expansion or can capital be obtained for expansion if needed? Is the company's organization and manpower adequate to handle the current business and possible growth?

## 3.22 Setting Objectives and Goals

Once a full analysis of the current state of the business has been made, it will be possible to decide what objectives and goals should be pursued. The situation analysis or business definition has provided answers to the question 'What are we doing now and where do we stand?'; objectives or goals indicate where the company should be going in the future.

Although one might think that every company knows exactly where it is going, the fact is that only very few have a clear idea of their objectives and fewer still have even made an effort to determine in writing what their objectives should be short-term, long-term, in general or specifically. Many also confuse intentions with objectives. A statement declaring that the company 'plans to export', is not an objective suitable to guide planning but merely an indication of a wish or a desire.

Objectives or goals should be written down, as clearly, completely and specifically as possible. A statement of objectives useful for planning and guiding a company's activities and commitments should include these points:

(a) Product(s): Does the company propose to continue making and marketing its current products or will new or modified products be introduced? (A company about to begin exporting will almost inevitably have to modify or adapt its products if its effort is to succeed.)

(b) Market(s): Will the company continue to serve its existing markets (either domestic or foreign or both) or is the aim expansion into new markets – i.e. new countries and/or new areas of demand?

(c) Sales and Profit Goals: What sales volume and profitability does the company want to achieve in the near (1 to 3 years) and in the more distant (over 3 years) future? What market position or 'market share' does the company aim for in its existing and/or new markets?

Note that the statement of objectives is only concerned with end results, but not with the ways and means to achieve these end results: selecting and deciding on ways and means or 'strategy' is the concern of the following planning phase, programming.

Before a statement of objectives can be adopted, however, it must be checked for its validity: the question to ask is whether the objectives stated are sensible, realistic and attainable, given the company's situation and resources. There is obviously no point in setting objectives which are so ambitious that they cannot be attained with the resources available, just as there is no point in objectives which do not fully use the company's potential.

Assessing the validity of objectives and goals is especially critical in export marketing because:

(a)  Too ambitious export objectives may put such a strain on the company's resources and organization that its domestic business suffers and the entire future of the company could be in danger;
(b)  The situation in export markets often changes rapidly and unpredictably as the result of fluctuations, devaluations in rates of exchange, new import regulations or sudden changes in demand.

Specific questions to probe the validity of objectives and goals before they are adopted and become the base for further planning work are:

(a)  Are the existing strengths of the company being used fully?;
(b)  Are weaknesses taken into account realistically or are they being overcome?
(c)  Are the resources required to achieve the objectives available or can they be obtained at acceptable cost?;
(d)  Are the objectives such that they will not put undue strain on the company's existing activities?;
(e)  Are the objectives in line with national export promotion policies?;
(f)  Is there an assurance that government or other outside assistance needed to reach the objectives will be forthcoming?;
(g)  Are the objectives and especially the sales and profit goals realistic and achievable?
(h)  How reliable, complete and up-to-date is the information – especially the market information – on which the objectives are based?;
(i)  Are the objectives stated clearly and not likely to create misunderstandings or differing interpretations?;
(j)  Are the objectives consistent with the company's overall aims or is there any risk that they will create controversies between different departments in the company?

### 3.23 Programming Marketing Operations

Planning work in this phase is concerned with three main areas of decision: selecting those marketing activities which are thought to be best suited to achieve the marketing objectives or in other words, deciding on the specific 'marketing mix' or the 'marketing strategy' that will be used. (Very often the term 'marketing mix' and 'marketing strategy' are used interchangeably to describe the marketing activities of a company. Sometimes a distinction is made between the two: 'marketing strategy' indicates the aims of the marketing effort, 'marketing mix' describes the marketing effort or marketing activities.) This naturally leads to establishing individual strategies for product, distribution, advertising/promotion and pricing and to the 'Plan of Operations'.

The second area of decisions involves the timing and the sequence of the activities to be undertaken. A time schedule is established and incorporated into the plan of operation.

Finally, decisions about the allocation of resources – budget, manpower, production capacity, materials etc. – and about the specific contributions and responsibilities of the different departments of the company and of those outside – distributors, advertising agents etc. – have to be made.

The Export Marketing Plan is the main planning instrument. Ideally, it should be in the form of a written document containing:

(a) Basic market data;
(b) Clear statements about the objectives and aims to be achieved;
(c) A description of all the measures and activities planned to reach these aims; and
(d) Budgets and time plans.

The responsibility for writing the plan will most likely be that of the exporting firm or its marketing consultant. Both should be able to bring to bear their general knowledge of marketing techniques and their specialized experience in a given market. In any event, responsibility for preparing the marketing plan should be assigned to the man or the organization best suited for the job; but the final authority for approving the plan and authorizing its execution remains with the exporting company's managers.

There are several sound reasons for going to the sometimes considerable effort involved in working out a written marketing plan. The first reason is the need for information: many people are involved in executing the plan. Someone is responsible for producing the product in the required quantities; aims and objectives set by the plan must be realistic rather than merely wishful thinking and different objectives must be related to each other rather than be at cross-purposes; they must be given weight in accordance with their true importance. Lastly, it demands that the measures and means proposed must be adequate to meet the objectives. If this is not the case, scaling down the aims to realistic levels or using different means is the only alternative.

The main steps in working a Marketing Plan can be visualized as follows.

*Fact Finding*
The first stage in developing a marketing plan is concerned with finding out as much as possible about the market, the product, the distribution, the consumers. Limitations at this stage are immediately apparent: it will not be possible to get all the facts – that would be too costly and time consuming. Also, some of the facts and figures found will be more important and pertinent than others. At this stage, therefore, completeness is less important in itself than the ability to look for and find those elements which are decisive for the subsequent stages of drawing up the plan.

Another aspect of fact finding is qualitative in nature: there is always the danger that information obtained is taken at 'face value', or worse even, opinions are taken as fact. To avoid the obvious risks of basing a plan on wrong data and unverified opinions, there should be a conscious effort at this stage to ensure reliability through verification, cross-checks and in general, a healthy scepticism. Fact finding would cover these points (see Figure 3.9).

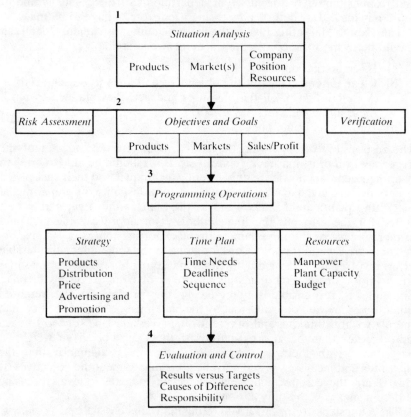

Figure 3.9  Marketing Planning Steps

(a)  Product. Characteristics and advantages/benefits, quality in relation to competition, cost and prices and price structures, packaging and package design, alternatives and substitutes, new technical developments.

(b)  Market. Size of the total market, market trends, seasonal variations and regional differences, shares held by the different brands and manufacturers and significant changes in these.

(c)  Distribution and Distribution Channels. Types of distributors, retailers selling the product and their relative importance, turnover ratios and stock levels in different types of outlets, frequency of 'out of stocks' situations. Importance of wholesalers, brokers, buying associations, etc. Strength of own and competing sales organizations. Transportation facilities (overseas and inland) and transport cost.

(d) Consumers and Users – Habits and Attitudes. Who are the consumers (age, sex, income group, city/rural etc.), when, how frequently and where do they buy? How do they use the product, why do they buy it and what do they think of its quality and benefits? How well known is the brand name and how well is its advertising recalled?

(e) Competitors. Who are they, which products do they market? What are their areas of strength? (Price, quality, distribution, advertising). Have new products been introduced lately and with what success?

(f) Import Rules and Regulations. Customs duties and taxes, quotas and licences, product standards, packaging requirements, trademarks and labelling.

(g) Prior Marketing Activities and Results. This is a summary of the preceding marketing plan, its objectives and the activities undertaken, and an assessment of the results achieved.

*Evaluation of Facts*

Once all the relevant facts are in hand, verified and found to be correct, they have to be put into perspective, to be weighed according to their relative importance and to be translated into a realistic assessment of the market potential of the product in question; the pricing levels and the problems and possibilities in the distribution area, the possibilities of advertising and sales promotion at different expenditure levels are identified and evaluated. It is important to realize that the following steps can be meaningful only if at the evaluation stage all facts, whether favourable or not, are looked at objectively. Areas of opportunity are usually readily apparent while finding weaknesses and 'problem areas' may be more laborious, but the additional effort is needed and will be justified later on.

*Future developments*

Fact finding and evaluation primarily deal with the past, establishing what the market is, who the competitors are, etc. The marketing plan however, will operate in the future, and therefore it is important that, in analysing problems and opportunities and in assigning priorities to them, realistic assumptions as to future developments are made.

Such assumptions and forecasts will concern the total market development, changes in market shares, consumer attitudes, distribution patterns, competition, price levels, etc. Very often, existing trends will continue and the forecasting is a relatively simple matter. More difficult to assess, and more dangerous to the success of the plan if overlooked, are those future developments which are not readily discernible from existing trends.

Determining marketing objectives or marketing goals means that clear and concise decisions must be formulated as to what the marketing effort – the product's design and packaging, pricing, distribution, advertising and sales promotion – should accomplish. The emphasis is on aims and purposes rather than on ways and means. The need for clearly separating aims and methods or 'objectives' and 'strategies' is evident: it is not really possible to agree on a plan of action before the aim of the action is defined.

It is useful in practice to distinguish between long-term and short-term objectives. A long-term objective is a broad aim, a desired end result which need not be quantified and related to a time period. Thus, 'market dominance' or 'increasing sales and profits' are long-term objectives. In contrast, short-term objectives need to be both quantified and given a time-scale. To 'increase sales by 15% in 1983' is a short-term objective.

Furthermore, there must be a clear distinction between general marketing objectives on the one hand and specific objectives for advertising, product design and packaging, distribution and sales, etc. on the other hand. This distinction is critical for a number of reasons: firstly, each marketing instrument – such as sales, advertising, product design, etc. – has a definite place and function within the total marketing mix, it can accomplish certain things that the other instruments cannot accomplish. Secondly, without specific objectives and measurable tasks for each of them, how will it be possible to tell whether the increase or decrease in sales is attributable to advertising, to product improvement, to a better selling effort, to price changes, etc? To ensure that results achieved can be measured and attributed to the element of the marketing mix which caused them – or failed to cause them – these specific objectives need to be stated in 'short-term' language, i.e. specific as to time and to degree. Thus, a proper advertising objective would be 'to increase consumer awareness of the product from 25 per cent to 40 per cent this year' rather than 'to communicate the idea that the product tastes better than its competitors'. Little will be gained by setting aims so high that achieving them is virtually impossible within the time period covered by the plan and with the means available.

In order that this relationship between objectives and proposed action is clearly visible for all concerned, the Plan of Action sections of the marketing plan document should have a separate chapter for each objective outlined in the preceding 'Marketing Objectives' section. The following principles help to ensure that the objectives stated govern the selection of activities:

(a) Concentration. It is dangerous to waste time and resources by planning too many activities, each of which creates the need for additional expenses, staff administration and control. It is much better to plan only a limited number of activities – and to choose those that promise the greatest effect.

(b) Magnitude. In deciding which activities to concentrate on, look to the potential results, not the size of the task. Do not waste time and money on activities which, even if successful, would have limited results. There are usually one or two problems whose solution would bring more results than all others combined. Select activities which will offer maximum return; a careful study of the 'Pareto' effect (the '80–20' principle) is important at this particular stage of planning.

(c) Adequacy. Any force must be proportionate to the job it is to do. There is an irreducible minimum required to carry out most marketing activities. If that minimum in resources is not available it would be better to concentrate on other activities that can be undertaken within the limits of the budget.

(d) Compare alternatives. In selecting activities careful consideration should be given to the relative costs versus the prospective results that can be obtained by various methods. To do so, these questions need to be asked:

What alternative activities can be used?

What is the cost of each alternative?

What is the size of the anticipated results from each alternative?

*Plan of Action Budget and Time Schedule*

Once the 'what' of the plan has been established in general terms – long-term and short-term marketing objectives – and specifically – product design and packaging objectives, sales and distribution objectives, advertising – it is necessary to determine how these objectives will be met. The key principle in selecting and deciding on marketing activities in the different areas is that the objective must govern the means, that no activity can be justified unless it is clearly and demonstrably related to the accomplishment of an objective.

From the description of the plan with all its details a budget needs to be developed covering in as much detail as possible all the expenditures necessary for the execution of the plan.

There are several methods to determine marketing budgets, each with its own advantages and disadvantages. More often than not the size of the budget, the sum of money available for different kinds of marketing activities is a management decision and hence a given fact for the marketing planning work. Furthermore, there is very rarely a true 'marketing budget' covering all facets of the marketing mix from product and package design through distribution to advertising and sales promotion plus marketing research and testing. There are in modern corporations budgets for all these activities, but typically the product design budget and sometimes the package design budget as well are part of a manufacturing budget and thus not under the control of the marketing department. Similarly, the sales and distribution budgets are under the control of the sales department. But the fact that these budgets are not always under the control of the marketing department does not mean that the corresponding activities should not form part of the marketing plan.

In writing up a budget as a part of a marketing plan certain ground rules apply. Their importance goes beyond the need to make the budget document clearly understandable and useful for the marketing man, the salesman, the advertiser and the accountant:

(a) Reference to objectives: Any given marketing activity is the result of a specific objective set out in the marketing plan; sometimes several activities serve one objective – or one activity may correspond to more than one objective. At any rate, showing activities and their objective helps to call attention to the priorities previously established – and shows how these priorities are being observed.

(b) Specification and Cost Detail. Indicating how the total cost for a given activity is arrived at helps two ways: firstly, the budget becomes more readily understandable to those who have to approve it, there are fewer questions of detail that remain unanswered. Secondly, budget adjustments that may become necessary at a later date are more quickly and easily effected if sufficient details are indicated.

(c) Spending Plan. It shows not just when the money will be spent but establishes the link between a detailed month-by-month sales forecast and the advertising and promotion activities planned.

*Control and Evaluation*
The final but crucial step in planning is control and evaluation. Whether a marketing plan is an effective one may be known only once it is put into operation and has had a chance to run for some time. But, unfortunately, even a well-thought-out plan may run into difficulties because the situation in the market has changed since it was originally worked out. In any event, it is necessary to set up a mechanism which permits the comparison of actual performance with planned performance throughout the planning period. If the proper controls are carried out regularly and start as early as possible in the plan period, adjustments and changes which become necessary can be made more effectively and at less cost.

Obviously, it makes little sense to have a plan with neatly quantified objectives and aims only to neglect the comparing of the actual results. Even though this is recognized, many otherwise excellent marketing plans omit to plan for controls from the start. Control and follow-up are therefore dealt with in more depth in Section 3.7.

There should be a mid-year comprehensive review of the state of the business not only for the purpose of modifying the current plan if needed, but also to act as a guide to the following year's plan. Sales can be only one yardstick for determining a plan's effectiveness or lack of it. In addition to regular sales reporting there should be specific controls for each individual activity proposed in the plan. Thus, the regular measurement of distribution effectiveness and distribution intensity should be included, together with procedures for measuring the penetration and effectiveness of advertising. In practice, the plan of operation in itself will dictate the controls which have to be instituted. Plan control and plan reviews thus serve a dual purpose: they enable corrections to be made in cost, advertising, spending and distribution efforts, throughout the planning period, and also supply additional raw material, as it were, for the preparation of the subsequent plan. Schematic illustrations of the export marketing planning process in action are contained in Figures 3.10 and 3.11.

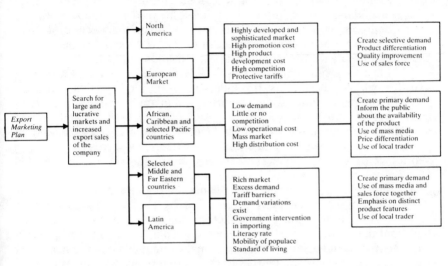

Figure 3.10  Schematic Illustration of Export Marketing Plan

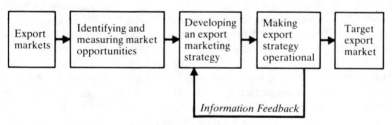

Figure 3.11  Strategic Export Plan
Source: Root, F. R. *Strategic Planning for Export Marketing* (International Textbook Company, New York, 1966, (Adapted).

## 3.3 Product Design and Development

Product innovation and design, by internal development, acquisition, licensing or other method, is a significant part of the marketing mix, and is clearly related to the extent of price and non-price competition discussed in Section 3.4. Much research and analysis have been undertaken on product policy and the product life cycle (this latter aspect is mentioned in Section

5.6 in relation to advertising). Further, there is also a direct relationship between product policy and market segmentation since it is often the policy of management, particularly in multi-national corporations, to segment the total world market according to the positioning of the product in the life cycle in different countries. An industrial product on the 'decline' stage in North America, for instance, can be on the 'growth' stage in developing countries entering the first phase of industrialization: indeed, an unsophisticated industrial product may be more cost-effective in countries with poor logistics and low labour costs. It should not be inferred from this, however, that product innovation and development are in any way the monopoly of large, well-resourced corporations. A small metal working and vehicle assembly company in the British Midlands for instance, has produced an armoured Land Rover, aimed specifically at security forces in the Third World, at prices these governments can afford (a security service and training programme to go with it is also being developed).

Another highly apt example of segmentation of overseas markets according to the product life cycle is provided by the household appliance industry. If one looks at the past market for hand clothes mangles in UK one finds that due to the ownership of electric washing machines, this product has reached the end of its life. However, in the mid 1960s, a manufacturer of various consumer durable items in Portsmouth produced a miniature mangle primarily for the caravanning and holiday market in the United Kingdom. This innovation created a new life cycle for such a product. However, this product did not last long and did not give sufficient quantity to the manufacturer to warrant further investment in the U.K. However, the manufacturer looked at other world markets for similar products and found that in South America and particularly Argentina and Brazil, there were no less than 60,000,000 women whose only method of washing clothes was by hand, and no appliances were in use. Consequently, he was able to market that product very successfully in Argentina, Brazil and other South American markets. These markets proved attainable, accessible, had the ability to afford such a product, which did not contravene any religious or cultural practices within these countries, and was developed profitably.

The promotional problems in respect of this product were relatively simple. No adjustments were required to the product, under test conditions, minor adjustments enabled the product to be used in 'bush' situations, and the introduction of that product to the market only required the use of local press media, aimed particularly at the trade. There was, at that time, a shortage of such products in that market, and consequently the middle men at both wholesale and retail level were very happy to take on such a product for their market.

There is also the vital point that a carefully differentiated product remains a very powerful competitive weapon. For example, the personal computer of Sinclair Company penetrated the Japanese market through reputation and uniqueness; another industrial company has developed an electrical probe for fine measurement, more accurate than any other on the market: this U.K. company's workforce grew from 5 to 150 in six years, and 85% of its sales are in export markets.

The basic question facing management is one of product policy, and particularly innovation, and standardization or adaptation. Whilst these policy matters are further, and appropriately, explored in Section 3.7 dealing with the marketing mix, some aspects of product management require discussion now as, of course, the whole process of design and product planning rests on policy decisions. The most important of course, is whether the company should design a product which is standard for all markets or should it match the product to the special needs and nuances of each market? And it has a very practical importance in relation to the product itself. The decision taken at the product design stage can determine the pattern of the firm's marketing effort for many years to come. A mistake at this early stage can make a major difference to the firm's fortunes. Whilst it is always very tempting to seek to standardize the product, as every international businessman knows, it is not always possible to do so. On the other hand, as a general rule, to differentiate where market conditions allow for total or partial standardization is certainly a very extravagant policy. For Kodak to differentiate its range of 'instamatic' cameras in different parts of the world would be a policy of indescribable wastage. At the same time it is difficult to see how a typewriter manufacturer can afford not to differentiate, in order to accommodate the special needs of language and script variations in different countries. It is unlikely that a typewriter that contains Germanic letters only will gain popularity in the French market.

The advantages of product standardization can be summarized as follows:

(a) Economies of scale in production, stock control and servicing policies can be quite significant;
(b) Product standardization is an essential forerunner to the wider aim of developing a marketing mix standardization. Without a standard product the other ingredients of the mix do not lend themselves to such a policy;
(c) The chances of attaining a rapid investment recovery are greatly enhanced where a standard product exists throughout the world;
(d) A firm that markets standard products internationally is invariably an easier company to manage both in terms of organization and control procedures. This is of course quite an attractive attribute to aim for.

On the other hand, it is relevant to mention a number of disadvantages that a standardization strategy entails:

(a) Marketing flexibility is often lost in foreign markets through an inadequacy to match the product to detailed local requirements;
(b) Standardization often discourages creativity and innovation especially among personnel of local companies (as their main role is to sell effectively they gradually lose the motivation to contribute ideas to product improvement and innovation);
(c) Linked with (b), one often finds that personnel in foreign

subsidiaries tend to seek their fortunes in other companies where total marketing jurisdiction including product design is possible.

These points must not be overlooked when planning a new product for overseas markets. The ultimate product decision may indeed, on occasions, be based on considerations of company resources and organization, not just on marketing; for example, if the quality of the organization will suffer as a result of a radical standardization policy the management at the decision point must be fully cognisant of the indirect implications before taking such a step.

One other major policy aspect is the provision of resources for developing and designing new products to maintain a competitive and broadly based product range. This highlights the difference between invention and innovation, particularly in technical products and industrial equipment etc. It is one thing to invent a new technical process, quite another to bring it to the market as a commercial proposition. So often, the design function can act as the link between invention and innovation in the market; if it is set up by management not only to be creative, but to be market-responsive. Indeed, many products are largely bought on the basis of design: fashionwear, glass, wall coverings, china, carpets, etc. There are also, of course, many companies worldwide which have secured a high reputation for design, and this has undoubtedly created a favourable image and allowed them to increase their sales in selected markets. Illustrations of this reputation for good design can be drawn from Danish furniture manufacturers, Italian leatherwork companies, British china manufacturers, Ford Motor Company, German food machinery and packaging manufacturers: consistent investment in new designs and in developing design management have brought about high reputations and business success.

Allied International Designers researched[4] a complete re-design for Ever-Ready Company (now Berec) of a lamp for motorists, with impressive results. This research project repays some further attention. The old lamp for motorists, was a solid square object designed originally to take a square battery. The designers could certainly have re-styled that, by changing the colour, altering the handle and so on; the square batteries were not widely available, particularly in overseas markets, and because the lamp itself was bulky, it was difficult to keep and was usually damaged by being knocked about in the car boot. New, foreign products, cheaper and more compact, were beginning to take sales from the manufacturer. What the designer did was first to redesign the lamp to take ordinary batteries available everywhere. Second, at the expense of the swivelling beam, they made the lamp flat so that now it can be kept in a glove compartment and, as an added attraction, the handle has been made to move to form variable legs. Third, they simplified the manufacturing process to attack costs. The old lamp had 72 parts and 49 assembly operations. The new lamp has half the number of parts and only 28 assembly operations. It costs 25% less to make and, even with an improved profit margin, it meets the price of comparable products. Sales of the new lamp doubled in the first year and export prospects look bright.

Interestingly, the company had already analysed the market before this complete re-design was launched; models were used to test the new proposition and the company even value engineered the product before tooling. So management knew how the product had to be positioned when the time came for investment. This is unusual in many engineering firms in the U.K., where technical staff are expected to develop new products, which production makes, and at a stage patently too late, the export marketing staff are then involved in promotion and selling (This question of teamwork is developed in Chapter 4.)

Some reference has already been made to the continuing development of new products to maintain a broadly based product range. In most companies operating in overseas markets, an examination of their products' performance will probably show a number of areas where the classic Pareto's Law would apply. Pareto, a nineteenth century mathematician, propounded the theory that, in most situations, eighty per cent of total results could be attributed to twenty per cent of total activity. Thus, an industrial chemical firm has found that eighty per cent of its sales are handled by twenty per cent of its salesmen. An airline has discovered that twenty per cent of its routes generate eighty per cent of its revenue. This is a very useful tool for management to identify those products generating the greatest volume of business overseas.

Before management can consider dropping existing products, it must attempt to quantify the total performance of each product in overseas markets. A focal point must be developed to collate information from all markets regarding the sales and contribution performance of the company's various products. The aim is to identify the international value of products to the total firm rather than monitor individual market's performance. Procedures must be laid down in order to evaluate the way a product is progressing in the various markets that the company is serving. Such procedures need not be complicated. However, they must clearly specify what is wanted from local managers and, where the market effort is conducted in a decentralized fashion, it is important that local personnel are adequately motivated to respond to what appears as an additional bit of bureaucracy. In this connection, an explanation of the underlying thinking is probably a useful aid to motivation. A full understanding of the product life-cycle concept, and its implications to the international situation, should remove any residual doubt regarding the legitimacy of such procedures in the effort to identify dying products on a global scale.

The important implication of everything that has been said in connection with product deletion is that some sort of product control must take place in a company marketing its products overseas. Whilst this comes quite naturally to a centralized firm, it is slightly inconsistent with the freedom that decentralized firms enjoy. Nonetheless, it is important that products are not allowed to drift on and on just because a few overseas markets still want them.

All this, then, must be the outcome of careful and quantified product planning in the context of all the company's overseas markets; planning which derives directly from policy considerations discussed earlier. The maintenance of a competitive range of products must not be overlooked in the detailed stages of dropping ageing products and adding new ones. The importance of this is shown in the recent case of a Scandinavian manufacturer of light agricultural machinery that had been unable, despite substantial marketing investment, good service and extensive sales force coverage to improve its share of the United States market. Following some research activity among buyers and industry suppliers, it was found that the manufacturer had failed to provide the breadth of product line required in U.S.A. American customers for agricultural machinery are often per- suaded by dealers to trade from cheaper to the more expensive model in a manufacturer's range. The Scandinavian company had no low-priced products to secure customers: it offered only a top-quality product. Accordingly, the company introduced an economy range to penetrate this key overseas market. Within less than two years, its share of the U.S. market had risen by 100%, and the profit contribution from its U.S. sales had tripled.

Thus, at the planning stage, management must set out clear and quantitative guidelines about the maintenance of a competitive product range, and the sales targets and profit contributions expected of each product. Figure 3.12 illustrates a marketing approach to product innova- tion, development and control.

There remains the vital question of ensuring in the design and development of products for overseas markets, that adaptation and product promotion are kept at a competitive level (including packaging); adaptation to meet foreign tastes and requirements, and packaging to attract consumers in an environment very different to that in the home market (see checklist, pp. 111–13). The following illustrations from actual business situations will make this point clear:

(a) Refrigerator manufacturers from Western countries initially encountered great difficulty in selling their products in Japan: the problem was that the refrigerator motors were too noisy for typical Japanese homes which were built with paper-thin walls. Sears became a successful exporter of refrigerators to Japan by develop- ing a motor for use in local conditions;

(b) In Australia, the manufacturer of 'Aim' toothpaste was taken to Court by one of its competitors because of an Australian law that prohibits the sale of competitive products in similar packages. Strict interpretation and enforcement of this law forced the foreign manufacturer to change the package having already spent £3m on promotion;

(c) A U.S. tyre manufacturer built a new plant in France with insufficient research, though having previously done well in sales to the French market. Due to changing driving habits of the French, new kinds of tyres were required, and costly adjustment became necessary;

(d) Flowers are used on many packages, but even here caution is required: certain flowers and their colours convey hidden messages.

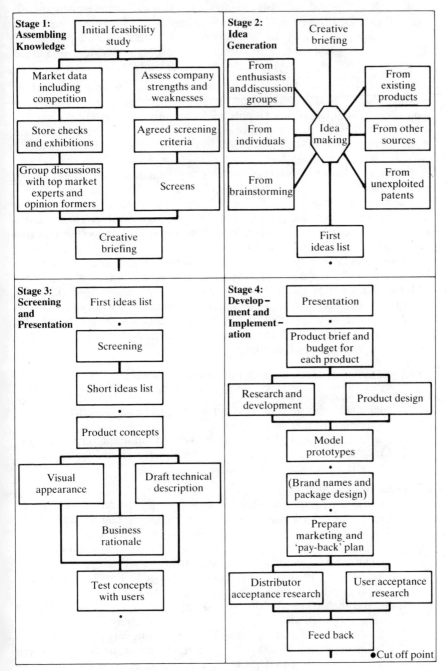

Figure 3.12 Marketing Approach to Product Design, Development and Planning[4]

In France and in many countries which have experienced British influence, the white lily is often used for funerals. Mexicans, though, use lilies to lift superstitious spells. A purple flower symbolizes death to a Brazilian or disrespect in Mexico. In France and U.S.S.R., the yellow flower signifies infidelity.

These illustrations also relate to one other but important aspect of product design and development, and that is what is known as Gap Analysis: the identification of a potentially lucrative segment of the market not as yet served by competitors. For instance, two Swiss chocolate manufacturers, Nestle Company and Interfood Company have identified different segments of the total world market for chocolates on the basis of 'gap analysis'. In some overseas markets, a substantial gap in usage of the product has been identified (less chocolate being consumed than population and income levels would indicate): this has required programmes to increase primary demand (as opposed to increasing a product's brand share at the expense of competitors). A fall in consumption of chocolate in North America in the 1970s as a result of concern about health and calorie intake prompted Nestle Company to identify another gap in that market: for promotion of chocolate as a pleasant, easily digestible source of energy for athletes and sportsmen. In tropical climates yet a further 'gap' has been identified in the potential sales for sweetened chocolates which are made to a formula that will not melt. In short, 'gap analysis' is a concept that requires techniques of identification and exploitation of new and relatively uncrowded segments of the total market.

*Product Design, Adaptation and Presentation Checklist*

(1) *Product Design*
    1. Make sure the product is fit for its purpose and efficient;
    2. Make certain it is safe and reliable;
    3. Make sure it meets the regulations to be found in the target market;
    4. Make sure there are no features which might offend the customer;
    5. Make it as attractive as possible.

(2) *Product Adaptation*
    1. Should the product be changed to meet the customer's preference? For example, colours, fashions, tastes and social customs vary. White is a sign of mourning in Malaya, for instance.
    2. Should the way the product works be changed. A hand-operated machine might be adapted to work from r.i electric motor.
    3. Should the size or measurement be changed? Products may need adaptation to suit metric units or feet/inches.
    4. Should the product be changed to suit different regulations? Health and safety regulations vary from country to country.
    5. Should the product be packaged in a different way or in a different quantity? Products may be sold in different units in different countries. Some countries use grams and kilograms and others use pounds and ounces, though there is a general move towards grams and kilograms.

(3) *Product Presentation*

Product presentation has three main purposes
1. To catch the customer's attention;
2. To give the product a 'brand image';
3. To identify the company that made the product.

Packaging is very much part of product presentation and has four main uses:
1. To identify the product and make it attractive;
2. To make it easy to buy or transport or handle;
3. To say what the product is and how it is used (the final seller may be unable to explain); most countries have regulations about food products – what they weigh; what they must have in them; where they come from and other details may have to be printed on packets;
4. To protect a product from damage, or pollution, or deterioration.

## 3.4 Price and Non-Price Competition

Before assessing price as a factor in the competitiveness of a company, and relating price to other significant non-price factors in securing some competitive advantage, it is essential to place cost analysis correctly as a factor in profitability. There has been much analysis of the applications, for example, of marginal costing to export pricing, and its contribution to profit in export operations. Marginal costing allocates only those direct costs per unit incurred in production for export; this is explained fully later with worked examples. If, however, standard costing (full absorption cost) is used, additional sales overseas can provide higher profits if there is no possibility of increasing domestic sales even at lower prices. Therefore, if standard costs are used to evaluate export business, this can aid management in its assessment of profits because if, for example, volume increases 10%, absorption of fixed costs increases 10% (yet actual fixed costs will remain constant); the result is that in the analysis 'over-absorbed' cost will show in the cost system as favourable capacity or volume variances. Specifically, therefore, one of the following will apply under standard costing:

(a) selling price equals standard cost plus general overhead plus a small profit;
(b) selling price equals standard cost plus general overhead and nothing available for profit;
(c) selling price equals standard cost, no general overhead, no profit;
(d) selling price is below standard cost.

The first worked example is shown in Table 3.8.

Here we see that the company can increase its production from 800 units to almost 1,400 units by selling the first 800 units at £2.00, an additional 200 units at £1.70, a further 200 units at £1.40 and the other 200 units at £1.35, and increase its profits from £400 to £470. Once the 1,400 unit level is exceeded, the overall profit will decrease because the differential cost is greater than the differential revenue.

## Table 3.8
### Effect of Volume on Profit

| Output | Differential Output | Total Cost | Differential Cost | Differential Unit Cost | Differential Unit Revenue | Total Revenue | Total Profit | Marginal Profit or (Loss) |
|---|---|---|---|---|---|---|---|---|
| Present 800 | | $1,200 | | $1.50 | 2.00 | $1,600 | 400 | |
| Proposed 1000 | 200 | 1,480 | 280 | 1.40 | 1.70 | 1,940 | 460 | 60 |
| Proposed 1200 | 200 | 1,750 | 270 | 1.35 | 1.40 | 2,220 | 470 | 10 |
| Proposed 1400 | 200 | 2,020 | 270 | 1.35 | 1.35 | 2,490 | 470 | 0 |
| Proposed 1600 | 200 | 2,290 | 270 | 1.35 | 1.30 | 2,750 | 460 | (10) |

Column 8=Column 7 minus Column 3
At the point where differential cost (or marginal cost) equals differential revenue (or marginal revenue), the 'Best-Profit' output is achieved.

Indeed one of the problems of cost analysis, particularly in relation to export prices and unit profit margins, is the treatment of items such as overheads and the differing interpretations that can be drawn from the same sets of cost figures.

A research study by Barclays Bank International[5] illustrates this aptly from cost data drawn from two exporting companies, one in textiles and the other in engineering. The two companies had a very similar construction; half the costs were fixed, and the other half variable; they also had a limited range of products which they exported. After an experimental period of more than 2 years of exporting, neither company had succeeded in getting as high a price for its products abroad as on its home market.

(a) *Engineering Company*
It sold (in round figures) 100,000 units at home at $2.50 average price per unit and 40,000 units abroad at only $2.10 per unit. Revenue and costs were as follows:

| Units Sold | Revenue | Costs | Profit |
|---|---|---|---|
| 100,000 at home | $ 250,000 | $200,000 | $50,000 |
| 40,000 exported | $ 84,000 | $ 80,000 | $ 4,000 |
| 140,000 | $334,000 | $280,000 | $54,000 |

Of the above costs 50 per cent ($140,000) were fixed and the other half variable (unit cost=$1 fixed+$1 variable).

After two disappointing years of not getting a better price abroad, the engineering company decided to discontinue exporting altogether. With the effort previously devoted to exports, it succeeded in increasing its sales in the home market by 20 per cent. Thus, its sales now amounted to 120,000 units=$300,000 revenue ($250,000 before).

It found its new cost and profit situation as follows:

| Units Sold | Revenue | Costs |
|---|---|---|
| 120,000 at home (now 120,000 units carry $1 per unit variable cost, item-fixed costs remaining constant) | $300,000 | $140,000=fixed<br>$120,000=variable |
| | $300,000 | $260,000 |

Having discontinued less profitable exports, total profit now is $40,000 compared with $54,000 before.

(b) *Textile Company*
This company followed an entirely different course and far from giving up exporting, decided to double it. (This is not an unrealistic course given the difficulty of achieving an increase in market shares at home; export markets in general present greater opportunities for expansion).

Originally they sold 100,000 units at home at $2.50 and 40,000 abroad at $2.10.

| Units Sold | Revenue | Costs | Profit |
|---|---|---|---|
| 100,000 at home | $250,000 | $200,000 | $50,000 |
| 40,000 exported | $ 84,000 | $ 80,000 | $ 4,000 |
| 100,000 at home | $250,000 | $140,000 fixed | |
| 80,000 | $168,000 | $180,000 variable | |
| | $418,000 | $320,000 | $98,000 |

Thus, having doubled 'less profitable' exports, profits are $98,000 compared with $54,000 before.

The exporter director of a successful German company was quoted in this Report, explaining why it was in his company's best interests to continue with 'less profitable' exports: 'Take away these exports, and you would reduce production volume by over a third, unit costs would go up significantly, we would be less competitive with imports, and would probably have to lay off some ten thousand employees'.

Indeed, on the basis of this analysis, more companies in the U.K. should consider the applications of marginal costing to their export pricing; for marginal costing allocates, not the full cost but only the incremental portion of cost incurred in increasing production to fulfil overseas orders. This research by Barclays Bank International (now 5 years old) found that three out of four German companies employ the same system for home and export costing; but there is an important 25% (mainly large and medium-sized companies) that uses a more discriminating method. This involves the more logical allocation of individual cost items: instead of including all the items in management overheads, they separate home management from export management overheads – for these may be many times greater than the other – and allocate them accordingly. Furthermore, they add to basic unit production costs only such sales overheads as may be demanded by the actual selling costs in overseas countries concerned. If, for example, sales operations are more expensive in one country than another, appropriate adjustments can be made to costs and prices.

Clearly, therefore, this has an important lesson for both finance and marketing staff in identifying and apportioning more accurately direct costs of export operations in different markets. Furthermore, management is in a better position to know what are the limits of national price competition and whether or not they will be making a profit on a contract overseas. There is a strong argument for finance and marketing to work more closely together in adopting this approach to cost analysis; and in contracts with some leading export companies made by the author, there are indications that some major British exporting companies do calculate the more important items of cost (e.g. overheads) separately for exports.

This is not to say of course that British companies should be 'guided only by their costs' when deciding what prices to charge in overseas markets; it must be the market overseas which mainly determines the price, not the cost accountant or shipping manager, as in some companies. It is, of course, essential to bring to bear on the market other factors such as quality, delivery and design to gain acceptance for the product in preference to that of the competitors. As non-price elements gain in importance, reflecting, for example, higher product quality and improved after sales service, so it becomes more feasible to charge a more profitable price.

Cost analysis leads directly to consideration of what is the optimal pricing for the market which a company should set. It has, of course, been apparent for some years that, in both consumer and industrial goods, considerations other than prices and costs have become increasingly important in overseas markets: design and styling, reliability, performance, promotion and market follow-up are some. In the capital goods sector, credit terms, delivery dates, performance bonds, technical service and development assistance have become steadily more important to secure business. But these absorb or tie up larger funds, hence the need for closer liaison on the best marketing use of the finance available.

This does not mean that price is unimportant: indeed the manufacturer selling overseas on, for example, quality or technical sophistication often has the opportunity to charge a higher price and should do so. Certainly, it is widely recognized in industry that severe price competition can become self-defeating and hinder rather than promote the revival of international trade; one has only to cite the severe price cutting of some Italian domestic appliance manufacturers some years ago, which ruined not only the Italians but a number of other European companies trying to match their price cutting.

The problem of implementing more profitable pricing in many British companies often arises from the 'cost plus' pricing approach of the accountant. Indeed, the author recently encountered one of the largest British-based pharmaceutical groups where the company has always had its selling prices determined by accountants; it is only this year that regular consultation with marketing staff is being set up. Other empirical evidence will be adduced in this section to indicate that 'cost plus' pricing is still prevalent; that British companies in some manufacturing sectors are 'under pricing' their products overseas as a result and that closer working liaison between finance and marketing can do a lot to rectify this situation. Price must therefore, be seen as a means of achieving the company's objectives in overseas markets in relation to its opportunities rather than, as at present in some companies, a means of covering costs by a given margin.

Root[6] has singled out the shortcomings of this 'cost plus' pricing:

(a) It completely ignores demand in the target market;
(b) It ignores competition;
(c) It uses arbitrary allocation of overhead costs which are not affected by current sales;

(d) It involves circular reasoning because price influences cost through its effect on sales volume;

(e) It offers no guidance to maximize profits or reach other profit goals.

Root concludes 'the proper use of cost pricing is to measure the profit contributions of different projected prices'.

Let us therefore concentrate on the most vital aspect of export pricing which seems to be overlooked by some companies: the need to determine realistic price thresholds of customers overseas for your products, rather than to price on a 'cost plus' basis. The BBI Report found that more British companies tend to quote the same price in every country than do their German counterparts. The analysis is as follows, and the survey responses are worth quoting in full:

*Do you charge the same price in every country*

*% of all companies*

|        |     | FRANCE | U.K. | GERMANY |
|--------|-----|--------|------|---------|
| Small  | Yes | 24     | 50   | 35      |
|        | No  | 76     | 50   | 65      |
| Medium | Yes | 40     | 37   | 30      |
|        | No  | 60     | 63   | 70      |
| Large  | Yes | 23     | 29   | 19      |
|        | No  | 77     | 71   | 81      |

It is clearly mainly the smaller British companies which deprive themselves of flexibility. This directly raises the important question 'Pricing to whom': agents, retailers, or consumers, for example. Frequently, the prices to the agent are in the form of a standard price list which is fairly uniformly quoted to all agents, with only minor modifications; simplicity and fairness in non-discrimination are claimed to be the merit of this approach, and it is often, in fact, the one adopted by the accountant. In contrast, other companies make a special study of at least their ten or twenty key markets and quote what the market will bear in each country. (The Ford Motor Company, for example, charges twelve different prices in twelve European countries for the same model.) Some companies with a very large range of products and selling in numerous markets, consider this approach too complicated and costly; to some extent, therefore, they must hope to offset slim margins in some markets with high margins in others. It does result, however, in a pricing policy which by definition, is insensitive to market conditions.

But this still leaves open the important problem of the 'ultimate' price, i.e. not the price at which the export department invoices the agent, but the price which the final consumer pays. Quite often companies know at what price their agents sell to customers; and with consumer products they even know the final selling price paid by the consumers in the shops; but as a rule, this only covers their most important products. Again, the statistics compiled by the BBI Report are worth quoting:

*'Do you know at what prices your products are sold, not to your Agent or Distributor but to the final purchaser?'*

## % of all companies

|  | FRANCE | U.K. | GERMANY |
|---|---|---|---|
| Yes | 77 | 56 | 77 |
| No | 8 | 32 | 12.5 |
| Sometimes | 15 | 12 | 10.5 |
| Total No. of Companies | 120 | 120 | 120 |

Too little attention is paid by the British to the study of competitors' final prices in overseas markets. Frequently companies have a tacit understanding with the agents that a product will be sold at approximately such and such a price. However, agents have been know to add 100% or 200% to his own (delivered) price – instead of 20% or 30% – simply because, having studied competitors' prices, he concludes that the market can bear it. What conclusions, at this stage, can be drawn from the statistics quoted?

First, pricing realistically and profitably overseas requires sensitivity to and analysis of what the final customer in that country is prepared to pay, and this is where companies often miss out on market opportunities: they have only a limited knowledge of the individual markets. What frequently happens is that neither the agent (because he has too many products to look after) nor the company (because it has too many markets to cover) knows in sufficient detail competitors' prices (or even the prices of the most important competitors). But where trouble is taken to find this out it is often found that an extra 10% (and not infrequently even 20%) added to the company's original prices would be quite acceptable to the market. Indeed, there are instances suggesting that even the bigger companies could secure better prices if more time and concentration were devoted to it in all the major markets. Quite often a 5% price mark-up can imply a 10% higher profit margin, or even more.

Second, closer collaboration between finance and marketing would ensure that in many cases high profit margins would accrue from more market-sensitive pricing. At present, pricing tends to be determined in ignorance of what the final purchaser overseas is paying.

Three recent examples of under-pricing illustrate this. Otherwise successful and well-established British companies were found to be under-pricing by between 15% and 20% high quality products to the final customer in some export markets and thus losing the incremental profit of a higher unit margin. These cases involved:

(a) A manufacturer selling high quality reproduction furniture to West Germany where the customer is a highly fastidious buyer of quality;
(b) A manufacturer selling all forms of car accessories (rear window-heaters, etc.) to U.S.A. Taking into account the quality and range of accessories on the market, American consumers were prepared to pay more;
(c) A manufacturer selling well-proved security and emergency lighting

systems to Scandinavian industries where complete reliability is the priority among Swedish buyers to comply with strict legislation; they associated reliability and safety, in the light of other offers, with a higher price threshold than that charged by the British exporters.

These are just three examples where companies have failed to research the actual price thresholds in these markets, and as a result, made a far lower unit profit margin than they could have done, without, it must be emphasized, achieving any greater volume of sales as a result. The point is not that they obtained orders, but that they did so almost entirely on price, thus running the danger of under-rating the product in the eyes of the customer, and leaving little or no margin for reinvestment in technical improvement. Furthermore in (a) and (b) they have given to the distributor or agent in these markets the opportunity to increase his margin on sale to the consumer at the expense of the exporter.

It is therefore vital that management, particularly financial management, understands that the higher the price sensitivity abroad, the greater the opportunity there is to take advantage of demand elasticity to increase profit margins and overall profitability. Factors which companies should take into account in setting profitable export prices are contained in Appendix 4.

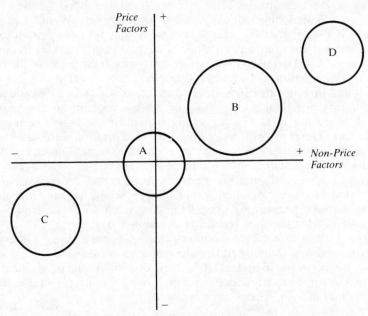

Figure 3.13  A Competitive Map for an Export Market

A = Our company, with the lowest sales
B = The largest supplier, based locally, strong on delivery and servicing
C = The largest importer, selling on low price, with poor service and quality
D = A small importer, selling at a high price on high quality, but restricted in volume by delivery constraints.

Some authoritative research on Non-Price Competition (NPC) under-taken by NEDO[7] claims that the major weakness in U.K. exporting has been reliance on price competition, and that non-price variables such as design, quality, personal selling, after sales and other service are more important, to establish export market shares than price. There is no doubt that non-price competition can be highly effective: for example, a small U.K. firm located in Gloucestershire sells a million camshafts a year to West Germany and Swedish automobile manufacturers purely on the basis of technological expertise and high quality reflected in extremely low customer rejection rates. One valuable analytical approach for manage-ment, therefore, is to construct a competitive map which highlights price and non-price factors in competition (Figure 3.13). This analysis may be an 'in-house' study, use distributors, or involve market research, but it will put the focus on the company's market position and the resultant 'market price' that may have to be changed.

## 3.5 The Marketing Mix

Recent research and analysis[8] of export performance of companies has paid special attention to the management of the elements of the marketing mix: principally (and traditionally): price, promotion, product policy and distribution; but there are other elements of this mix which apply especially in exporting: design, credit, service and selling. Each of these elements is accorded detailed attention in terms of operational effectiveness overseas. At the point where the company's home-based management is setting up and controlling export operations, it is essential to discuss and explain the 'mix' in its totality and how it is incorporated in the planning, assessment and evaluation process. Indeed, the research cited has also focussed on competence in managing the elements of the marketing mix as a major determinant of the company's long-run performance in and commitment to international operations.

What is clear from this and other research is that whilst it is one thing to discuss the 'optional' mix in conceptual terms, it is another matter altogether to put such an optimal mix into operation.

The problems of deciding upon such an optimal mix and then implementing it in different overseas markets can be resolved only if management can identify some of the key elements of the mix country by country, and the extent of the difference between home and each overseas country. These must include for example:

(a) Differences in cost and pattern of distribution;
(b) Adaptation of the product required to place it competitively in overseas market;
(c) Differences in design and specifications;
(d) Differences in selling methods, particularly negotiation and sales promotion methods;
(e) Cost additions brought about by some of the above and other factors such as tariffs which affect price at which company place it overseas;

(f)  Lack of suitable, available media to generate volume demand for product to achieve unit cost reductions;
(g)  Changes in consumption levels in some segments of an overseas market;
(h)  Higher levels of service required to maintain market position;
(i)  Longer credit terms required to obtain new business; also essential for maintaining market share, and/or position, particularly in relatively high growth markets.

The basic policy options facing management, therefore, are:

(a)  To determine the degree to which 'standardization' of the mix is likely to be feasible in each overseas market;
(b)  To identify precisely in which elements of the mix the company is able to ensure competitive advantage.

Before we discuss these two operational aspects (which indeed provide the focus for this chapter), the concept of the marketing mix raises a dilemma fundamental to the management of the exporting company. However the elements of the mix are determined, they will fall between two extremes: market the same product that is being manufactured for the home market and incur heavy promotional costs in educating the overseas customer, or alternatively incur heavy development costs to adapt the product to each export market in which it is to be sold. However, much detailed marketing data is required before a quantification analysis along the lines in Figure 3.14 can be carried out.

| Cultural Variables | Marketing Functions | | | | |
|---|---|---|---|---|---|
| | Product | Price | Promotion | Distribution | Market Research |
| Material culture Education Language Aesthetics Political attitudes, values Social organization | | | | | |

Figure 3.14 External variables related to 'mix' elements

The degree of standardization must clearly be related both to market potential and level of competitor activity. Since investment in highly 'non-standard' items only makes sense in marketing and profit terms if the assessed sales potential is higher in that than in other overseas markets. This is not merely a question of product adaptation (important though this element of the mix is), but of identifying and sharpening the company's competitive advantage in one or more elements. This is essentially the main application of the macro-concept of 'differential advantage' at a national level. Indeed, observation of current market practice shows that some companies have built up strong brand images, others have a reputation for excellence in design and quality, others for offering outstanding value for money, and so on. These reflect consistent investment, over the years, in part or parts of the mix in which, as a result, these companies have special expertise, resources and reputation.

The practical implications of 'competitive advantage' are also particularly pertinent to the management and control of the mix. Consider, for instance, the scope for extending, even putting some initial investment in this competitive advantage:

(a) Product: performance, consistency overall quality;
(b) Price: outstanding value and use of price to indicate quality, price thresholds, sophistication of price structure to achieve high margin sales;
(c) Promotion: creativity of copy and concepts, display support, direct mail, use of symposia;
(d) Distribution: level of service, reliability, response to orders;
(e) Design: innovation, aesthetic appeal, technical excellence;
(f) Credit: terms and use of foreign currencies;
(g) Service: Pre-sale; during installation and commissioning, after sales service; management training;
(h) Selling: project/task face approach to key customers, negotiating and bargaining skills, buyer research.

As far as putting some of these approaches, particularly the last mentioned, into operation, a straightforward use of indexation or weightings can put management in a better position to quantify and, therefore, sharpen competitive advantage in key overseas markets. The two parameters in such an exercise are those elements of the mix in the overseas market which need special attention and activity if the company is to improve its market position, and the company's resources to do this successfully in the light of competition.

The analysis in Figure 3.15 requires a critical assessment not only of Country X but of the strengths of major foreign competitors in the market. It will reveal the exporting company's strengths and weaknesses but, significantly, it will show where the company has competitive advantage in those elements of the mix which are known, by research, to be of special importance in that market. Of course, the analysis can be done, and used, only on the basis of sound research and analysis (discussed in depth earlier in this chapter and Chapter 2) and in the light of management's objectives, its assessment of market potential, and the company's resources to exploit that potential.

An illustration of the management of the mix in overseas markets in action is provided by the operations of the Timex Company in West Germany, reported in the business press and quoted by Terpstra[9].

| A | B | C | | | | | D |
|---|---|---|---|---|---|---|---|
| | Weight | Competitive Resources of Exporting Company | | | | | |
| Marketing Mix Element | Assigned to Country X (Maximum 10) | Very Strong 10 | Strong 8 | Fair 6 | Adequate 4 | Poor 2 | Rating B×C (Maximum 100) |
| Price | 6 | | * | | | | 48 |
| Promotion | 4 | | | | * | | 16 |
| Product Policy | 8 | | | * | | | 48 |
| Distribution | 9 | * | | | | | 90 |
| Design | 4 | | | * | | | 24 |
| Service | 4 | * | | | | * | 32 |
| Selling | 8 | * | | | | | 48 |

TOTAL RATING 306
(Maximum 700)

Figure 3.15 Weighting Matrix – Marketing Mix

*Product Strategy*
This company studied the competitive situation and found existing producers selling primarily high- and medium-priced watches – as status items. There were also sales of low-priced, low quality watches, sold without guarantee and with the initial repair costing more than the price of the watch. The company felt that its products filled a gap between these two segments, both as to price and quality.

*Service*
To beat the low-priced competition and to meet the high-priced competition, Timex provided service arrangements at moderate cost. Service was free during the guarantee period. After that, a new movement could be purchased for one-half to one-fourth the price of the new watch. This helped upgrade the image of the inexpensive or 'cheap' watch.

*Guarantee*
The company offered the first inexpensive watch with a guarantee. In fact, the guarantee was as liberal as those on high-priced watches, with free service or repairs during the first year. This was important in persuading a sceptical public about the quality of the inexpensive watch.

*Price*
Timex stressed its low prices but at the same time emphasized the quality and the guarantee. The company's prices were generally a step above the

low-priced competition, but well below most of the high priced competition. Other pricing decisions were to use resale price maintenance and to give retailers the same margins as on high-priced watches (33⅓ per cent).

*Distribution*

Distribution strategy was one of the major elements in the Timex programme in Germany. Since jewellers sold 75% of the watches, Timex needed that channel. However, the company also felt it necessary to use the large department stores and mail-order houses. Others who had tried this earlier had been boycotted by the jewellers. Timex was successful in persuading jewellers that its business was too profitable to ignore. The elements of persuasion were:

(a) Giving the same margin as on expensive watches
(b) Saving repair work by having the watches sent to the Timex factory in France, while giving the dealer 25% commission on the charges to the customer
(c) Using resale price maintenance to protect the jewellers against discounters, and
(d) A heavy publicity and advertising campaign (more than twice what all German competition spent). This made Timex the best-known watch in Germany.

*Promotion*

A heavy advertising campaign double the total competitive outlays, initiated the 'hard-sell' approach. Dramatic 'torture tests' were used as the advertisements. Competitors called these undignified but later on some began to imitate them. Eighty per cent of the company budget went for television because of its coverage and dramatic effect. In a separate promotional effort, a missionary selling force toured Germany, explaining to retailers the advantages of handling Timex.

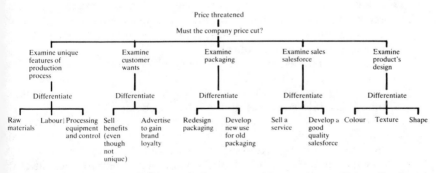

Figure 3.16 Product Differentiation as an Alternative to Price Cutting

An analysis by Hague[10] of Business and Market Research, shows that, particularly in the industrial goods sector, price often comes third as a buying factor after assured quantity and high quality; this analysis can be illustrated by Figure 3.16 which was part of the research listed.

Managing the marketing mix, therefore, is primarily an activity to strengthen the competitive edge of the exporting company, where the market potential is there, and where it has the resources to do so. Product design, development and pricing, both key elements of the mix, have been discussed in depth in Sections 3.5 and 3.6. The importance of service competition must be underlined and these apt illustrations show what can be achieved with some creativity.

(a)  A supplier of material for military uniforms faced increasing competition from low-cost suppliers. Unable to equal the competitors' low costs, the company started supplying overseas customers complete uniforms and advice on styling (differentiated by an increased service element).

(b)  A leather supplier, unable to sell its product to the high quality, prestige, leather-covered furniture manufacturers, established a new sector of the overseas market by adding a service: cutting leather for fabric upholsterers using their own patterns.

(c)  Manufacturer of airport fire tenders also reacted, successfully, to price competition by designing, and selling a complete, packaged programme of operator training, maintenance scheduling and efficiency targets for its customers worldwide, linked to a terminal technical qualification for staff examined in U.K.

(d)  A fibreboard supplier facing competition from lower quality material, held 1 day seminars in overseas cities to educate his customers in the technicalities of the product's manufacture, and its uses, to educate key overseas buyers.

### 3.6  Export Marketing Action Plan

(a)  Identify key markets and then select target markets carefully before making financial and manpower commitments.

Key markets have large sales volumes, above average growth rates and intensive consumption, but also usually more intensive competition, lower price levels, fewer opportunties for newcomers to enter and to gain a share.

Target markets are those markets which offer the exporter the best chances of success either short-term or long-term. Sometimes they are identical with the key markets, but very often a smaller market with less competition is a better choice.

(b)  Be ready to adapt product and packaging to market requirements, to adjust prices to the prevailing level, but only after a critical investigation of the necessity, the cost and the sales potential.

Very often exporters adapt their products, only to find out that the modified product is too costly to produce – or cannot be produced with existing plant equipment. Or they find out too late that price adjustments reduce their profit margin too much or even produce a loss.

(c)  Recognize that markets are rarely alike and static and be prepared to use different strategies and plans.

Even if a plan worked well at one time or in one market, there is no grounds to assume that it will work again in a different market or at a different time. Doing the same thing everywhere and all the time is rarely, if ever, a guarantee for long-term success.

(d)  Copying what competitors are doing can be as successful as inventing a new way to market a product or inventing a new product.

Although innovation and invention – products, marketing techniques, promotion methods etc. – are much more talked about and often considered to be alone decisive for success, more profitable business is being done by companies who do exactly what their competitors do – only better or faster.

(e)  Limit your risks, especially in the early phases of an export programme by testing, by small-scale operations and by trial agreements.

All business risks are a matter of available information; the less information available when decisions are taken, the greater the risk of failure. Conversely, risks decrease as more information becomes available.

A company seeking to step up exports will rarely have sufficient information to hand to make low-risk decisions. This is why product testing and market testing is important for exporters: it permits them to assess their products' market potential on a small scale before they make important financial commitments. For the same reasons, trial agreements with distributors, or agents, or large buyers are often preferable.

(f)  Make an estimate of the cost to the company of becoming an exporter – and of the additional sales revenue and profit expected. Keep revising both estimates as more information becomes available.

When deciding to export, most companies have no idea at all – or a very vague one only – of the cost of additional staff, travel, research, investment in fixed and working capital that exporting will entail. Export sales forecasts are made by quite a few companies, but they tend to be less than reliable. The result is very often that the real cost of gearing up for exports remains unknown too long, and is not controlled.

(g)  Usually there is more than one worthwhile aim in exporting, just as there are different ways to achieve a given aim. Investigating alternatives and trade-offs between different aims and methods is important.

Examples of alternative aims are short-term profit vs long-term growth or high unit profit vs large sales volume. Examples of alternative activities are product adaptation vs new product development or the use of one distribution channel in preference for another. Each alternative considered involves certain costs and 'rewards' in the form of sales and profit. Choosing between them is a matter of comparing costs and rewards.

'Trade-off' problems arise when decisions about different marketing activities are to be taken. Thus, there is a trade-off relationship between granting credit to customers and the cost of interest on capital tied up as a result: granting credit will increase sales, but from a certain point on, additional sales due to credit will become too expensive in interest and capital tied up. Trade-off problems thus arise whenever the best 'dosage' – such as credit terms – is to be determined. Other trade-off problems involve finding the best combination between two or more marketing activities such as determining the effort to be allocated to personal selling and advertising – or between the higher cost of airfreight and the advantages of faster deliver to the customers.

(h)  The need for permanent and systematic marketing information.

Many exporters make the mistake of collecting marketing information only once; when they prepare their initial marketing plan, they forget that markets are rarely static and unchangeable. In this way, they lose the possibility of adjusting their plans as market conditions change – and are unable to determine whether their plans work as forecast.

(i)  Good marketing plans can break down because the company's internal organization and procedures are defective.

Typical 'breakdown' risk areas are product quality control, production scheduling, order handling and shipping, collection and customer service. Some of these are activities which are usually not under the direct responsibility of the export management, and therefore difficult to supervise and control. The areas mentioned – and others not directly related to the company's marketing function – need to be investigated early in the marketing planning process to discover weaknesses and defects so that the necessary changes in organization and procedures can be made before the plan itself goes into operation.

(j)  Select your local associates – distributors, advertising agents, consultants – carefully, listen to their views critically and follow their advice only if it is supported by convincing reasons.

Many exporters follow the suggestions of their partners in the export market almost blindly, thinking they know the market best and their advice will therefore be in the exporter's best interests. But this is not always so: distributors and advertising agents, and also consultants tend to have their own interest at heart and that does not always coincide exactly with the exporter's needs and aims.

## 3.7  Control and Follow-Up

Control tends to be taken for granted – with the undesirable result that not enough importance is attached to it; or again, control is considered as something foreign to a modern enterprise where people work together as a team, agree together about goals and objectives and are sufficiently motivated to work intelligently towards their achievement.

Both attitudes are dangerous, because they lead to insufficient or unsystematic, occasional control and this can only have negative effects on the organization and its stability – without any compensating positive effects on the attitudes and motivations of the people working in it.

Control can be described as the process by which actual results and planned results are compared in order to find out any discrepancies and to take corrective action. To do this, control must be organized in such a way that:

    (a) Information on actual results is available as soon as possible. In the context of budget control this means that information on expenditures, their type, amounts, and timing must flow rapidly to those responsible for the budget. Also, information on the results achieved – sales or tourist arrivals – must become available rapidly;

    (b) Deviations from the budget, whether they concern expenditures or revenues, are investigated to find what caused them and whether there are good reasons for them or not;

    (c) Corrective action can be taken in time, early enough to avoid losses or to take advantage of new opportunities.

The main requirements for a good control system are reliability, speed, completeness and responsiveness:

    (a) A control system that produces information which is not accurate and therefore needs constant verification, is dangerous, because it can lead to corrective action where none is needed – or the reverse.

    (b) If control information is only available with considerable delay, the time for necessary corrective action may be long past and the only solution is to accept the inevitable.

    (c) The requirement of completeness does not mean that every small detail needs to be 'controlled' but rather that the critical areas of control must be identified and a system devised to cover them.

    (d) Finally, a control system which does not lead to corrective action when needed, is almost worthless.

The main difference between control and auditing is that control is a permanent activity while auditing is undertaken only periodically.

Four steps are involved in setting up and operating a budget control system for promotion:

    (a) Establishment of control points and control measurements;

    (b) Establishment of control standards;

    (c) Collection and dissemination of control information;

    (d) Analysis of information and corrective action where indicated.

## 3.71 Control Points and Measures

Although the budget is one of the main items to be controlled, control points and standards are not limited to expenditures only, but need to be

*Table 3.9*
*Control Points and Measures*

| Control Point | Control Measurement or Data |
|---|---|
| Sales Analysis | Weekly or monthly sales revenue, broken down by:<br>— Customer type (commercial and tourism)<br>— Product<br>— Terms of sale<br>— Order size<br>— Sales revenue per customer |
| Sales vs. Target | Sales vs. Target<br>— Cumulative sales to date in percentage of target and percentage of time<br>— Cumulative sales vs. same time a year and a month ago |
| Promotion Budget Analysis | Separately by market and promotion activity:<br>— Expenditure to date<br>— Commitments for expenditure<br>— Uncommitted amounts |
| Market Development | This section should contain information on major developments in the key markets which are likely to influence demand for the exporter's product(s) |
| Competitive Activities | This section should cover the promotion activities of the main competitors, new promotion campaigns, new introductions of products, price ranges, promotions |
| Promotion Activities | Advertising:<br>— Placement and publication of media advertising in accordance with schedule<br>— Timing and execution of post tests for effectiveness control<br>— Progress on creation of new advertising campaign:<br>    Message development<br>    Media selection and media schedule<br><br>Sales Support:<br>— Progress of production and distribution of sales support material vs. time plan<br>— Control of distribution<br>— Other sales support activities<br><br>Public Relations:<br>— Preparation of P.R. activities vs. time plan<br>— Evaluation of P.R. measures |

established for sales, market shares, competitor's activities and the firm's or organization's own promotion activities (Table 3.9). An exporter might thus establish these control points and control measures.

Control standards of the following types are needed:

(a) Quantitative performance standards (sales revenues, number of visitors, occupancy rates, etc.) are used to compare actual performance with established targets. They can be expressed in absolute numbers, in ratios (e.g. actual sales vs target sales) or in the form of indexes (e.g. index of sales this month vs last month or vs the same month a year ago).

Expenditure standards indicate the amounts of budgeted expenditure for promotion activities and their timing. Their main purpose is to indicate whether actual expenditure (and also commitments for later expenditure) is within the limits of the budget and the spending plan (the latter is a part of the budget which indicates when the expenditures are going to occur).

(b) Time standards: since there is usually a certain 'lead time' required to prepare a promotional campaign in all its details and different functions and activities need to be performed, a time schedule for campaign preparation is needed to indicate the various deadlines. These deadlines are in effect the 'time standards' and the object of control is to ascertain whether deadlines are kept or not.

Control standards have two aspects: the first and obvious one is straightforward comparison between actual data, such as sales figures, expenditures, dates and the respective standard. The second aspect is that of acceptable deviation from the standard: it would be unreasonable to expect that standards will be met perfectly – and it would be uneconomical to take corrective action if a standard is overshot or undershot by a small amount. There should be, therefore, for each standard a range of acceptable deviation or a 'tolerance range' within which normal, acceptable performance should lie.

### 3.72 The Collection and Dissemination of Control Information

Actual performance is gauged from the various types of information gathered. In spite of the crucial role of information in the control process, only recently has management begun to think systematically about information economics, design, and management. Such information-manipulative company operations as accounting and marketing research highlight the heavy costs of collecting, processing, storing and transmitting information. The great cost makes it desirable to assess carefully the information needs of various executives. Specifically, it should be established who needs what information, when, where, and in what form. The challenge is to design a company information system where the value of the information is maximized for a given expenditure or the cost is minimized to achieve a given mix of information.

Information is needed on actual performance to check against desired performance. The comparisons may be made continuously (daily field reports) or intermittently (quarterly profit reports). Where many performance indicators are involved, much time may be required just to make the comparisons. For example, the promotion budget usually involves dozens of items. After the period is over, all of these items must be compared for unusual budgetary variances.

### 3.73 Analysis and Corrective Action

The final step of the control process is the analysis of the control information by comparing actual performance with the standards, identifying items and positions where deviation goes beyond the acceptable tolerances, establishing the causes of these deviations and taking decisions about corrective action.

Whenever a deviation is noted, the principal question to ask is 'What caused it?' A deviation may be due to human error, a failure in communications, a lack of information when needed, a weakness in the organization or to changes in markets, the action of competitors, but it may also be due to faulty measurements and standards or to deficiencies in the basic promotion plan itself.

After the causes of a deviation have been investigated and a satisfactory explanation has been found, various options are open for corrective action: some of these options might be:

(a) To do nothing until faults or possible errors in the information gathering and reporting systems have been investigated;
(b) To wait for a certain time to see whether the condition will correct itself;
(c) To establish new performance standards and tolerances in the light of the information;
(d) To revise the basic promotion plan either in part or entirely – perhaps by putting into effect a contingency plan previously developed.

Throughout the control process, information is the main element. Deciding which information is needed for control, how to gather it fast, economically and reliably, how to determine useful standards against which to compare it and, finally, how to analyse it, are the key problems of control.

### 3.74 Follow-up

Control is closely related to all aspects of market follow-up. An exporter or export manager who has visited his markets, contacted agents, analysed the competition and taken orders often feels that the task started by the market analysis and carried on during the period of the market visit comes to an end when he returns to his office and hands over his orders (those not sent by telex to the home office during the period of market investigation) to production. It must be recognized that for an export manager that task of assessing market potential, appointing agents or beginning a series of trial agency agreements and booking initial orders is only the beginning of the long-term process of exporting.

The export manager must try to convince the general management of his company or government enterprise that exporting should be regarded as a priority activity. This process is not especially difficult in those cases where a large proportion of the final product is exported: bulk food, grains, oilseeds, raw materials, fibres, minerals and oil, but it is difficult in the case of manufactured goods or processed food where exports will constitute only a small percentage of total sales volume in the initial stages.

Primarily an export manager on his return must try to explain to senior management the problems they will face as the company develops its key markets. They will be dealing with clients thousands of miles away; language difficulties will arise; delivery problems may become acute – in particular the problem of conflict between domestic and export sales will have to be resolved; and there will be many problems in the financing of export sales. Not only must senior management assign export orders top priority in terms of financial and manpower resources, they must ensure that export sales staff are trained in negotiating and financial techniques (see Chapter 4). Above all, effective 'follow-up' in export operations must be carried out at all levels of the company. This section explores some ways of ensuring effective 'follow-up', without which there can be no long-term profitable export market development.

Maintaining contacts with agents and importers overseas requires prompt and courteous replies to queries as well as orders: a telex query requires a telex reply; a cable requires a cabled reply and an airmail letter requires a reply by airmail. All enquiries should be replied to on the day of receipt, or at least on the following day. Even if an immediate reply to any communication is impossible, an interim reply should be sent indicating that a detailed response (e.g. a quotation) will follow as soon as all the relevant information has been collected. Staff at all levels (managerial, clerical, technical and reception) in the company who have any 'interface' or contact with overseas customers must be trained to react courteously and accurately to enquiries about new designs, orders pending and despatch, prices and payments, delivery data, supplies or promotional material, etc. This appears simplistic, yet it is all too often the weakest part of a company organization.

Communications can and should be used intelligently by the company's management to set up a 'dialogue' with overseas agents, importers and key customers to keep them informed (e.g. by well-edited newsletters) of new designs, new technical developments, new staff appointments; at the same time inviting comments, criticisms (for improvement) of the company's products and services in each overseas market. There can be competitions, incentive schemes (visits to the U.K. and E.E.C. as prizes) with the focus on continuing improvements in design, quality and service to customers. Agents' reports should be studied, acknowledged and commented on: not just for control, but to ensure that 'dialogue' with the Agent makes him feel that he is a part, and an important part of his Principal's organization. Market 'follow-up' itself lends to creative thinking, and it is still neglected by the management of even well-established exporting companies in the U.K. (Table 3.10).

*Table 3.10*
*Market Follow-Up Analysis*

| Item | Overseas Market/ Customer | Information Communicated | Information Originator | Follow-Up Action | Executive Responsible |
|------|------|------|------|------|------|
| Quality | | | | | |
| Delivery | | | | | |
| Design | | | | | |
| Performance | | | | | |
| Promotional Support | | | | | |
| Order Levels & Re-order | | | | | |
| Payments | | | | | |
| After-Sales Service | | | | | |
| Competitor Activity | | | | | |
| Maintenance | | | | | |
| Local Technical & Staff Training | | | | | |

There is also a particular need for 'follow-up' in checking that delivery dates or schedules promised are being kept (this applies to supply of display materials as well as to the product itself). The export market may require changes in the product, its purity, its finish or its design. It is important that the export manager should not promise major changes during his market visit if it is likely that these changes cannot be easily made by the production staff. (Any sensible market visit is preceded by detailed discussion between the general manager, export and production departments designed to ensure that any offers of change to the existing product line can be matched at reasonable cost within some definite time period). The export manager, must, of course, thoroughly understand the implications of production changes and their likely costs for the enterprise, and discover the effects of these and other technical changes on the agents' business, and on customers; this aspect of 'follow-up' is, in practice, not always put in hand (but is particularly important if these changes result in increased costs).

Follow-up overseas visits must be made to markets with prospects, and to agents who are fulfilling satisfactory sales orders: there is a tendency by export managers to concentrate attention and visits on problem markets to the detriment of those doing well. Observation and analysis are essential if 'follow-up' is to be effective (see Chapter 2).

There is also much scope for developing and refining after-sales service, not only in the provision (in plenty of time) of spares, replacement parts and equipment and replacing faulty consumer products, but in providing training to agents and importers in business management, basic accounting techniques and promotional methods (including demonstrating and presentation skills). In the case of technical and industrial and capital goods, 'follow-up' and servicing will be stipulated, in detail, in the contract: and in the case of consumer products which are faulty or rejected, local commercial law may require certain 'follow-up' actions by the principal or his agent (and prosecution in default).

The focus of export market 'follow-up', therefore, is communication skills development, quality of service, delivery, innovation in developing design, specifications, etc. in the light of customer reactions and use. Without 'follow-up', this vital aspect of export management will be neglected and long-term market development stunted, to say nothing of a loss of image and reputation by the exporting company worldwide. Follow-up is a particularly significant part of the 'total export concept' mentioned in Section 4.1.

In heavy industrial sectors, follow-up has, of course, become part of the contractual relationship particularly in the supply of services. For example, in Poland, Massey Ferguson supplied after-sale management and engineering resources. Both these are increasingly important aspects of follow-up which apply to all types of consumer goods, particularly needed are logistical expertise to improve the efficiency of distribution overseas, and training of distributive staff and those in display support. The basic lesson of 'follow-up' is clear: in helping Agents and importers to develop their business, the exporting company is by definition strengthening its market position and prospects for profits.

## References

1. 'International Economic Indicators, 1980', *U.N. Statistical Yearbook and World Bank Atlas* (U.S. Department of Commerce International Trade Administration, 1982).
2. *World Bank Developments Report* (1979). *World Bank Atlas* (Washington DC, 1980).
3. Yankelovich, D. 'New Criteria for Market Segmentation', *Harvard Business Review*, March/April, 1964.
4. Allied International Designers, *Marketing*, December, 1978.

5. Barclays Bank International 'Factors for International Success: Export Development in France, Germany and U.K.', *I.T.I. Research*, 1979.
6. Root, F. A. *Strategic Planning for Export Marketing* (Forlag: Copenhagen, 1975).
7. National Economic Development Office *International Price Competitiveness, Non-Price Factors and Export Performance* (NEDO: London, 1978).
8. Weinrauch, J., Donald, J. and Rao, C. 'The Export Marketing Mix: An Examination of Company Experiences and Perceptions', *Journal of Business Research*, October, 1974.
9. Terpstra. V. *International Marketing*, (Holt-Saunders International, New York, 1980) pp. 457–8.
10. Hague, P. 'How to Avoid Competing on Price', *Industrial Marketing Digest*, **2**, No. 2, pp. 52–9.

# 4. *EFFECTIVE MANAGEMENT ORGANIZATION*

## 4.1 Supply and Shipping

An early research study[1] published by the Royal Society of Arts first highlighted the problem of supply capacity which many companies still seem to encounter, particularly in U.K., though the supply and delivery performance of British companies has improved markedly in recent years, and is now generally much more competitive with European counterparts.

Nevertheless, this BETRO report singled out lack of production capacity as being the most serious limitation on export sales growth. It reported supply shortfalls and irregular flow in companies as responsible for many bottlenecks, and cites instances where 300% higher prices were being paid for imported components – to speed up orders to overseas customers (the lack of adequate steel supplies, for example, was singled out as frequently responsible for unduly long delivery dates and loss of overseas orders).

Also mentioned in this Report is the need to improve the level of shipping and freight handling services for U.K. exporters; a need highlighted by recent correspondence in the financial press by exporters reporting unsatisfactory service by these agencies (some goods not loaded on to the correct ship, or even shipped to the incorrect destination in spite of documentation being in order including Clean Bill of Lading).

Whilst the supply position has undoubtedly improved in the U.K. (no doubt due in many sectors, such as construction, to the fall-off in domestic demand producing surplus capacity for export) since this research was done, there are still indications that supply management requires a thorough overhaul and, above all, much closer integration with marketing planning and operations (the all-important question of management organization is discussed fully in Section 4.2). A survey by the British Institute of Management (BIM) found that 80% of orders from British suppliers were not received on time; whilst too much should not be read into one set of research data, there are two particularly important aspects of supply/production which relate to overseas customers:

(a) Supply, shipping and service are a vital part of export operations and they can make or break a company's competitive edge overseas;
(b) What are the perceptions (if any) that overseas customers have of British supply and delivery, and how do these influence buying decisions?

Indeed these two points raise another general one: there is no point in an exporting company spending man-hours, resources and funds researching overseas markets, planning and implementing marketing programmes if, at the end of the day, the company is unable to supply goods on time and ensure shipping and a level of service at least as competitive as its major rivals. A recent report[2] in the U.K. financial press highlighted overseas customers' views of British exporting. Interestingly, the practice of marketing in the U.K. was highly rated and esteemed by respondents; but they still regarded as suspect the supply and delivery performance in their markets by British companies.

Now, it is certainly true that, anxious to obtain orders, export sales staff do, from time to time, promise delivery dates, terms of supply, special specifications, etc. which the home-based factory simply is not in a position to fulfill. But, with proper co-ordination by management, this problem should not arise at all; and if it does, all the pressure should be applied to production to supply what the customer wants. There is the further point that, in the eyes of overseas customers, a company's reputation stands or falls primarily on its ability to deliver on time precisely, quality and quantities ordered, rather than on marketing expertise (vital though this is). Such reputations for reliability take time to build up; they can be destroyed overnight by one short shipment, inaccurate documentation, etc. – short shipment not declared on the invoice, resulting in importer or agent wasting his (and the exporter's) time searching in Customs premises or airport cargo bays for a consignment lying in a U.K. port or at an exporter's factory. Indeed, such inadequacy can even damage the exporting reputation of an entire sector of industry and management must ensure by planning and co-ordination that it does not happen.

The role of the shipping manager in ensuring cost-effective and punctual delivery is particularly important and merits further analysis. As it is, export distribution still rates a low priority in many manufacturing companies, and the shipping manager tends to appear low down in the company's management organization. Yet the cost of shipping and distribution will almost certainly be much more significant in export than in domestic markets. Transport costs frequently exceed tariff costs. The cost of documentation can be considerable, even for a single consignment, and an export consignment can easily involve up to about 15 separate parties, and may require information for up to 50 commercial and official procedures. Thus, the shipping manager may well be responsible for expenditure averaging 10% of the company's total sales. If this percentage is applied nationally to the total overseas sales of U.K. valued annually at £40 billion, the result is a staggering £4 billion annually accounted for by distribution and shipping costs[1]. Senior management in many companies needs to become more directly involved in decisions and controls relating, not just to advertising and sales, but to shipping and distribution (too often the task of arranging international distribution is delegated to a junior member of staff). Shipping and delivery performance can, therefore, clearly be improved by more attention to cost and management organization.

The Institute of Export stresses the importance for management planning, shipping, delivery and service of the 'total export concept'. This identifies every stage or phase of the physical movement of goods by air or sea and, more importantly, assesses the effects of each on both company costs and customer requirements. The implication of this concept for management is that, for example, the designer should be taking into account the shipping space that the packed product will occupy, and the need to minimize packing, cost and risk. The manager responsible for setting up, or operating overseas distribution channels must realize all possible economy of operation, particularly in Europe, in siting depots and in route planning. For example, the exporter may not be able to generate return loads and another firm will; if transport staff are consulted at an early stage they may be able to indicate where the opportunities for return loads will be highest. Clearly, any movement of goods affects production, and this links back to design. There is yet a further link in this concept which concerns payment for the goods: the speed and extent of payment can be affected by how the entire transport operation has been handled. For example, documentation is normally done by the shipping department, but can be delegated to the freight forwarder: but payment methods require documentary evidence of the despatch or receipt of goods, and the efficiency of the shipping department is vital to the expeditious timing of receipts.

At this point it is timely to itemize briefly the principal cost headings involved in an export shipment:

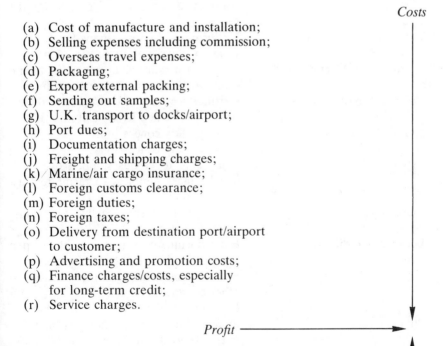

*Costs*

(a) Cost of manufacture and installation;
(b) Selling expenses including commission;
(c) Overseas travel expenses;
(d) Packaging;
(e) Export external packing;
(f) Sending out samples;
(g) U.K. transport to docks/airport;
(h) Port dues;
(i) Documentation charges;
(j) Freight and shipping charges;
(k) Marine/air cargo insurance;
(l) Foreign customs clearance;
(m) Foreign duties;
(n) Foreign taxes;
(o) Delivery from destination port/airport
to customer;
(p) Advertising and promotion costs;
(q) Finance charges/costs, especially
for long-term credit;
(r) Service charges.

*Profit*

*Market Price*

Further, the shipping manager is responsible for prompt and accurate preparation of the shippings documents for both expeditious transportation and payment. In principle, documents are required:

(a)  To satisfy government regulations both in the U.K. and overseas;
(b)  To invoice customer;
(c)  To receive payment.

*Table 4.1*
*Checklist: Shipping Documents*

| Document | Description |
| --- | --- |
| Pro Forma Invoice | Sent at quotation stage, to include payments and delivery |
| Export/Import Licences | Customs and Excise to advise requirements, e.g. Open or Specific |
| Certified Invoice | Sterling or foreign currency |
| Customs entry | Codes for national export statistics |
| Standard Shipping Note | Contains specification of the goods and indicates who pays port charges |
| Hazardous cargo declaration | Applicable to sea and air consignments |
| Bill of Lading | Contains evidence of shipment; it is also a contract of carriage and receipt for the goods |
| Certificate of Shipping | Notification of goods shipped |
| Airway Bill | Contains details of air consignment |
| Certificate of Origin | Required in some overseas markets and often on Chamber of Commerce form |
| Consular Invoice | Certifies accuracy of consignment details signed and sealed by Consul in U.K. |
| E.E.C. Certificate | To give Duty concessions |
| E.F.T.A. Forms | To give Duty concessions |
| TIR Carnet | Applicable to Goods shipped overland, and business samples, to facilitate Customs clearance |
| Bill of Exchange | Form of Payment legally demanding buyer to pay |
| Letter of Credit | Bank document more secure than open account or clean Bill of Exchange |
| Black List Certificate | Required by some customers hostile to other countries |
| Export Credits Guarantee Policy | Contains insurance against bad debts due to insolvency of buyer, non-payment due to government restrictions, trade dispute, civil war, etc. |

*Table 4.2*
*Checklist: Product Supply Analysis*

(1) Which product types are important foreign currency earners? Could their export potential be increased if they were:

(a) Produced in greater volume in their present form?
(b) Modified so as to adapt them more closely to the needs of present markets?
(c) Modified to meet the needs of markets to which they cannot be sold in their present form?
(d) Better distributed, sold, publicised or merchandised in foreign markets?
(e) Offered in a different form? For example, in sales packages instead of in bulk?
(f) Offered at a lower price?

If any of these measures are advisable, what are the barriers to their execution?

(a) Do the managements of the manufacturers concerned lack adequate information or expertise, or are they simply lethargic?
(b) Do the manufacturers lack adequate finance to make the necessary changes?
(c) Are supplies of essential personnel not readily available?

If barriers exist that the manufacturers themselves cannot overcome, or are unwilling to overcome, can the government take effective steps to improve the situation? If so,

(a) What would be the cost, and can it be afforded?
(b) Would the return justify the cost?
(c) How long would the process take?

Taking into account the answers to these questions, to what extent will the export potential of this product type improve in the short term?

(2) Which product types are sold mainly on the home market? Could the export potential of these product types be increased without damage to domestic needs if they were:

(a) Produced in greater volume in their present form?
(b) Marketed more energetically or expertly abroad?
(c) Modified to meet the needs of foreign markets?

If any of these measures are both feasible and advisable what are the barriers to their execution?

If barriers exist that the manufacturers themselves cannot overcome, or are unwilling to overcome, can the government take effective steps to improve the situation? If so:

(a) What would be the cost and can it be afforded?
(b) Would the return justify the cost?
(c) How long would the process take?

Taking into account the answers to these questions, to what extent will the export potential of this product type improve in the short term?

(3) Which product types produced elsewhere in the world could be made in this country at the present time?

  (a) Are there forms of industrial waste that are processed into marketable products elsewhere in the world?

  (b) Are opportunities neglected to market by-products generated by industrial processes?

  (c) Could more advantageous use of existing industrial skills and knowledge be made by the introduction of additional product types?

  (d) Would it be possible and advantageous to make the finished products, for which at present the country supplies the raw materials and components?

  (e) Would it be possible and advantageous to assemble finished goods from imported components, instead of importing the finished product?

  (f) Are opportunities being lost to make essential industrial supplies that existing factories at present buy from abroad?

  (g) Are there product types that at present are largely or wholly imported and that require no special skills or know-how to manufacture?

  (h) Are there neglected opportunities to exploit low overheads or low labour costs?

If the answer to any of these questions suggests that the country's present product potential is not being effectively exploited, what are the barriers to the introduction of suitable additional product types?

  (a) What part must the government play in their introduction?

  (b) What would be the cost and can it be afforded?

  (c) Would any of the additional products be exportable?

  (d) Would the return justify the cost?

  (e) How long would the process take?

Taking into account the answers to these questions, to what extent will general and export product potential improve in the short term as the result of any action that it is intended to take?

(4) Which product types could find a ready market in this country and in the surrounding region but could be manufactured only with the aid of extensive assistance from outside sources?

If such product type exist, what is the present situation with each of them?

  (a) Have the sizes of the home and export markets been carefully calculated and a persuasive case been established to attract outside investment and assistance?

  (b) Have approaches been made to international sources of assistance, or to foreign governments, bankers or suitable manufacturing organizations?

(c) Are these negotiations likely to be successful?
(d) If so, how long will it take to conclude them?

Taking into account the answers to these questions, to what extent will general export potential improve in the short and middle term as the result of any agreement that might be made?

(5) What resources remain unexploited, or are poorly exploited for lack of investment or expertise that at present is available only from outside sources? Use the same checklist as for the previous question.

## 4.2 The Task Force and the Work Force

The BETRO Report (published by Royal Society of Arts and cited earlier) made a number of important points about manning for export and manpower policy and, in particular, commented on the relative 'under-manning' by British companies of their overseas sales operations (this will be referred to again in the light of more recent research in Section 5.5). But it is not only the sales operations that are considered here: undermanning in one vital sector is a direct consequence of inadequate management organization to cope effectively with increasingly sophisticated demands of overseas customers in a competitive world. And this report does actually cite many companies, where, not only is one of the sales staff responsible for enormous areas of the world (operating almost always through Agents), but where almost the entire export effort revolves round one man (including some exporting 50–80% of turnover) who has to attend to sales administration too.

This report strongly urges the adoption of a new manpower policy by exporting companies, and in particular increased and better paid and better qualified staffing in export operations as compared with the high level of manning in the home market. Of course, manpower is only one of the total resources that the company's management is prepared to put towards successful export operations. But it is without doubt the most important resource and in this sector, more effective organization of manpower for exporting is therefore the focus.

Much must depend on the level and quality of commitment that the management has to export operations. Whilst it is difficult to quantify such a concept as commitment, there are certain operational indicators that show what stage of involvement in the resourcing of export operations a company has reached. Levels of commitment are therefore illustrated in Figure 4.1 and require, and indeed repay, some detailed study by management (each successive stage includes the activities of its predecessor). Effective management organization for exporting can be achieved by:

(a) Setting up Task Forces which can be deployed in key overseas markets, and which are made up of sales staff supported by design and technical staff. These can respond to customers' requirements as a team and present a 'package' to overseas customers which is technically up-to-date, competitive in design and range etc.

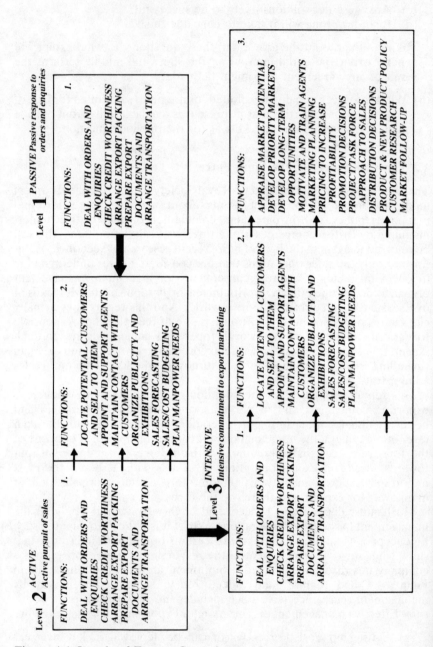

Figure 4.1  Levels of Export Committment by Management

Source: International Trade Centre UNCTAD/GATT, Geneva. Analysis of Export Marketing Training Needs

(b) Ensuring a much closer interface in all overseas operations between the finance and marketing functions.

Policy and organization under (b) are dealt with later in this section, but the entire concept of building Task Forces and setting up teamwork in overseas markets must of course encompass the financial as well as other functions. At this stage, one practical example will point the way: a British company manufacturing pre-fabricated building materials and components for sale to the Far East, having previously used only sales staff abroad, decided to send out a senior designer to accompany sales staff. The result was that customers' special requirements could be re-drawn overnight, and new design concepts introduced and discussed on the spot avoiding lengthy correspondence and consultation with the home base. Technical service and design quality for customers improved substantially, and within three years the company had doubled its export turnover in this region by penetration at the expense of competitors.

Management organizations, both traditional and Task-Force-orientated, are illustrated in Figures 4.2 and 4.3.

Furthermore, authoritative research[3] undertaken at University of Wisconsin, U.S.A. on export management has shown conclusively that:

(a) The financial and marketing implications of export policy need to be set up in a co-ordinated way;
(b) The typical management structure leans towards 'separation' rather than 'integration' of these two functions;
(c) Export marketing staff need to have greater financial expertise and support if they are to develop profitable business overseas.

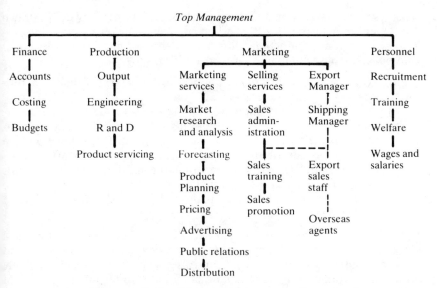

Figure 4.2 Traditional Management Organization

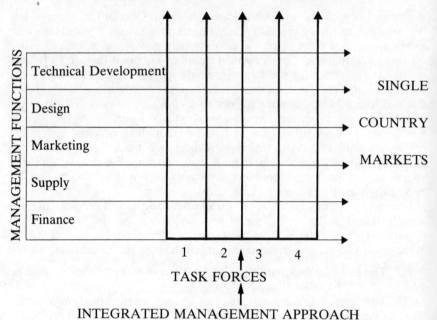

Figure 4.3 Task Force Organization for more Competitive Export Marketing

This research also demonstrates, on the basis of empirical evidence drawn from management practice, that when companies achieve a close integration of management functions directed towards specific export objectives and policies, these companies are more likely:

(a) To achieve a higher penetration in export markets than competitors;
(b) To have higher staff motivation at all levels to succeed;
(c) To share expertise from different disciplines in policy implementation. Thus, closer working liaison among the different functions can make some contribution towards improving the performance of industry. And as international trading conditions improve, profits can be restored to a level where companies can put into reserve more for investment in new plant and technical processes, and in market development.

Particular attention must be paid to the interface between technical development and marketing; new technology such as robotics and microcomputer-based designs and controls now make it possible not only to maintain volume production and quality but to offer more varieties of product of consistent quality at comparable unit output costs. There is also the extent to which Information Technology (IT) is being used effectively by management for analysis and worldwide communications (e.g. accessing International Product Codes and data retrieval). The implications of these for marketing management's planning are highly significant and further research is needed to identify the extent to which company competitiveness can be sharpened by closer interfaces. There is also the interface between supply and marketing: surveys reported by British Institute of Management and *Financial Times*[4] suggest that poor supply performance by U.K. firms reduces promotional effectiveness.

The importance of this 'task force' or 'integrated approach' has also been stressed at the highest level of industry. Sir Kenneth Corfield, Chairman of Standard Telephones and Cables has called for new standards of leadership in export.

> "Management is itself insufficiently aware of overseas markets – and more particularly of how the design, engineering, manufacturing and selling disciplines have to be integrated if overseas markets are to be taken . . . A major task lies ahead for Britain in creating technically literate, professionally skilled and internationally experienced management at all levels in our companies. . . . The breadth and experience necessary to open trade routes has to pervade all levels of a company so that its culture is international."[5]

And Rensis Likert, the American management and organization writer, has suggested that the 'best' management style that a manager can adopt is to form his staff into a group, who must interact with him only as a group, and then use a consultative approach to decision-making in which this group is expected to participate. The group in this sense only acts as a group in the decision-making situation, and for the rest of the time the members act as individuals carrying out their jobs. As a method of decision-making it has been criticized for its inflexibility, as some research has shown that certain types of decisions (namely those for which one manager has at least all the necessary information and a high degree of certainty that his decision will be accepted by subordinates) can be more effectively taken by one man than opened up to a group discussion, which can cause delays. Boards of directors have traditionally worked as groups in many companies, and although there are exceptions, it is interesting to note that the shared responsibility and co-operative effort of a team seems to be preferred as a method of operation at this level in organizations for at least some activities.

So far the focus of attention has been the deployment of project/task forces to improve the manning of export sales activities, and thereby to sharpen the penetration of key export markets. This has been done in the context of raising the level of corporate commitment to exporting. What must now be considered in this context is the relationship between management and the shopfloor. Reference has been made in the last section to quality, delivery, supply capacity, and technical adaptations, and shipping to ensure customer satisfaction: it is impossible to analyse improvements in these sectors without reference to the work-force who make and deliver the goods. Their interest in the company, their productivity and motivation, their attitudes to visiting overseas customers, their awareness of the importance of exports to the company's livelihood – all these are, or should be, of vital concern to management.

Clear and continuing communication between management and work-force is required about the company's overseas activities, and the importance of these to the livelihood of all the staff. In the U.K. the initiative of Export Year was followed up in 1978 by Export United to achieve just this in many British manufacturing companies. The creation of a sense of commitment to export at every level within a company is an effective description of the Export United concept. Sponsored jointly by the British Overseas Trade Board, the Association of British Chambers of Commerce, the Confederation of British Industry, the Committee on Invisible Exports, the Institute of Export and the TUC, Export United followed 1977's Export Year, during which companies all over Britain undertook to improve export awareness amongst their work force. Export Year was a limited success and rather than let the benefits it brought to its enthusiastic supporters dwindle and fade, Export United was created to continue the aims of Export Year indefinitely.

Export United campaigns varied according to the size and nature of the individual company. The scope is wide and many firms have shown enormous ingenuity in thinking up ideas to stimulate interest in export. Export evenings, outings and competitions are popular and Export United posters, charts, badges and beermats number among the endless possibili-ties. Most companies find it helpful to appoint an Export United organizing committee or representative whose job it is to co-ordinate the Export United activities and keep enthusiasm for it high within the company.

To illustrate this concept in action, Victor Products & Co of Wallsend, Tyne and Wear, have always placed emphasis on communications between management and shopfloor. The company is split into three divisions responsible for three main areas of manufacture – hazardous area lighting equipment, cable connecting products and portable drilling equipment, around 25 per cent of the company's £8.5m annual turnover was from exports, at the time of the scheme.

In addition to the monthly meeting on company activities attended by every employee, a working party of four shop floor workers, one trade union representative and a factory manager has been set up to co-ordinate the Export United campaign. The company are proud of their delivery track record – production works a month ahead of the delivery schedule and no delivery has ever been late; the company attributed this as much to the efforts of an enthusiastic and flexible work force as to efficient management. Export United can only enhance working relations, particu-larly as all the schemes introduced have been popular in this particular company.

The philosophy behind the Export United campaign was simple – greater export awareness means improved export performance. This, in turn, means greater prosperity for everyone within the firm. The reasons for setting up an Export United campaign can vary from company to company. Victor Products stress the unifying effects of the campaign, other firms hope to improve particular aspects of their export performance such as delivery or product quality. A checklist of Export United campaign ideas for companies to consider was contained in the publicity material available from BOTB. Basically, whatever form a campaign takes, its aim must alway be to keep everybody in the company in touch with the export operation. Only then can they be aware of how vital export performance is to both the company and to themselves.

Another task force approach is illustrated in Figure 4.3 involving group structures of managers and specialists, and is sometimes referred to as 'matrix' management. As illustrated, this involves setting up teams to work together on a particular project (for example developing a new product and setting up the production and marketing activities to make and sell it). These teams are drawn from any level of the organization and any specialist team. Firms which use the technique are cautious about their recommendation of it across the spectrum of industry; whilst most enthusiastic about its potential for achieving rapid and effective results, there are problems which can arise due to the uncertainty about lines of accountability and authority.

There is still also the basic organization decision which management has to resolve: whether to have an 'international division' providing research and other services and planning and control across a spectrum of overseas markets, or whether these functions should be dispersed, with full management accountability, to export companies or operating subsidies trading with different regions. Some companies which formerly had international divisions, have now disbanded them, for example, Baker Perkins of Peterborough; such divisions can be found to be too remote from the markets they serve and become bureaucratic in planning and control. Other companies have dispersed export expertise to subsidiaries, for example, Reckitt & Colman; others, such as Glaxo concentrate their exporting and shipping expertise in an export company. Often, it is the return on assets employed over an assessed period which will determine the type of management organization most appropriate (such a ratio might be very different in Africa and North America). A simple matrix covering these points is contained in Figure 4.4.

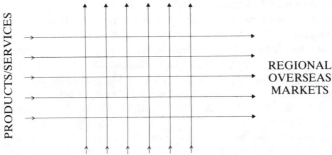

EXPORT OPERATIONS DISPERSED TO SUBSIDIARIES

PRODUCTS/SERVICES

REGIONAL OVERSEAS MARKETS

UNIFIED/CENTRALIZED EXPORT COMPANY

Figure 4.4 Simple Matrix for Overseas Operations

**4.3 Financial Aspects**

Of special significance, therefore, particularly in the stepping up of profits in export operations, is the interface in the management organization of the finance and marketing functions.

The provision of medium-term and long-term credit can play a decisive role in exports. Significant national differences exist, though the recent international credit agreements are intended to lessen the severity of credit competition. Indeed, the provision of credit is frequently more important than a competitive price and there are examples of companies having success in Eastern European tenders by offering very attractive credit terms but inflating their bid to cover the additional cost of credit. Conversely, there are instances of a British manufacturer's marketing staff losing a contract almost at the last minute because they were unable to match the interest terms (the actual rate of interest and the term period over which repayments are completed) of foreign manufacturers, particularly the Japanese.

Credit must be used as a key element not only in the total marketing mix, but as a way of maintaining margins. There are, of course, specialist agencies which can advise and support credit offers such as banks and ECGD. Indeed, 31% of British exports are now financed with the aid of credits from government funds, a figure second in the E.E.C. only to France's 74% and well in front of Germany's 11%.

The important question also arises here: are British companies as efficient as they could be in credit collection on overseas sales. Clearly, in addition to price, profitability also must depend on the time it takes for a company to receive monies owing to it by overseas customers. Even though a certain time element is implicitly calculated into the export price, nevertheless, the more a company can improve on the average time (by collecting money from customers faster) the more profitability can be improved; this is often a problem, particularly when interest rates are high. Whether a company can collect its outstanding funds quickly or slowly depends to a large extent on the national composition of its markets. Some countries are prompt payers, others are slow. Export marketing staff need to be constantly alerted by financial management in this regard before undertaking new business abroad.

Of course, all marketing staff are concerned to retain customers and increase orders: the problem, however, can arise where marketing staff overseas offer longer credit to important customers to take business from competitors. One recent example occurred of an industrial chemicals company where the export representative extended the credit period of a customer from ninety to one hundred and eighty days to secure a volume order. To the financial controller, mindful of the cost of money, this is tantamount to 'giving the goods away'. Another problem which arises is the overseas customer whose credit limit, set by ECGD, has been exhausted; the result is that ECGD is unable to provide cover for new orders taken by marketing staff who should be alerted to this, wherever possible, before they go overseas.

Therefore, a sound credit policy demands much closer liaison between finance and marketing so that the company can ensure that:

(a) Its credit terms are financially sound;
(b) It is not losing business because its credit terms are no longer competitive;
(c) The cost of collecting debts internationally is fully taken into account in pricing policy.

It is, of course widely recognized that export pricing under a floating currency presents both problems and opportunities. If an economy is in trouble, 'floating' can be a timely way out for governments; and the currency profit from exporting can also be useful. Moreover, as the sterling inflation rate has tended to be higher than that of other major currencies, this is itself a good reason to invoice in foreign currencies. But currency instability and the changed role of sterling in international trade payments underline the vital point about adopting a policy towards exporting, which closely associates finance and marketing. This is still not grasped by many British manufacturing exporters. Currency fluctuations can destroy a company's profitability overseas; moreover, the recent downward move in sterling is not entirely welcome; it makes the cost of imported materials and components high, and it creates problems even when 'value added' is well above the average and where costs rise at once, but the cash recovery follows six to twelve months later. Indeed, where companies maintain their sterling prices hoping to see a reduction in the price of their products overseas, their hopes seldom materialize.

Given the substantial advantages in terms of profits in conducting export transactions in foreign currencies, what use do British companies selling abroad make of the facilities available? The Department of Trade undertook a survey in 1980 which shows that less than 30% do so (Table 4.3).

*Table 4.3*
*U.K. Exports: Analysis by Commodity Group of Foreign Currency Invoicing*

| Commodity Groups | % by value Shipments 1979 |
|---|---|
| Food, beverages and tobacco | 16 |
| Fuels and basic materials | 48 |
| Chemicals | 58 |
| Textiles | 21 |
| Metals and articles of metal | 30 |
| Electrical machinery, apparatus and appliances | 16 |
| Other machinery | 15 |
| Transport equipment | 15 |
| Other manufactured goods | 38 |
| TOTAL | 29% |

Management can also take advantage of the liberalization of U.K. exchange control by operating a 'reservoir of foreign currency'; this can provide a regular flow of cash from the overseas market which eliminates the foreign currency overdraft as payments are received. In this way, overdrafts in the U.K. can be replaced by those raised in foreign currencies at an interest rate lower than that in the U.K. Indeed, many of the new banking services are only becoming available as a result of the lifting of all foreign exchange regulations. Freedom to operate in foreign exchange markets can offset the impact of inflation, the fluctuating pound and high overdraft rates. Clearly these raise vital considerations for marketing staff making competitive quotations to overseas customers.

But companies in, for example, engineering consider understandably that their expertise lies in engineering rather than 'banking', and there is reluctance to get involved in foreign exchange markets; yet companies can acquire the appropriate expertise and there are instances when profitability can be greatly enhanced. An engineering company in the Midlands, for example, had a total turnover of £25m of which 60% was in export markets; yet in the first two years of invoicing in foreign currencies and using the foreign currency markets, the company made a trading profit on its currency dealings alone of £100,000.

Another complaint by exporting companies has been the incidence of high domestic interest rates; the answer is, in this case, not to fund these exports in sterling. There is also sometimes a strong reaction among established exporters that selling overseas in currencies other than sterling is unpatriotic. In fact the opposite is the case. Every time British industry sells overseas in sterling, it has to 'sell' sterling, and as approximately 70% of U.K. exports are invoiced in sterling, we are currently having to 'sell' sterling to the value of approximately £25,000m for the purpose of paying ourselves. This should be compared with the situation in Japan where they have always transacted the bulk of their exports in currencies other than their own, mainly U.S. dollars. Consequently, they have virtually no outflow of Yen but a huge inflow of currencies.

How, in practice, can companies improve both the profitability and marketing impact of their export operations by foreign currency management? There are three principal approaches:

(a) Selling or buying the foreign currency 'forward'
   This entails fixing the rate today at which the bank will exchange that currency into sterling, or vice versa, at some agreed time in the future. By adopting this technique, the exporter removes the risk of the exchange rate moving against him between the time he accepts the order and the time he receives the currency or is due to pay in currency. Moreover, he is able to quantify the amount of any premium or discount and either take advantage of any such gain in his marketing or include any loss in his onward selling price.

(b) Borrowing foreign currencies
   While the use of foreign currency borrowing for medium-/long-term

investment purposes has increased considerably over the last few years, the use of such currencies for financing exports on both short- and medium-term credit is still rare. If a buyer in, say, Germany is taking 90 days credit, there may be considerable advantage in financing this sale by borrowing 90 day Deutschemarks as opposed to sterling, and provided the sale is invoiced in Deutschemarks, there is no exchange risk.

(c) Offsetting imports in one currency with exports in the same currency
This can be done by (i) Exchange Commission: the use of the same currency to finance both transactions can reduce the cost of exchange commissions both to the exporter and to the importer. (ii) Holding Accounts: in order to minimize the cost of exchange commissions as well as the premiums involved in the 'forward' purchase of currencies, it may sometimes be desirable to operate a 'Holding' account into which a certain currency is placed and out of which payments in that currency may be made.

It is, of course, essential for financial management to provide up-to-date intelligence of currency interest and exchange rates; this will help export marketing staff:

(a) To up-date currency trends for costing and selling purposes;
(b) To be briefed fully for overseas negotiations;
(c) To quote in foreign currencies;
(d) To meet and beat foreign competitors' quotations;
(e) To assess extra profits made by overseas distributors buying in sterling and selling in local currency; and
(f) To reduce buyer resistance, if any, to switching out of sterling.

It will also provide essential facts for: calculating foreign currency price lists, keeping records of their own and/or competitors' currency margins and assessing the amount of cover to buy under the ECGD extended currency insurance.

Foreign buyers who insist on paying in sterling are also taking a gamble on the parity of sterling going down against their own currency during the period of the contract. Thus, from a marketing viewpoint, if the exporter is in a highly competitive market, he can well have the edge simply by resolving the problem of fluctuating exchange rates for his buyer overseas. Moreover, one of the best arguments for a British exporter to sell in foreign currencies is price stability. The salesman's nightmare is having to go to his buyer every month only to tell him that the sterling price has gone up (currently by about $\frac{1}{2}\%$). By the same token, most buyers prefer to know that the price is likely to remain stable over a reasonable period, and using this argument alone British exporters should switch a large proportion of their sales into foreign currencies.

A recent example of how a British exporter could have helped his French buyer is well demonstrated as follows: the exporter had sold to France in sterling and the period from date of order to date of payment was approximately six months. The French buyer, wishing to cover his exchange risk, approached his bank in Paris in order to buy the sterling forward six months. He was told, however, that he was only allowed to buy forward up to two months and he was thus exposed to an exchange risk for the remaining four months. The British exporter, on the other hand, should have invoiced in French Francs and sold forward on the London Money Market up to twelve months, if necessary; had he done so, he would have secured the order in the first place whereas in fact the French buyer delayed confirmation, with a resultant loss to the exporter. Another example, with a more successful outcome was well demonstrated in January 1980 by a British exporter who, although requested to quote in sterling, was encouraged by his advisers to quote for a large contract in Germany both in sterling and D-marks. At the time, the three-year-forward premium on the D-mark was equivalent to no less than 15% on the face value of the contract and so the exporter was able safely to reduce his D-mark quotation by 5%. Confronted by the two quotations, the Germans converted the sterling price into D-marks at the spot rate and were then surprised to find that the D-mark quotation was cheaper than the one in sterling.

In addition to the extra flexibility in marketing which the use of foreign currencies provides, it can have a direct bearing on costs and pricing, particularly when the currency of the exporter is weak. British exporters have direct access to the London Money Market (more so than their foreign competitors) but do not make the fullest use of the services available for their own benefit; the services are detailed in Appendix 3.

This section has concentrated in some detail on currency management as this is one sector in which, in many companies, there is practically no systematic working liaison between finance and marketing; as a result both financial and marketing benefits are lost. It is, therefore, appropriate to summarize some of these major benefits:

    (a)   Depreciating Value of Book Debts
         When inflation in U.K. is at a higher rate than in other industrialized countries, the advantage of having receivables in currencies which are depreciating at a slower rate than sterling is self-evident.

    (b)   Price Stabilization – Cost Escalation
         The same considerations as in (a) would apply to invoicing in sterling; export price increases need to be smaller or even unnecessary when invoicing in currencies with low inflation rates.

    (c)   Additional Flexibility in Marketing
         The salesman with knowledge of the usage of the forward market can give a price based on a firm rate of exchange. If needs be he can use the forward rate as an inducement to obtain sales. He can also sell in a third currency if the situation demands it.

    (d)   Buyer Preference for Own Currency
         In the great majority of cases the customer prefers to buy and to be invoiced in his own currency. It is better marketing and saves the buyer the trouble of conversion. It also makes payment simpler for him.

(e)  Additional Profitability
     Where other trading currencies are at a premium against sterling, this premium can be realized by using the forward market which will provide additional sterling yields on sales.
(f)  Additional Flexibility in Financial Management
     By invoicing in other currencies the exporter may be able to borrow that currency on the Euro-Currency market at considerably lower rates of interest than sterling, with no exchange risk. This fact in turn may enable him to obtain 'Pre-Shipment' finance at very low cost.
(g)  Offsetting Imports with Exports
     Once an exporter is selling in currencies he may be able to use those currencies to pay for his imports, thereby saving himself exchange commission and a proportion of the cost of buying the currency forward.

What are the implications of these points for financial and marketing management. As has been seen, management is having to operate under conditions of increasing uncertainty in export markets: political risks, commercial risks and competition from newly industrializing countries (NICs); added to this are financial uncertainties, particularly in the movements of interest rates and currencies.

These external factors alone demand the closest possible collaboration between the finance and marketing functions: the financial implications of alternative export marketing strategies must be set out in terms of offering not only an attractive product range but a competitive set of financial offers. Indeed, planning marketing activities for overseas demands the most careful financial interpretation of the objectives set and the means of achieving these objectives. This approach is essential

(a)  to 'out-market' competitors with a superior 'total package', and
(b)  to secure improved financial returns to the exporting company.

The financial package offered by the company has become a vital part of its offers to customers, and there is clear evidence that the nature of competition has been changing and that management tasks and organization need to be re-appraised. Longer credit terms are essential to sustain a position overseas: this is an investment decision (tying up money) as well as a marketing decision. Furthermore, the financing of additional capacity or the setting-up of subsidiaries abroad means investment on a more substantial scale.

The net effect of these considerations is that exporting must increase demands on the company's financial resources under conditions worldwide where the profitable use of these resources is less certain. Of course, the effect can be offset to some extent by government services in making exporting more profitable through the provision of low-cost finance, remission of some internal taxes, financing of exports, credit insurance and facilitating international transactions. But it is up to the company to organize its export operations more profitably, using the guidelines set out in this section, and it can do this only if analysis and planning draw on the joint expertise in the company. Consider, for example, the assessment of long-term prospects of an export market and the expected return on the company's investment over a given period, the impact of inflation on pricing policy, the relationship between major economic and financial indicators and market potential – these and other vital questions require both financial and marketing expertise to resolve. Yet, in many manufacturing companies management organization is such that there is woefully insufficient dialogue between finance and marketing staff, let alone joint decision-making on export policies.

Export staff take orders but find they are unable to match interest rates or credit terms offered by their competitors and, as a result, the order is not confirmed; or they accept orders on unprofitable terms. More detailed briefing by financial staff can often avoid such lapses; and by using government financial support for visits and missions overseas, companies can extend their budgets.

Take, for example, Schedule 2 of the ECGD which is sent regularly to policyholders; this Schedule is a confidential document containing vital information on:

(a) Credit and foreign exchange status of all export markets covered by the policy and their financial prospects;
(b) Lines of credit available to finance bi-lateral trade agreements and the markets concerned.

In practice, many exporting sales staff never see, let alone consult, this document which is sent to and held by the financial controller; some have never even heard of it.

In the light of these and other instances of management 'separation' companies should seriously consider setting up 'overseas task forces' which bring together operationally managers in key sectors such as marketing and finance, (one might add design and supply) so that a total policy to penetrate markets and to maximize profits and cash collection can be set up and implemented. Management should, therefore, consider taking steps to ensure that their companies gain from a policy of integration rather than separation. These steps can include the following:

(a) Set out marketing objectives, methods of penetration, pricing and market follow-up with the full financial implications;
(b) Review full sales potential of each overseas market so that financial returns can be maximized without damaging the company's market position or prospects;
(c) Analyse and remain alert to improvements in the price thresholds perceived and accepted by overseas customers in the light of non-price benefits and of competitors' offers;
(d) Act on the application of marginal costing to exporting pricing;
(e) Set up and maintain closer working relationships among financial management and export staff and, where appropriate, export supply and design so that the company has a controlling overseas

project group responsible for total implementation, including major contracts;

(f) Set up or buy in management expertise so that the company can get and offer the best terms in foreign currency dealings, and knows what it is doing;

(g) Ensure that all marketing staff working abroad are better equipped (i) to understand their customer's business and provide advice on business development (ii) to undertake negotiations successfully with overseas customers, using financial as well as sales expertise;

(h) Implement appropriate management training.

This section has examined how profitability in exporting can be improved by better co-ordination and decision-making between the finance and marketing functions. The possible extent of improvement in various key tasks has been set forth in some detail with the focus on improving the terms offered to overseas customers so that the company's competitive position is strengthened and profitability ensured. As the company's involvement overseas grows in the more successful markets, so investment decisions in new plant, direct representation and larger-scale financing have to be made.

The important question remains: who is to ensure that this closer liaison between finance and marketing is brought about? Of course, this must be the top management or direction of the company, whether the managing director or the chairman himself. It must be emphasized that 'integration' does not involve any loss of executive authority on the part of either financial or marketing management; it does require a broader but stronger basis of joint assessment and planning in setting up export policy. This will not happen unless the Board of the company recognizes why it is important: hence the need to get acceptance by top management of this Task Force approach to export operations.

A critical Path Analysis showing financial decision making is contained in Appendix 7.

## References

1. BETRO Trust and the Royal Society of Arts 'Concentration on Key Markets – A Development Plan for Exports'. *ITC Research*, 1965.
2. Davies, G. *How Shipping Hurts Deliveries*. Study Group for Export Distribution, Manchester Polytechnic, 1980.
3. Bilkey, W. N. J. 'An Attempted Integration of the Literature on the Export Behaviour of Firms'. *Journal of International Business*, Summer, 1978.
4. 'Traveller's Tales from Overseas' *Financial Times*, 30 August, 1979.
5. 'World Communications: Tomorrow's Trade Rates'. British Computer Society and Department of Trade and Industry Conference, 1984.

# 5. EFFECTIVE REPRESENTATION OVERSEAS

### 5.1 Role of Trade Commissioner/Commercial Attaché

The Commercial Officer posted overseas represents his country's trading interests in his country of assignment; this is his principal role. The Commercial Officer is not involved directly in setting up trade policy, this is, of course, the responsibility of his home government.

The focus of his work should be export promotion, in all its phases; nevertheless, he will become involved in some staff work relating to trade negotiations (the actual negotiating is normally done at a more senior level), commercial regulations or access of his country's exporters, and in fostering sound and harmonious trade relationships with his counterparts overseas. He is also concerned with commercial intelligence, both reporting market opportunities back to exporters in his home country and spending some time at home acquainting himself with the output of products and services and export market coverage of his home-based manufacturers.

A more detailed, critical appraisal of the Commercial Officer's major tasks is now required as follows: Market analysis: markets for specific products have to be identified, and actual trade opportunities uncovered. Finding markets, however lucrative does not necessarily mean that the exporters will have automatic access to them. Barriers to trade must be detected. Tariffs, quotas, preferential arrangements, quarantine restrictions, packaging regulations, or technical requirements may eliminate or limit the prospects for his country's exporters' products. Access may need to be negotiated, and may require diplomatic work outside the scope of export promotion.

Commercial intelligence also has an important part in securing business: for once a market is identified, access has to be facilitated. Shipping services and freight rates, financing terms, import regulations and related matters connected with local requirements or international practice require accurate reporting and constant review. In more specific terms, therefore, commercial intelligence involves the following:

(a) Handling local trade enquiries about manufactured goods from distributors, end users, etc; the Commercial Officer must check that manufacturers at home are in a position to supply the export market on time; they may have varied their production range, changed the nature of their activities, or even gone out of business. They may already be represented in the market, limited by franchise from

128

competing with associated companies in the market, or committed forward in other markets to the extent of their productive capacity.

(b) Enquiries about exports to Commercial Officer's home country, and in cases, such as the following, direct assistance may be appropriate: essential materials for agriculture or industry that are in short world supply and known to be in demand in the home country; a source of supply that is cheaper than those existing, thereby providing savings for home importers; return cargo for a shipping line that is heavily dependent on cargos (and freight charges) from Officer's home country; maintain good will with leading or prospective importers of home country's products who seek some reciprocity.

(c) The last aspect of this commercial intelligence concerns tender opportunities. In some countries, government dominates or monopolizes the import trade. In most, government purchasing is significant (see Section 1.5). For some product types, official bodies are the only buyers. Central, regional and local government authorities, as well as public utilities and other institutional and private organizations and developers, frequently seek their supplies by calling for international tenders. Their requirements and the particular problems involved in this type of trading, require the particular attention of the Commercial Officer, who must keep informed of tenders (called and, if possible, imminent), and keep in close touch with tendering bodies, ensure that his country's suppliers are on the tender lists, and above all, keep his home trade department fully informed and up-dated. In the U.K. all this is processed by EIS on Calls for Tender Notices; it is of interest to add that, in notifying his home base, the Officer should include these details: nature and present status of the project, its prospects of implementation and anticipated costs; financing arrangements, likely extent of foreign participation, and the possibility of home exporters supplying any part of the requirement; anticipated date of tender notice and from whom documentation can be obtained; any special procedures or conditions e.g. whether bids may be submitted direct or only through an agent, method of payment, tender bonds (if any). Follow-up is also important (details of successful tender, reasons for acceptance, possibility of subcontracting to successful bidder).

The Commercial Officer also has to attend to trade relations: this involves regular contacts with government officials and with industrialists in the Commercial Officer's host country: it may be necessary to influence these sectors to improve export promotion procedures or improve trade relations with host government. Specifically, these activities can include: liaison with foreign government officials; acting on behalf of his own government to improve access and sales prospects for his country's products: assisting delegations to international organizations such as UNCTAD, GATT, U.N. Economic Commissions etc.; assisting with staff work at bi-lateral and multi-lateral trade negotiations as required. Also, the Commercial Officer in his relations with the business sectors must ensure that they understand that he will facilitate but cannot participate in these negotiations and dealings; it must be understood too that the Commercial Officer is not a sponsoring body, does not guarantee the outcome of his efforts, and does not accept any responsibility for the standing or practices of any firm or person that may be subject of the Officer's proposals or comments. Of course, the Officer's local contacts and knowledge of his overseas market's prospects are vital in helping him to provide visiting businessmen with guidance and assistance.

As will already be clear, the promotional role of the Commercial Officer is particularly significant as, given the availability of products for export, the Officer is well placed to pursue penetration of the market, and, of course, to advise and assist his own business community as to the most effective promotional methods of achieving this. This aspect of the Officer's work requires initiative, some creativity, but above all, persistence in such activities as traders' and technical symposia to publicize his country's products and services by sectors; fair participation, store promotions and trade displays, social receptions for local business leaders and senior officials, arrangements for local media coverage of promotional events, guidance and support for national trade visitors and missions; and some public relations work. The Commercial Officer must also ensure that he travels widely and gets to know the local business community; he must make tours as appropriate, particularly of new industrial development or tax-free zones, and he must actively publicize new industrial and technical developments of his own country in the local press. In short, the Officer should exercise creativity in planning new promotional events such as national weeks devoted to his country's heritage and achievements, etc. and in creating a favourable climate for business contacts and developments.

There is one further point requiring elucidation: what, in general terms, is the organizational and operational effectiveness of Official Commercial Trade Commissioner services. In the U.K. the Central Policy Review Staff[1] examined this aspect as far as H.M. Diplomatic Service is concerned but did not make any far-reaching conclusions as to its future structure; though it accepted that there was a high degree of dedication among many U.K. Diplomatic Posts towards export promotion it questioned the continuing emphasis still placed in some posts on political work in terms of status and career development. What is certainly required in the U.K. is a formal, sustained programme of training in export marketing for Commercial Officers. CPRS also commented favourably on some aspects of the Canadian and Australian Trade Commissioner Services. These are differently organized to that of U.K. in that they appoint (usually on contract) a cadre of senior, experienced businessmen to commercial posts: the advantage is that they have business in many cases, marketing expertise, speak the businessman's language, and are more readily effective and better trained to pursue business opportunities; but they have little or no political expertise, and there is no career structure for them which will take them up to ambassadorial or ministerial posts. In this latter respect, the general concensus is that U.K. Diplomatic Service is better structured: it must be borne in mind that many obstacles to trade, many issues affecting trade policy and relationships are politically based: therefore some political expertise is vital. A more important point, though, is that in the U.K. Diplomatic Service more ambassadors are becoming actively involved in general trade promotion and policy and this is changing the traditional career pattern, for the ambassador clearly has the contacts, the influence, the wide experience and indeed the authority to promote trade and ensure the highest possible representation at promotional events; Trade Commissioner Services lack this, and are likely to prove increasingly ineffective in the long term.

*Check List of Data Summaries to be Provided by Commercial Officer*
(1) Data Foreign Importers require about exports and exporters of Officer's country
  (a) Illustrated brochures (accurately translated, if necessary);
  (b) Samples;
  (c) Prices and credit terms;
  (d) Achievable delivery schedules;
  (e) Supply capacity;
  (f) Uses for the product;
  (g) Attitudes to the distribution system;
  (h) Details of previous agents/importers (if any);
  (i) Information sheet on exporter;
  (j) Arrangements for visits by exporters or visits to exporting company in Officer's country.

(2) Data required by Officer's own Government and Export Community
  (a) Contacts established, status reports and details of agents;
  (b) Effectiveness of or prospects for bi-lateral or multi-lateral trade agreements;
  (c) Country's foreign exchange position;
  (d) Arrangements for traders' symposia;
  (e) Market conditions for specific products (e.g. consumption trends, domestic and foreign suppliers, prices, consumer expectations in regard to taste, design, quality, packing, colours, etc.);
  (f) Details of forthcoming trade fairs and exhibitions;
  (g) Assistance available and/or given to trade delegations/missions from home country;
  (h) Important changes in industrial standards/specifications;
  (i) Major capital projects and details of forthcoming tenders and trade enquiries;
  (j) Financial aid (if any) from international agencies;
  (k) Results of any local market research initiated or supervised by Officer.

All Data should be up-to-date, double-checked for accuracy, with sources stated, together with any specific recommendations for stimulating exports (occasionally there may be some value in reporting trade rumours, particularly if they concern major acquisitions or large-scale tenders).

## 5.2 Organization and Operation of Trade Fairs

These events are used nationally and internationally as a means of generating personal contacts among key buyers and sellers from many different countries, and as a means of market testing, promotion, and market entry or penetration. Of course, there are many types of fairs, though most are described generically as exhibitions: these have become particularly used by governments in recent years as a means of assisting exporters to promote their products. There are, for example, general fairs such as the Canadian National Exhibition, and Japanese International Trade Fair, where there are attractions for both industrialists and consumers. There will also be pavilions at these events for special sectors of industry and national pavilions where countries can display a broad range of their exporters products such as IMPO/EXPO (organized by U.K. Trade Agency). There are major industrial fairs such as that at Leipzig and permanent trade fair sites such as at Hanover, and National Displays such as British Trade Pavilion in Tokyo. There are consumer fairs such as Ideal Home Exhibition and Boat Show annually in London; there is the Food Fair in Paris (SIAL) which also attracts mostly consumers: indeed a few years ago 2,800 exhibitors from 65 countries participated in the largest ever European Exhibition of consumer goods, also in Paris. Then there are store functions, shopping weeks for consumers promoted by a particular sector of an overseas country in one of its major export markets.

Minor trade fairs such as the U.K. Toy Fair and Men's and Boys' Wear Exhibition, Cologne Household Goods and Hardware Fair, attract mostly retailers who are looking for new lines to put into their shops. Solo exhibitions are mounted by a country, which takes a theme and groups together some exporting companies in the same trade, or they can be put on by a single company, whether at its own cost or government-sponsored. In fact, most governments provide financial support to exporting companies participating in trade fairs overseas; this usually takes the form of limited free 'stand space' where the exporter is provided with a 'shell' in which he builds his own display and there is also a contribution to the exporter's costs of travel and accommodation.

For the exporter of industrial goods and services, and for those exporting all types of products to key institutional and buyers, the major industrial and trade fairs are by far the most important events, the scope of these is indicated by a recent industrial/trade fair in Milan: there were 306 exhibition days in a 12 month cycle of 54 specialized trade shows, with 31,200 exhibitors from 90 countries and buyers from 137 countries. Usually they are more specialized and are devoted to one sector of industry, such as Construction and Building in Stuttgart, SAE (car components) in Detroit, Instruments, Electronics (Electronica) and Automation (IEA) and Packing and Packaging Equipment (PACWEX) in U.K. Many of these are sponsored by the appropriate Trade and Industry Associations. In some parts of the world, notably Eastern Europe, the industrial fair is the only way of establishing personal contact with major buyers and subsequently obtaining orders. Of special and growing value to industrial exporters is the Symposium or Seminar where experts in particular technologies or product applications present papers to major industrial users and consultants (using sophisticated communications, CCTV, micro-computers etc). This can be a highly effective way for the sponsoring body to get new technology or new industrial applications explained and promoted to key audiences; the measure of success of a Symposium is not the number but the quality of personnel attracted to the event.

Trade fairs can have a number of advantages. They can attract a concentration of buyers from a wide area and thus offer a special opportunity to display products, make valuable contacts, find new representation and distribution channels and support existing agents. Specially, therefore, these events can be effectively used to:

(a) Generate personal contacts with key buyers and specifiers;
(b) See at first hand competitors' products;
(c) Find suitable agents or representatives;
(d) Test overseas markets for product acceptability and positioning;
(e) Facilitate joint ventures and licensing arrangements;
(f) Stimulate interest in the products displayed by attractive audio-visual presentation.

Thorough preparation cannot be over-emphasized: for instance at a store promotion in West Germany a few years ago, a foreign cake mix was being demonstrated; unfortunately, the demonstrator failed to realize that German flour is heavier than that used in other countries and the mixture came out looking like porridge.

Trade fairs are often not used effectively by participants, because of a lack of planning or follow up or, more seriously, because participation is not part of a planned, logical and targeted export promotion campaign. If a Fair is integrated into a broader export promotion plan and is designed to achieve specific objectives, if it is based on the proper groundwork and is well-executed and followed up, it can achieve satisfying – even dramatic – commercial results, which might take longer to achieve by other means. Unfortunately, such is often not the case. Participation in trade fairs and the staging of exhibitions are often prompted by motives of national prestige, which may be perfectly valid but without commercial impact. When there are commercial objectives, they are often totally frustrated by inadequate preparations, and opportunities created by them are often subsequently lost through failure to pursue them.

One of the most common mistakes made by governments, for example, is going into trade fairs without the active support and personal participation of the companies whose products they display. No matter how well briefed they are, government representatives cannot replace company people when it comes to answering technical questions and actually making business deals.

And there are many cases of countries choosing the wrong trade fair for their needs, or of making the mistake of going into fairs or staging exhibitions when other promotional techniques would be cheaper and more effective. For example, if a country wants to promote commodities for which there are only a handful of buyers, or whose distribution is controlled by a small number of firms, exhibiting at a trade fair would probably be less useful and more expensive than direct correspondence and sales calls. Yet countries are continually showing at trade fairs when they face precisely this situation. Mistakes like these represent more than opportunities lost; and they can have a really negative impact on the country's export promotion achievements, for fairs can consume large amounts of time and foreign exchange; they can also drain budgets and distract Commercial Officers from other, more productive duties.

Before recommending participation in a particular trade fair, every Commercial Officer and exporter should satisfy themselves that it really is a suitable vehicle – that the fair itself is a highly reputable one, and that it is consonant with the particular situation of the exporting country. The business of staging trade fairs has become highly competitive, and the number of fairs has proliferated. To some extent this is healthy, because it reflects the need for more specialization. But it has also resulted in exhibitors having to choose between too many fairs. Despite their sponsor's enthusiastic claims, not every fair represents value for money. They are certainly not of equal value. The Commercial Officer should be careful to evaluate a fair before recommending it.

The Commercial Officer and the exporting company should be able to get a lot of basic information about a fair from the authority or company that puts it on. They should supply statistics on audience and exhibitors for a number of years. These can give an idea of the fair's 'health' – has it been growing or shrinking? Many fair operators emphasize numbers. The quality of the audience, and of the exhibitors, is at least as important as the number. Some fair companies can give a breakdown of the audience and exhibitors by function and origin, which reveal what proportion of the audience is from the trade, at what levels, and from which areas or countries. The fair's catalogue should be checked for previous years to see if the leading firms in the particular field have been exhibiting at it regularly and if any have dropped out. The Commercial Officer, too, can find out from the fair management the charges involved and what kind of support they give exhibitors, particularly publicity support; he can ask important buyers and others in the trade how important they think it is, and why, and talk to participants about their reasons for taking part, the problems they have encountered, and their results. Finally, the Commercial Officer must go to each fair, talk with exhibitors and visitors, study the exhibits, and evaluate it as an export promotion method. After this kind of investigation, both the Commercial Officer and the exporter should be able to judge a fair with confidence.

There is one final point regarding government financial assistance to exporting companies participating in trade fairs, and missions (see Section 5.4); two specific benefits can be derived by companies:

(a)  It enables companies to break into or at least test new export markets who would otherwise be deterred by high initial costs of travel, accommodation, initial distribution, set up costs, etc.

(b)  It enables companies to extend their operating budgets and send technical experts, designers, as well as sales staff, to meet key customers direct, discuss requirements and work out suitable presentations and terms on the spot.

### 5.3  Selecting and Managing Overseas Agents

The management of overseas operations has already been discussed in general terms (see Chapter 4), and probably the most important decision the management of a company has to make is the appointment and control of agents to sell its products in export markets. There are, of course, other methods of distribution overseas, and these should be carefully considered, though generally, they are taken up some time after an overseas agent has been in operation (they are discussed in detail in Section 5.4). In outline, direct methods of overseas distribution comprise:

(a)  Acquiring or setting up a subsidiary company overseas;
(b)  Manufacturing locally through a wholly owned subsidiary;
(c)  Supplying through a joint exporting venture;
(d)  Deploying own sales force, usually under an overseas regional office;
(e)  Licensing.

Joint exporting agreements (c) and direct selling (d) are of special significance and consequently are dealt with separately in Sections 5.5 and 5.6. The point is that these direct methods involve substantial planning and investment in finance, manpower, plant and inventories; clearly, the long-term sales potential of the market has to be assessed and, as far as possible, quantified by market research and risk analysis, before these investment decisions can be considered.

Before discussing in detail representation through overseas agents, some practical illustrations of direct representation as summarized above in (a) and (d) are appropriate, as these are drawn from actual business situations and show some of the problems encountered. A volatile political situation overseas can make it most inadvisable to enter into a joint venture with a local company currently in favour with the host government, but running the risk that a change of regime can damage business prospects. Just such an experience afflicted Massey Ferguson in Turkey when after entering into a 51% ownership venture, the company had to withdraw from the market and terminate the venture due to political instability and lack of Turkish Government support. Licensing agreements are also highly inappropriate where world market potential has not been thoroughly researched, and these examples show why: A U.S. manufacturer not only licensed the manufacture and sale of its products to a U.K. firm but granted it exclusive right to sub-license U.S. expertise to other countries. At the time of this decision, the U.S. manufacturer was not interested in expanding overseas, and believed it was best simply to collect the royalties without having to provide additional investment money. Within a few years, worldwide markets for U.S. firm's products developed, but it derived little financial benefit. In another case, a U.S. electronics firm was approached by a foreign firm interested in setting up a jont venture in Asia. In this case, the product potential overseas was researched and appeared high, and the manufacturer was anxious to establish the joint venture quickly before any competition could be enticed into the Asian market. An agreement was accordingly signed, but with insufficient time to do a full market analysis (particularly distribution requirements, marketing costs etc.), or to investigate partner's experience, technical know-how and operational procedures. Consequently, operational problems which should have been resolved at the outset continued to beset this joint venture for some years. Finally, there is the example of a foreign company which decided to change the name of a newly acquired Spanish subsidiary company in a way which impugned the competence of the previous Spanish management; this led to bad publicity in the Spanish press, a 'go-slow' by the workers and some harassment by the local authorities, all making normal business operations difficult and unprofitable.

In some industries, such as pharmaceuticals, it is common practice to have an appointed agent in export markets and at the same time to deploy its own salesforce to support the agent with sales calls, displays and other forms of promotion. Again, in the automobile industry, it is usually necessary to appoint distributors or stockists in the localities to support the sales efforts of the main agent or concessionaire. A distributor overseas normally buys, stocks and re-sells on his own account whereas agent sells on commission the products of his principal (the exporting manufacturer).

There are other types of intermediary which the exporting company can consider depending on its commitment to long-term market development. These others include:

(a) Foreign buyers employed by state or commercial traders resident in the exporting country;
(b) Foreign companies licensed to sell locally or to manufacture the product under contract;
(c) Commission or confirming houses, which are usually home-based, specialize in buying goods on behalf of overseas clients, paying the manufacturer, dealing with transport, documentation and customs for a commission usually of between $3\frac{1}{2}\%$ and $8\frac{1}{2}\%$.

In making these decisions about how best to distribute, sell and promote its products overseas, the management of the company must make a careful evaluation of the following:

(a) Company's production capacity;
(b) Logistics systems in the market;
(c) Short-term and long-term sales potential of market;
(d) Company's level of export manning and expertise;
(e) Financial stability of market;

(f) Existing trade contacts in the market;
(g) Promotional requirements of the product (e.g. demonstrations, displays, etc.);
(h) Technical sophistication of product;
(i) Market follow-up required;
(j) Extent of competition by local and foreign suppliers;
(k) Profit targets and sales targets for first three trading years;
(l) Likely price levels and gross margins;
(m) Sales support needed to realize full sales potential of market;
(n) Level of and nature of market risks in relation to company's investment;
(o) Estimate of direct costs of setting up sales and agency operation;
(p) Availability of local, trained manpower in market.

So, basically, therefore, an agent acts on behalf of his principal, who is responsible for what the agent does within their contract. The principal also retains title to the goods until they are sold by the agent to a third party, whereupon the agent collects the commission. Some agents, particularly in consumer goods, buy and stock like wholesalers; many agents have their own sales staff; some prefer sole selling rights to certain products, while other will act as general agents and stock competing lines. As explained, an agent who cannot cover the whole market, can operate in the localities with the principal's sales staff covering the whole region. In fact, over half the world's trade is handled by export agents.

The first step, though, for any company is to improve its motivation and support for the overseas agents in existing key markets. Where new agents are sought, some kind of screening is essential; a company usually chooses an agent in the first place because of:

(a) Lack of resources to set up own operations;
(b) Insufficient production capacity to supply large-scale importing organizations direct;
(c) Little, or no knowledge or expertise relating to market conditions.

As it is increasingly difficult to dismiss agents in many countries, mention has already been made of the support, training and development increasingly required from principals, and this aspect will be developed later in this chapter. Nevertheless, this highlights the need to make satisfactory first appointments usually from a shortlist derived from contacts at trade fairs, on overseas visits, export directories, banks or direct advertising. Sometimes it pays to contact potential customers who can recommend an agent who sells efficiently complementary products to them. One British exporter of printing materials went direct to an agent who had given his own representatives a lot of competition, to find that the agent was unhappy with his current principal and looking for a change; he was offered the new agency and was an outstanding success.

BOTB operates an efficient agency-finding service in U.K. (but in no way guarantees performance or results). In making, or indeed reviewing an appointment, the exporter must take account of the agent's financial stability, his trade and customer contacts and product knowledge, the products, both complimentary and competing that he already stocks, his manpower and sales knowledge in relation to the market and other factors. The exporter must not make an agency appointment solely because of a large first order, or because the agent has technical expertise (it will be order No. 3 that really counts, anyway). Once the agreement is being worked out with the agent chosen, the following points must be clearly understood by both parties: clear definitions of products and territory, promotional duties, method of payment (usually commission at an agreed rate), information reporting (e.g. orders taken from customers direct by principal for sales follow-up by agent), length and termination of agreement, law and language to be used, especially duties of the agent in terms of sales targets, promotion, administration (e.g. import licences) whether he is 'del credere', so guaranteeing that the exporter gets payment from customers; also duties of the exporter in terms of promotional and sales back-up, inventories and delivery terms, price negotiation, and training, consultation about market conditions and prospects and sales targets.

The exporter gains from an agency operation: payment by results, local market knowledge (particularly about competitors) and expertise to promote his products, coverage of all key customers in the locality. The agent gets some measure of market exclusivity and promotional support for established products with a minimum of investment in stock, personnel, etc. and a commission related directly to turnover. The exporter must, however, be alert to the tendencies of some agents: to stock too many lines (particularly competing ones) and represent too many other principals with inadequate resources, and some agents concentrate too much on short-term business and quick returns to the detriment of long-term market development (it has been known for an agent to take on an agency not to develop sales but to stop a competitor taking it on in his territory); this can apply especially to large agencies in the Middle East.

Recent research on overseas representation at Manchester University International Business Unit shows that a common mistake by exporters is to use an agent because he fulfills one important requirement (e.g. having technical expertise); but if the exporter expands his product range, such an agent may prove too specialized to cope with more products or longer-term market development. Another hazard shown up by this is the under-estimation of the size of the geographical area the agent claims to cover (in West Germany it is prudent to appoint agents for different regions; the same applies in Benelux and Yugoslavia).

The research[2] also showed that the most effective exporting companies were those who exercised the tightest control over the activities of their agents, but supported them by frequent, planned visits and reporting, particularly of new product developments; also, the agent should be involved if the market justifies setting up a manufacturing subsidiary, but not just a branch office (which the agent may see as a threat). There should also be a 'no competition' clause in the Agency Agreement, and those exporters which closely monitor competition, and have contingency plans, can more effectively cope with a situation where a competitor enters the market with a cheaper product leaving the agent with unsaleable stock.

Finally, the management (not just the sales staff) of the exporting company must understand that they are responsible for developing the market and gaining the agent's co-operation. Export departments in U.K. are frequently under-staffed (see Sections 4.2 and 5.5) and many agents overseas are just not serviced properly. If the agent's performance declines; the management should ask itself:

(a) Has he been visited by a company representative in the past year?
(b) Has he been consulted about market conditions and sales targets in the last year?
(c) Has he visited the home company in the past two years?
(d) Has he been informed of new product developments and promotional proposals in the last year?
(e) Are his orders and queries attended to as efficiently as home orders?

The Institute of Export, London has published specimen agency agreements[3].

## 5.4 Trade Missions

These Missions represent a concerted effort nationally to develop exports in target markets. They are basically structured in one of two ways:

(a) Outward Selling Missions by exporting countries;
(b) Inward Buying Missions from importing countries;

They have the primary objective of improving the flow of bi-lateral trade, sometimes to rectify agreed imbalances between the two trading countries, sometimes to raise the level of trade in specific commodities, or sometimes on a basis of goodwill and cultural exchanges, to promote consumption internally of both countries' principal export goods.

Outward Missions are usually assisted in some form by government agencies, which agree to meet a proportion of the cost of establishing and sending out the Mission. The initiative can come from Industry associations, chambers of commerce or trade; if representing one industry it can be regarded as 'horizonal', but if representing a range of industries, organized by a trade chamber, it can be regarded as 'vertical'. The main purpose of an Outgoing Sales Mission is not only to take orders, but to assess profitable viable export market sectors, and to develop long-term sales opportunities. Horizontal missions are not always popular among businessmen who find themselves competing against each other overseas (call on the same buyers, promoting similar products, etc.).

The benefits to be derived from the Sales Mission can be direct for the Mission members in that they can negotiate contracts and supply terms and actually bring back orders. The indirect benefits are more relevant to the entire business and exporting community in that mission members bring back with them first-hand and up-to-date export intelligence. Clearly, much administration and logistical work and briefing are required beforehand in both the home and host countries if such a Mission is to be worthwhile and make an impact.

Inward Purchasing Missions comprise visits by foreign buyers and importers from one overseas country to exporters in the host country. The advantages to be exploited by the exporting community are a favourable disposition by the members of such a mission to evaluate new plant and machinery, and to see demonstrations of entire product ranges in the host country. However, members of an Inward Mission are under no obligation to buy. Such a Mission is usually structured on a 'vertical' basis therefore trade or industry associations usually play an important part in both staffing and hosting these Missions.

The steps in setting up and implementing an Inward Purchasing Mission involve:

(a)  Selecting and briefing exporting firms in host country;
(b)  Inviting and briefing the Mission members themselves.

It should be noted too that these Missions are often going on to visit other host countries and therefore the emphasis may be on long-term sales development rather than immediate order taking.

Both Outward Sales and Inward Buying Missions require carefully planned and vigorous follow-up if contacts and enquiries are to be converted into orders, and if market entry opportunities are to exploited competitively through export promotion activities; some governments synchronize Trade Missions with Trade Fairs and Exhibitions.

It is also important not to overlook the need for an in-depth and detailed briefing of Mission members well before departure. This applies particularly to Inward Missions, but is often overlooked; these members require details of quality and design ranges of products, production capacity and location of plants, prices, freight routes and costs and other details of potential suppliers, particularly those they will visit in the host country, well before their arrival.

When they are aimed at well-conceived goals and are properly planned and executed, Trade Missions are an important export promotion method. The Commercial Officer is involved with assisting Trade Missions; he may, in fact, be the instigator of Missions or he may advise on whether a particular Mission is advisable. Of course, Trade Missions vary in composition. They may consist entirely of government officials, or of private enterprise traders, or of representatives of official trading corporations, marketing boards or trade associations. They may be a blend of these, and include representatives of other organizations not involved directly with buying and selling, from such fields as banking, transport and tourism. Their composition should reflect their purpose.

The purpose of Trade Missions also vary. The aim may be to establish goodwill, to purchase essential imports, to attract investment or manufactures under license, or even to negotiate access for specific commodities or a wide-ranging trade agreement (although an official group involved in this latter form of government-to-government activity is usually described as a 'delegation' rather than a 'mission'). In common usage, therefore, the term 'Trade Mission' is applied most frequently to a group concerned with either market exploration or development, with surveying prospects and methods of conducting business, or with appointing agents and promoting or actually selling goods. What are the specific advantages of Trade Missions? A selling mission can, if the groundwork has been done – achieve immediate sales, which can cover the cost of the Mission; more important, it can lay the foundation on which to build future business.

Trade Missions can undertake some of the tasks performed by the commerical Officer or the individual visiting businessman, and can sometimes perform them more effectively. For example, a Trade Mission can set out to perform market research, exploring a number of markets to see which would be the most rewarding or study specific product sectors within a single market; it can, collectively, bring far more man-hours to the investigation than an individual can spare, and often more technical expertise. Indeed, a well-organized Mission can also make a greater promotional impact on the market than an individual (whether an official or a businessman) is likely to in the same time. A Mission collectively carries a certain news value and can serve as the platform for trade publicity. This, in turn, can focus attention on the home country as a supplier and can attract the attention of buyers otherwise hard to identify. A Mission can also gain access to high-level business and Government Officials whom the individual businessman might find difficult to reach, and generally provide him with wider and deeper contact coverage than he can easily achieve on his own. Trade Missions can also make a substantial impact in the home country. If they are well-publicized at home in advance, they can attract participation of key businessmen and representatives of firms new to export, who otherwise might not visit export markets. The findings of a self-interested group of businessmen who have been personally involved in a Mission and have 'seen for themselves' are more likely to stimulate their own future export efforts, as well as their colleagues', than would a market report mailed home by a field representative. Moreover, a Mission can be an important educational experience for inexperienced Mission members; even the ones who are experienced in exporting can profit from exchanging notes with fellow Mission members. And if a Mission has been successful and properly publicized, it can help contribute to general consciousness in the home country.

As has been indicated, there are various types of Trade Mission, each suited to achieving different purposes. Before a Mission is proposed, a number of related aspects should be carefully considered. Trading conditions might call for a 'country survey' Mission, to focus on a market largely untapped by exporters. They may not be aware of the prospects, and their country may not be known in these markets as a potential supplier. The evidence may suggest that there are possibilities for a range of products, but the precise knowledge available may be insufficient to enable practical export action. A country survey Mission, made up of businessmen capable of exploring and reporting to their Government and traders on every relevant facet of the market potential for those products, might be the most appropriate form of initial action.

Other situations might suggest an 'industry survey' Mission. A particular product or a range of products in one or more industry groups may figure largely in a country's export trade. It may appear from the evidence available that there is scope for achieving a greater share of the export market for these products. Concerted action in the form of a specialized commodity or 'industry survey' Mission to research the market for them might be the logical starting point to determine how that potential can be translated into business. Such a Mission can not only pinpoint the scope of the market, but can also study prevailing distribution systems, promotional techniques, and pricing; clarify what product modifications might be necessary and develop other market intelligence.

In other cases, it may appear that there is scope for much better sales results for a particular commodity or a number of unrelated products, given effort on the part of the exporters concerned and knowledge of their products by local importers and consumers. A Selling Mission, specialized in an industry sector or representative of all product categories involved, can be an appropriate way of bringing these opportunities into focus and obtaining quick and substantial results.

### 5.5 Effective Selling Overseas

It has been pointed out (Section 4) that the different methods of ensuring effective representation overseas are by no means mutually exclusive. Many companies find from experience that, however vital the role of the agent, he can be made more effective in sales coverage and promotional impact if he is supported by some form of direct sales organization. Indeed, as sales develop, many companies conclude that it is time to establish their own sales office in the market. Some can have specific reasons for dissatisfaction with the agency system: research cited earlier also indicates that:

(a) Companies relying heavily on agents risk losing control of the selling process; agents often prove less flexible than direct sales staff in coping with competition and are relatively expensive in areas where sales volume is high;

(b) Productivity and performance of agent's staff are generally lower than company's own staff in terms of obtaining orders, handling customer problems/complaints, product knowledge and technical support and demonstrations.

Indeed, some companies find that the agency works at its best when controlled and supported by on-the-spot company representation; the agent ensures specific expertise in knowledge of the language, local competitors, regulations and knowledge of some localities, while the company representative promotes its sole interests, ensures that the agent is giving appropriate priority to the products and provides some training and motivation. One major Italian paint manufacturer selling worldwide treats its agents as an extension of its own sales force. Sales offices and agents alike are expected to submit monthly progress reports, which are put into a computer for analysis; a video display system enables the company's management to check what stocks key customers have bought and the price paid; if an agent's sales fall off, the management can quickly identify the problem area and send one of its senior sales staff to investigate.

Companies in industrial sectors generally favour direct selling, particularly where market growth is slow or where negotiating with key clients is a necessary part of the sales process. Advantages claimed by companies doing this include:

(a) Close relationship with customers who prefer to deal direct with manufacturers;
(b) Increased confidence in supplier where technical problems can be sorted out directly with technical sales staff;
(c) Sounder base for longer-term development and sales planning;
(d) More accurate and fuller reporting back to exporter of price levels, competition, changes in specifications or buyers' organizations.

In many countries, personal selling takes on special importance where restrictions on advertising and lack of media availability restrict the advertising an exporter can do. Again, low wages in other countries enables the company to hire a much larger local sales force than at home. Though there is no substitute for the trained and experienced home-based sales representative, a local force of sales assistants can, of course, cover a particular market effectively; this is the sales organization favoured by some major cigarette manufacturers in developing countries. Depending on the type of product, sales support staff are often drawn from nationals of the overseas country. IBM, for instance, use national representatives in each of its markets; whereas in the case of export sales to large retail or wholesaleing organizations which handle their own important arrangements, it is common for the manufacturer's sales representative to sell across national boundaries. If, however, it is the exporter's policy to have local sales assistants who are nationals of each country working under the overall direction of senior home-based sales staff, either directly or through an agent, the management of such a force will have to be largely decentralized to each national market with home-based staff acting as sales trainers and advisers to national operations, contributing guidance and direction because of their special new knowledge, experience and authority.

In setting up and indeed running an overseas sales force, the company's management should undertake a sales profile analysis of the market (and should up-date it as appropriate); itemized it should include the points given in Figure 5.1.

This sales profile analysis is a vital, yet often ignored, step in establishing (and up-dating) realistic views of the sales potential (growth prospects, competition levels) of an export market. Whilst it will not answer all problems and, in particular, lacks the sophistication of demand forecasting techniques now used (usually with computer applications) by many multi-national corporations, it does at least guide management as to the most relevent and effective sales organization required by a particular market.

| | |
|---|---|
| Environment | Extent and topography of area to be covered |
| | Requirements of distributors as to sales support |
| | Expectations and attitudes of key customers to selling methods |
| Competition | Competitor sales audit |
| | Key points of effectiveness of competitors |
| | Competitor information on market prospects including strengths and weaknesses |
| Institutions | Organizations which support and/or recognize value of salesmanship |
| | Contract/Task Sales Forces |
| | Study of purchasing institutions |
| | Training (e.g. languages) institutions |
| Legal System | Laws relating to selling practices and transfer of goods and services |
| Economic | Market growth rates and other business indicators (e.g. stock levels) |
| | Credit terms, expected levels of trade solvency |

Figure 5.1 Sales Profile Analysis

In recruiting an overseas sales force, two problems can arise:

(a) Selling is a low status occupation in some countries, and therefore quality of training and competitive pay are vital in attracting high quality sales recruits;
(b) Finding people with the requisite educational and technical (and social) accomplishments is often difficult and time-consuming for management.

Both these points highlight the need for sustained effective sales programmes; even so, cultural and other differences (highlighted in sales profile analysis) affect sales organization: sales staff from one tribe or religious group sometimes cannot be employed to sell to another group in their own country or adjoining country (e.g. Hindu vs Muslim, Ibo vs Hausa, French-speaking versus English-speaking Canadians), and German sales staff have generally not been used in France. The importance of training is well illustrated by these examples from Japan. NCR Company has been in Japan for over seventy years but only in the past two decades has it been able to recruit college graduates; selling was considered low-prestige. Today, however, 80% of its sales force are college graduates. And a joint venture between 3M Company and Sumitomo has developed a sales training programme that has drawn much interest from Japanese firms. The programme includes initial training, dealer training, training for experienced sales staff, marketing seminars, a sales manual, and national sales meetings. New sales recruits from Japanese universities have two months intensive training, followed by ten months of general marketing and field training. Such a programme (attended also by agents and sometimes licensees) must of course be part of the exporting company's overall marketing and sales development plan, with a home-based resource team. Indeed, as the company finds new product applications, or enters new market segments, the sales tasks will have to be changed or sharpened, especially in such sectors as computers, chemicals, technical equipment, etc.

The differences of culture, environment, status and economics have similar impacts on management's methods of remunerating, motivating, controlling the sales force overseas. Clearly, non-monetary rewards will have more pull in different countries (status, foreign travel, recognition). Philip Morris of Venezuela publicizes the achievements of its best sales staff. Clearly, a mix of monetary (salary and/or commission) and non-monetary rewards appropriate to each overseas market must be set, which take account of local 'norms'. Further, where the sales profile analysis is done, and other well-proved sales management ratios used, and updated for each market, comparative evaluation of the performance of each overseas sales force becomes standard practice (the comparisons must be among groups of similar countries), and performance can be improved (particularly where some innovation is put in hand) overall by learning from experiences in the company's other markets. Added to this must be the continued streamlining of reporting and cross-reporting, between the home base and overseas.

What is of continuing concern to the company's management is the productivity of their overseas sales force(s), in terms of number of active sales staff, sales revenue, amount of customer contact time, call frequencies, value of order per salesman, unit profit per order, average cost of sales call etc.

Some research by Barclays Bank International[4] has compared the productivity and manpower of sales forces in France, Germany and U.K. This research found that in West Germany, for example the sales specialist often works together with his technical colleagues, they go on Missions together, negotiate contracts jointly, etc. while, in contrast, U.K. companies tend to rely on excellent salesmanship alone. This research also analysed the staffing and relative productivity of the home and export sales departments of companies in France, West Germany and the U.K. It found that the number of staff in home sales departments of large British companies is more than five times greater than in the export departments, yet they sell little more than twice as much as the export salesmen. In France, sales at home are more than twice as great as abroad, but the numbers in the home sales department are not nearly twice as great, and well below the British figure (and the British ratio). In West Germany, there is a somewhat greater degree of proportionality: sales in the home market are slightly lower than in exports and the home sales department is only about a third bigger.

The evidence would seem to indicate that the British, during the past two decades, have become too concerned about their home market and may have over-organized it to the point where diminishing returns are now realized. Nor does this excessive preoccupation with the home market place a company in a better position to compete against imports: an export-oriented approach with a strong product design bias is likely to be much more successful than massing all one's guns predominantly to defend a position in the home market.

The rational course for British companies would be to increase the number of export sales specialists up to the point where sales per man equal, say, the French levels – and also assuming diminishing returns up to the point where the French figures are reached – this could add substantially to the exports of British companies. (Since large British companies are said to account for over 60% of total British exports, the increase for the country could be anywhere between £1,000m to £3,000m per annum.)

This research highlights three significant factors in export sales performance: U.K. companies:

(a)  have larger home sales staffs than their European counterparts;
(b)  have a much higher ratio of staff employed in their home than in their export sales departments;
(c)  have generally lower staff levels in their export departments than their European counterparts.

This is particularly true of large-scale companies where implications should become very clear to British management:

(a)  Productivity of U.K. export sales staff is higher than in France or West Germany;
(b)  There must be potential in gaining incremental sales by raising the staffing levels of export sales departments.

The statistics quoted in this report are less significant for medium-size companies. As far as small-scale companies are concerned, this research indicates that there are even better prospects for growth than in large companies: typically, these U.K. companies have too many people in the home sales department, there is consequently scope for either a transfer to the export department, or for the existing staff to handle a much bigger volume of trade.

The argument for a redeployment on the British side of the personnel engaged in home and export operations becomes even stronger where this research examines the position of the sales specialists, as distinct from administrative and supporting personnel.

In home sales, a British sales specialist in a large company averages £1.5m sales per annum. But on the export side, the figure is £4.4m. Admittedly the two types of specialists are not interchangeable but their costs are very similar (and there are examples where the export specialist earned less than his home counterpart). A policy of endeavouring to reduce the home side and increase the export side of operations is likely to bring about an increase in the productivity of selling operations at home and an increase in export sales, even if export sales productivity were to drop marginally.

This research also postulates some reasons for the outstanding perform-ance and productivity of export specialists in large British companies, and these are:

(a) Many large British companies have production facilities abroad which frequently serve as a base for marketing operations. The value-output of British owned production units abroad has been estimated at about 210% of the total annual value of British exports. For France it is nearer 100%. Whilst, for Britain, investments abroad amount to 17% of G.D.P., for Germany it is only 3.5%. Sometimes these overseas subsidiaries are actively helping in the sale of British products, sometimes they provide advice and local knowledge which can be of considerable value.

(b) The larger companies in Britain are frequently very well-organized, more so than the medium companies against whom, as we shall see later, there is a stronger fiscal bias.

(c) The sales specialists are highly skilled and well paid – better, as a rule, than in the medium companies.

(d) Perhaps most important of all, the products they are selling are good. However talented a salesman might be, his success would be short-lived if he did not have good products to support him, year in year out.

The research indicates therefore that overall an increase in the export selling organizations of large British companies could add substantially to the volume of British exports.

However, these observations are not intended as categorical statements urging action along these lines. For conditions can differ considerably from company to company and however logical a proposition might appear, the realities of the situation may contradict it. Certainly the measures proposed in this research should not be undertaken without a careful examination of all the conditions that could influence a company's fortunes as a result of the changes. All that is intended is to suggest that comparisons of home and export productivity could be both stimulating and useful in alerting sales management to the realities of the changing marketing situations. All the more so because in all three countries investigated, such comparisons are hardly ever made.

In order to raise the effectiveness of selling operations overseas, management must therefore consider implementing the following among their export staff:

(a) Developing negotiating and bargaining expertise (wherever approp-riate to the product or service). Included in this is the need to improve presentation skills, particularly for sales presentations to committees and key buyers. Research[5] at Strathclyde University Marketing Department into the offshore oil industry has shown that, whilst British suppliers are highly competitive on technical specifications, they fall down on the quality of their sales and tender presentations. Effective use can be made of portable audio-visual presentation (whether slides or tapes) featuring the company's latest products and developments. The research quotes the experience of a number of major buyers of off-shore oil services and equipment to the effect that accuracy of specifications, quality of presentation by sales staff and negotiators, use of A/V materials, wording of scripts, impressing the client with the practical, verifiable track record of the supplier, bidding for the work, meeting deadlines for submission, translation of proposal into buyer's language, and provision of sufficient copies of proposal smartly produced for each member of buyer's group etc. are all important.

(b)  Development and refinement through observation and trade contacts of the 'typology' of the 'ideal customer' for the exporting company: his requirements, sectors of business, organization and attitudes, buying pattern and prospects; this typology can then be utilized by the sales force both to identify new customers who conform to this typology, and in helping existing customers to develop their own businesses more profitably by targeting growth sectors of the market.

(c)  Developing technical product knowledge, particularly more aware-ness of technical and aesthetic aspects of design, and competitors' designs.

(d)  Training in salesmanship particularly 'closing techniques' and 'benefits selling'. In industrial goods, the buyer's reputation is at stake and he must obtain reassurance with special emphasis on the requirements and attitudes of overseas customers, training should be ideally linked to a recognized terminal U.K. qualification such as the Certificate or the Diploma of the Institute of Marketing or the Certificate of the Diploma of the Institute of Export.

(e)  Some basic training in financial aspects of export transactions, particular credit terms, export credits, documentary credits and trade terms.

(f)  Some basic language training, particularly in one of the Romance languages (preferably French or Spanish) for those not already fluent. It is not always possible to achieve linguistic fluency up to the point of negotiating a commercial deal, where an interpreter is essential. However, export sales staff should speak well enough for everyday conversation; in the case of oriental languages such as Arabic (where long-term study is required) greetings and basic vocabulary are sufficient at least to create goodwill and get the business relationship off to a good start. There are a number of reputable language schools in U.K. and details are available from BOTB (many programmes are on audio tapes).

(g)  Providing export sales staff with well-designed sales support materials and documentation (translated as appropriate). Relying on salesmanship (and linguistic ability) is not enough; it is a common misconception by management that these two, together with a price list, air ticket and samples are sufficient; they are not (if samples are essential, sufficient must be taken or sent out in advance to leave with customers). Sales support includes short, portable A/V presentations (see (a)) to show to customers (in the appropriate language), sales aids which provide the salesman with material(s) which support him in making his presentation, such as 'cut outs' of a model machine or plant, flow charts with colour codes illustrating equipment, customized business analysis folder setting out the financial benefits to the customer of buying the exporter's product or service, a folder to complete for the customer on a brief statement of his requirements, problems, and the 'benefits' expected by him, and of him, by his own customers (the salesman is then 'aided' by having the opportunity of coming back to the customer with specific, worked out proposals delivering these benefits, and the terms). There are many other applications of sales support but it is one of the most vital, yet most neglected aspects of overseas selling, and British management must understand it, and then apply it, with some creativity and drive, to the particular conditions of their own sales operations. Support material is especially important where engineering, technical and precision products and equipment are sold: operator manuals, checklists, performance schedules and other specifications lend themselves to improved design layout, visuals, etc. and will repay attention.

(h) Some basic training in first-hand market reporting (trading conditions for customers and distributors, sales prospects) and in observational techniques so that time spent overseas is more productively used.

(i) Improved remuneration and benefits for export sales staff to encourage intake of more talented and better qualified trainees, and to compensate experienced staff better for loneliness and aggravation of overseas work and to reward them for earning Britain's livelihood.

It is not, of course, recommended that management implement all these steps at once: much will depend on their assessment of the strengths and weaknesses of their overseas sales operations and clearly some items will have a higher priority than others. But they should all be put together in a coherent and well-researched sales development plan, which should have as its focus:

(a) Key markets and key customers overseas to be targeted in the light of research and analysis

(b) Task force selling in appropriate markets where strength of competition requires it: this means supporting sales staff with technical, design and financial staff to win orders and to discuss requirements direct with customers;

(c) Critical review of manning levels in export sales departments with appropriate action (discussed earlier in this chapter).

Mention has been made in earlier chapters of the importance of assessing sales potential in an overseas market as an aid to sales policy. The basic trade dimensions of the market are, as has been explained:

$$\frac{\begin{array}{l}\text{Total imports}\\ +\ \text{Local production}\end{array}}{}$$

$$\frac{\begin{array}{l}=\ \text{Total exports}\\ -\ \text{Re-exports}\end{array}}{}$$

$$= \text{Total consumption}$$

But the company's management requires more specific data on sales volume, sales growth rates, stock levels and ordering patterns in each major sector of the market. This is essential if management is to train and deploy the optimal level of sales staff both home-based, and support sales staff overseas, and to plan sales campaigns and sales function budgets and programmes. The following simple matrix can therefore be used and adapted by management to quantify sales potential in its key overseas markets. It should be noted from Table 5.1 that sales effort is directly related to the company's share of the current market; the key factor is Column 4 where the potential extra sales can be quantified. It should also be noted that there is no indication in this particular matrix as to whether the total market is in decline or growing, and at what rate. For a more sophisticated treatment of market growth rates, refer to Appendix 6. Indeed, in determining the factor to be used in column 4 much will depend on management's assessment of market growth.

*Table 5.1*
*Export Sales Potential*

| Country | C.1 Total Market Size | C.2 Actual Market Share | C.3 Sales Effort as % | C.4 Potential Extra Sales C.3×C.1−C.2 (as appropriate) |
|---|---|---|---|---|
|  | £m | £ |  |  |
| A | 125 | 1,600,000 | 1.28 |  |
| B | 100 | 4.5m | 4.5 |  |
| C | 30 | 300,000 | 1.0 | Factor |
| D | 250 | 6m | 2.4 |  |
| E | 40 | 500,000 | 1.25 |  |
| TOTALS | £545m | CURRENT SALES POTENTIAL |  | depending on the factor used in C.4 |

Reference has been made to various forms of communication in personal selling: sales aids, A/V presentations, documentation, etc, but especially important in overseas selling is 'body language' or non-verbal ways of communicating correctly. A recent analysis[6] of this aspect demonstrates what is involved in different non-verbal aspects:

(a)  Appearance and physical attire and grooming can convey a stronger or different message than intended;

(b) Chronemics: timing of verbal exchanges; sales staff should not expect prompt responses where customers prefer slower response times;

(c) Haptics: use of touch while conversing is generally used more in Mediterranean countries than in U.K. or U.S.A.;

(d) Kinesics: movement of part of the body to communicate (in some cultures a lot of hand movement is normal);

(e) Oculesics: use or avoidance of eye contact for communication and this varies considerably among different cultures;

(f) Olfaction: the action of smelling, some cultures use specific odours to convey messages but their interpretations vary;

(g) Orientations: angles at which buyer and seller position themselves in relation to each other. A face-to-face position can convey friendship in one country but confrontation in another;

(h) Paralinguistics: the non-verbal aspects of speech which include emotional tones (compare the speech of a nervous person with that of an angry person), accents and the quality (and volume) of the voice. Chinese, for example, do not like to be spoken to at full volume;

(i) Postures: the many different bodily positions of standing, sitting, lying, etc. generally convey interpersonal attitudes which are culturally defined variously as friendly, antagonistic, superior, or other attitudes:

(j) Proxemics: Use of space in communication. South Americans, Greeks, Japanese feel more comfortable standing or sitting closer to strangers than do many other nationals.

Particularly important, too is the exercise of patience in sales visits and communications; putting undue pressure on customers can damage a company's business prospects in some overseas markets. Similarly, the 'improper' amount of touching or eye contact can leave customers feeling uncomfortable so that effective communication is hampered. Again, the 'incorrect' distance between individuals engaged in conversation can lead to the false conclusion that the other person is too aggressive and hostile or too cold and distrustful.

## 5.6 Effective Advertising Overseas

Media advertising is generally understood to encompass persuasive communications paid for by the advertiser and transmitted through one or more media and designed to secure sales or other behaviour by customers favourable to the advertiser. Of course, media advertising must operate in support of and sympathetic to other elements in the marketing 'mix'; management aspects of this 'mix' within overall exporting strategy have been discussed earlier in this chapter. Particularly important are the support that media advertising overseas provides for sales operations, especially sales promotion, and the connection with publicity and Public Relations (PR). It must be clearly grasped by management that so wide is the scope of all forms of promotion and publicity in exporting, that special attention is given to the planning and organization of numerous promotional activities elsewhere in this chapter, such as Symposia, Trade Fairs, and Missions, Store Promotions, Marketing Weeks, Trade Centres (e.g. Brazilian Trade Centre in London) and the services of the Commercial Officer. All these are designed to achieve objectives closely related to the practice of PR, publicity and sales promotion; that is, they are not necessarily all designed to secure immediate sales: they are designed and planned in the context of:

(a)  Long-term market development;
(b)  Creating a favourable export image of a country or a company;
(c)  Setting up conditions favourable to business dealings;
(d)  Communicating with key sectors of business and government overseas about the benefits of the product or service.

In this connection, the function of PR is to create and maintain a favourable relationship between an organization and the different sectors of society (i.e. its 'publics'); it will already be clear that the role of the Commercial Officer is particularly relevant to this (see Section 5.1).

Whilst PR therefore encompasses many activities carried out both by businessmen and Commercial Officers, there is also much that can be gained overseas by sponsorship, of cultural and sporting events, for example. Although its assets were expropriated in Peru, Esso Petroleum Company contrived to project a better image in Colombia by organizing a comprehensive collection of Colombian art and sponsoring its presentation in U.S.A. The acclaim this exhibition received there undoubtedly contributed to new understanding and respect for South American culture (and led to the Award of the Colombian Government's highest decoration for the company). Therefore, events such as sponsorship help to create a favourable climate for doing business and an improved image for the company among the public of the target overseas country.

Nevertheless, media advertising occupies a central role in the overall export marketing plan, and in terms of expenditure alone, must be accorded special attention. Added to this are decisions regarding appointment of and relationships with the advertising agency, media planning, buying and scheduling, evaluation of advertising campaigns, payment methods and the all-important creative aspects.

Advertising overseas presents the advertiser with opportunities for communicating with and persuading buyers among markets which can be more lucrative than his domestic market, but present special problems or differences of language, culture, distance, attitude and usage. There are also differences in the organization of media. Statistics are given in Table 5.2 opposite.

Figure 5.2 refers to the product life cycle, and to the term 'cognitive dissonance'; This is a concept which originated in other research into consumer psychology and it denotes the post-purchase reassurance which consumers seek from advertising and their desire to discount any

*Table 5.2*
Comparative Mass Communications in Selected Countries

|  | Telephones per 100 pop. | Pieces of Mail Sent (Millions) | Newspapers— Copies per 1,000 population | Radios per 1,000 population |
|---|---|---|---|---|
| United States | 74.4 | 88,970 | 287 | 1,882 |
| *Western Europe* | | | | |
| France | 32.9 | 11,382 | 214 | 330 |
| Germany | 37.4 | 12,368 | 312 | 329 |
| Italy | 28.5 | 3,031 | 113 | 232 |
| Spain | 26.1 | 3,578 | 98 | 259 |
| Sweden | 71.7 | 2,551 | 572 | 390 |
| United Kingdom | 41.5 | 8,840 | 388 | 706 |
| *Latin America* | | | | |
| Argentina | 9.0 | 620 | n.a. | 838 |
| Brazil | 4.1 | 2,178 | 39 | 158 |
| Colombia | 5.6 | 119 | n.a. | 117 |
| Ecuador | 2.9 | 7 | 49 | 279 |
| Mexico | 5.9 | 1,068 | n.a. | 301 |
| Peru | 2.6 | n.a. | n.a. | 129 |
| *Asia* | | | | |
| India | 0.3 | 7,421 | 16 | 24 |
| Japan | 42.4 | 12,186 | 526 | 530 |
| Pakistan | 0.3 | 502 | n.a. | 17 |
| Philippines | 1.3 | 630 | n.a. | 43 |
| Sri Lanka | 0.5 | 580 | n.a. | 58 |
| Thailand | 0.8 | 184 | n.a. | 131 |
| *Africa* | | | | |
| Egypt | 1.4 | 205 | 21 | 138 |
| Ghana | 0.7 | 58 | 51 | 105 |
| Madagascar | 0.4 | 22 | 9 | 74 |
| Nigeria | 0.2 | 959 | n.a. | 79 |
| South Africa | 8.3 | 1,383 | 70 | 96 |
| Zimbabwe | 2.9 | 112 | 18 | 39 |

n.a. not available
Source: *Statistical Abstract of the United States, 1980* (Bureau of The Census, Washington D.C., 1981)

information disparaging to the product purchased, and therefore to reduce any 'dissonance' resulting after the purchase is made.

Management of an exporting company clearly has neither the time nor the resources to undertake rigorous advertising research in all its overseas markets, though the concepts already quoted do have practical applications, which will be fully explained. As with sales operations, the primary task for management is to set up in many cases, with the appointed advertising Agency, an advertising profile analysis. Such an analysis has been formulated by Majaro and is illustrated in Table 5.3.

*Table 5.3*
*Advertising Profile Analysis*

| | |
|---|---|
| Environment | Language details; literacy levels; readership details; response to symbolism; general attitude to advertising; details of buyer, decider, influence patterns; various segments; demography |
| Competition | Identify competitive advertising practices; their expenditure and ratio to sales over a period. Research strengths and weaknesses of competitors' advertising policies |
| Institutions | Total advertising expenditure in country; media available and growth in expenditure patterns; technical facilities (e.g. colour) Media details – circulation readership and segments, media costs, frequency. Any special media; research bodies; code of advertising; various organizations |
| Legal System | Trade description legislation. Special rules pertaining to various products (e.g. cigarettes, drugs, fertilizers). Laws limiting expenditure |
| Economics | Levels of consumption. Disposable incomes. Ownership of radios, TVs. Readership of newspapers, magazines. Socio-economic class structure Degree of social mobility. |
| Language | Translation and 'Back Translation' |

Early research on how the advertising process works was reported in the journal of the American Marketing Association[7] and it has since been adopted as the standard concept on which most subsequent research on advertising effectiveness has been based. This search is illustrated in Figure 5.2 (adapted) which shows the main objectives of communication at various stages of the product life cycle.

The advertising profile analysis will highlight significant differences in the organization of advertising media in overseas markets, and in the types and levels of tastes, attitudes, spending habits, consumption, styles etc. of consumers. These differences should be noted by advertisers when selecting media and evaluating impact, and can aptly be illustrated by the following examples: Italy has by far the largest cinema attendances in Europe; Portugal has the highest level of commercial T.V. advertising; Sweden has the highest consumption per head of 'glossy' magazines and West Germany the highest readership of trade and industry journals. Householders in Belgium and Holland receive more pieces of direct mail per head than elsewhere in Europe; there is the highest expenditure per head in Belgium on posters/outdoor advertising; T.V. is relatively weak in

France, and some products such as textiles, books and furniture cannot be advertised there on T.V. The U.K. has the largest network and readership of national newspapers (and regional newspapers alone account for about one third of all U.K. advertising expenditure). Commercial radio and cinema advertising have relatively more impact in countries such as India, and Nigeria than in Europe. In the U.S.A. there are typically about 10 local and national T.V. networks to choose from in the localities (e.g. CBS, ABC, PBS, NBC, etc.) and almost as many Cable TV Channels as well (e.g. WGN, USA, HBO, WOR, Cinemax, Showtime, etc.). Also note from Table 5.2 that India has 16 copies of newspapers per 1,000 population, while another Asian country has 526 per 1,000. Mexico and Argentina have 5 times the commercial radio penetration of Brazil.

Figure 5.2 Hierarchy of Advertising Effects

| Product Life Cycle Stage | Main Emphasis of Message and expected Attitude/ Action by Consumers | Types of Communication Relevant at each Stage |
|---|---|---|
| Introduction | Awareness ↓ Knowledge ↓ | Announcements; descriptive copy; classified ads; slogans; jingles; sky writing; teaser campaign |
| Growth | Liking ↓ | Competitive ads; argu- mentative copy; 'image' ads; status; glamour appeals |
| Maturity | Preference ↓ | |
| Saturation | Conviction ↓ | Point-of-sale displays; retail store ads; special deals; price offers; testimonials |
| Decline | Purchase ↓ | |
| | 'Cognitive dissonance' removal (Applies throughout life cycle) | Argumentative copy; glamour/image ads; testimonials |

(Time ↓)

Table 5.4
Advertising Expenditures

| Per Capita Advertising Expenditure 1979 | | Advertising Expenditure 1975 % of GNP | |
|---|---|---|---|
| U.S.A. | $156.69 | U.S.A. | 2.07 |
| *Western Europe* | | Switzerland | 1.38 |
| Switzerland | $109.59 | Canada | 1.16 |
| Sweden | 91.81 | Denmark | 1.16 |
| Netherlands | 81.28 | U.K. | 1.13 |
| Germany | 48.56 | Australia | 1.05 |
| U.K. | 40.25 | Netherlands | 1.05 |
| Belgium | 29.73 | Finland | 1.02 |
| Italy | 10.69 | Austria | 1.00 |
| *Latin America* | | New Zealand | 0.91 |
| Venezuela | $19.36 | Japan | 0.88 |
| Argentina | 16.30 | Brazil | 0.86 |
| Brazil | 11.54 | Norway | 0.83 |
| Mexico | 7.71 | France | 0.79 |
| Nicaragua | 2.50 | West Germany | 0.79 |
| Bolivia | 1.79 | Sweden | 0.73 |
| *Africa* | | Belgium | 0.68 |
| South Africa | $13.11 | Thailand | 0.47 |
| Zambia | 2.24 | Zambia | 0.45 |
| Egypt | 1.52 | Kenya | 0.41 |
| Kenya | 0.93 | Egypt | 0.40 |
| Nigeria | 0.82 | Pakistan | 0.17 |
| Ethiopia | 0.03 | India | 0.14 |
| *Asia* | | Ghana | 0.07 |
| Japan | $43.06 | Nepal | 0.05 |
| Singapore | 22.04 | | |
| Taiwan | 10.36 | | |
| Korea | 5.21 | | |
| Philippines | 1.35 | | |
| India | 0.23 | | |

*Advertising Age*, 1979     *World Bank Atlas*, 1978

The positioning of advertising in relation to economic development in overseas countries must also be taken into account. Over half the world's advertising is placed in U.S.A. (about $38 billion in 1982); Japan is second, and Germany and U.K. follow. Table 5.4 contains some published data on this aspect.

In so far as advertising uses spoken and written words, clearly language (referred to in Advertising Profile Analysis) and the use of language need special attention by companies advertising overseas. Indeed, translation errors are commonly known to be the cause of many misunderstandings and lost sales. A recent analysis[6] of language problems (particularly in relation to advertising) cautions advertisers against three types of errors:

(a) Carelessness in translation (which can be humorous to overseas consumers, but highly embarrassing to the exporting company). The research quoted cites two pertinent examples of carelessness. A U.S. brand shirt manufacturer ran a series of magazine advertisements in Mexico with advertising copy in Spanish conveying exactly the opposite message to that intended. The advertisement, instead of declaring 'when I used this shirt, I felt good' read 'until I used this shirt I felt good'. A car manufacturer promoted its product in English-speaking markets by claiming that its product 'topped them all'; by careless translation of a key phrase, this came out in French-speaking markets as 'topped by them all'.

(b) Multiple-meaning words. Parker Pen Co uncovered and resolved this particular problem in using the word 'bola' to describe its ball point pen in advertisements in Latin America; in some countries 'bola' conveys the intended meaning 'ball' but in others the translation means, variously, 'revolution', an obscenity, and a 'lie', or fabrication.

(c) Idioms. To overcome this problem in advertising 'back-translation' is essential; many idioms simply do not translate directly into a foreign language, and any attempt to do this will damage a company's market position. Back translation requires that one person translate the message into the desired foreign language and another translate the foreign version back to the original language. Again, the research quoted cites three telling illustrations:
The Pepsi-Cola advertising slogan 'Come alive with Pepsi' came out in the German translation 'Come alive out of the Grave' and in Asia 'Bring your ancestors back from the dead'. A U.K. dental equipment manufacturer featured the English expression 'touch toe' to advertise 'touch toe' control of dental chair movement in U.S.S.R.; the translator put this idiom across in such a way to suggest that the Russian dentist would have to be barefoot to operate it.

Particular care also has to be taken in the selection and translation of company and brand names; more exporting companies now seek specialist advice from consultants and agents in devising new names, and indeed in protecting existing names and symbols. For example, General Motors was troubled with lack of enthusiasm among Puerto Rican car dealers for its recently introduced Chevrolet 'Nova'. The name 'Nova' meant 'star' when literally translated. However, when spoken, it sounded like 'no va', which in Spanish means 'it doesn't go'. This did little to build consumer confidence in the new vehicle; to remedy this, General Motors changed the name to 'Caribe' and sales increased. It cannot therefore be assumed that a name acceptable in the home market will have favourable impact overseas. As for company names, Sears, for example, was forbidden to use its unchanged name in Spain, although enjoying a high reputation there;

Castillian Spanish pronunciation of Sears sounded much like the name of Spain's largest car manufacturer and this forced Sears to incorporate the name 'Roebuck' on all of its products. For two other companies, careful research (some of it computer-assisted), enabled Kodak Company and Exxon Company to use their company names worldwide (pronouncable everywhere and with no specific meaning anywhere).

At this point, management must fully assess and act on the single most important aspect of overseas advertising: language.

Several other developments are also relevant: the growing use of English as the international commercial language (research by Advertising Association has shown that 90% of the world's mail is written in English and 54% of the world's business community use English as their main business language); nevertheless, the importance of the French-speaking and Spanish-speaking worlds should not be overlooked. Nor should preferences be ignored among consumers who may speak English, but nonetheless react more favourably and positively to advertisements in their native language (this is particularly so of Africa). Then there is language 'overlap', where multi-national advertising can be highly cost-effective for the advertiser: the German language covers Austria and most of Switzerland in addition to Germany; French covers parts of Belgium, Switzerland, Luxembourg and Monaco, as well as France; Swahili covers East Africa and, in addition, parts of Somalia, Zaire, Rwanda, Burundi, Mozambique and a small southern part of Sudan. Language overlap is directly related to media overlap such as occurs in the Benelux countries (where Belgium has become the test market of Europe), in North Italy and along the Ligurian coast.

The growing use of visual presentations in advertising is resolving some of the more intractable translation problems that advertisers have traditionally had to cope with; in some European campaigns advertisements are visual; showing a city or country scene, fantasy sequences, evoking a mood, and citing the company name; emphasis on pictures and illustrations also avoids part of the communication problems resulting from a high level of illiteracy in poor nations. Libby & Co made a commercial a few years ago for less than $20,000 to be used by its subsidiaries around the world. To avoid problems in localizing it, the commercial featured a clown pantomime, and the simple story of the clown enjoying Libby products.

The single most important operational decision by the management of an exporting company is the appointment of and partnership with the advertising agency, however it is structured; and this depends upon the strategy chosen and the composition of markets; one international agency may be appointed to handle the account through subsidiaries overseas, or each market may have its own agency (in some cases a competitor to that used by the head office at home). Of course, the availability of suitable agencies will vary and be directly related to a country's economic development and size; thus India, a poor nation in per capita income, offers several highly reputable agencies because its total market is so large; on the other hand, Ghana and Morocco have only one major agency each, although their per capita income is higher than that of India. Another important aspect in briefing and working with an agency is a realistic assessment of the state of consumer demand/sales potential (discussed in Chapter 3). Since media advertising is intended to stimulate this demand, the company's management must be familiar with these local market characteristics.

*Table 5.5*
*World's Biggest Advertising Agencies 1980*

| Rank | Agency | Total Billings (in Millions) |
|---|---|---|
| 1 | Dentsu | $2,721 |
| 2 | Young & Rubicam | 2,273 |
| 3 | J. Walter Thompson | 2,138 |
| 4 | McCann-Erickson | 1,682 |
| 5 | Ogilvy & Mather | 1,662 |
| 6 | Ted Bates | 1,404 |
| 7 | BBDO | 1,305 |
| 8 | SSC&B-Lintas | 1,203 |
| 9 | Leo Burnett | 1,145 |
| 10 | Foote, Cone & Belding | 1,118 |
| 11 | D'Arcy-MacManus & Masius | 1,045 |
| 12 | Dole Dane Bernbach | 1,004 |
| 13 | Hakuhodo | 927 |
| 14 | Benton & Bowles | 806 |
| 15 | Grey Advertising | 796 |
| 16 | Eurocom | 712 |
| 17 | Marschalk Campbell Ewald | 703 |
| 18 | Compton Advertising | 641 |
| 19 | Publicis-Intermarco-Farner | 579 |
| 20 | Dancer Fitzgerald Sample | 558 |
| 21 | N. W. Ayer ABH | 497 |
| 22 | Marsteller, Inc. | 440 |
| 23 | Wells, Rich, Greene | 411 |
| 24 | Needham, Harper & Steers | 411 |
| 25 | William Esty Co. | 390 |

Source: *Advertising Age*, 1981

In briefing and evaluating his Advertising Agency, the exporter will find a useful set of guidelines researched by Terpstra[9]; these are:

(a) Market coverage: Does the particular agency or package of agencies cover all the relevant markets?

(b) Quality of coverage: How good a job does this package of agencies do in preparing advertising in each market?

(c) Market research, public relations, and other marketing services: If the firm needs these services in world markets, in addition to advertising work, how do the different agencies compare on their offerings of these facilities?

(d) Relative roles of company advertising department and agency: Some firms have a large staff that does much of the work of preparing advertising campaigns. These firms require less of an agency than do companies that rely on the agency for almost everything relating to advertising. Thus a weak company advertising department needs strong agency, and vice versa.

(e) Communication and control: If the firm wants frequent communication with agencies in foreign markets and wishes to oversee their efforts, it will be inclined to tie up with the domestic agency that has overseas offices. The internal communications system of this agency network would facilitate communications for international marketers.

(f) International co-ordinator: Does the firm wish to have advertising tailor-made to each national market? Or does it desire co-ordination of national advertising with that done in other markets, and/or with the domestic programme? One of the major differences between agency groups will be their ability to aid the advertiser in attaining international co-ordination.

(g) Size of company international business: The smaller the firm's international advertising expenditures, the less its ability to divide its expenditures up among many different agencies. The firm's advertising volume may determine agency choice to assure some minimum level of service. A small volume multiplied by a number of markets could be of interest to an international agency even if it is of no interest to an agency in any one market.

(h) Image: Does the firm want a national or international image? Desire for local identification and good local citizenship might indicate that the firm should choose national agencies rather than an international one. This is the practice of IBM for example.

(i) Company organization: Companies that are very decentralized, with national profit centres, might wish to leave agency selection to the local subsidiary.

(j) Level of involvement: In joint venture arrangements, the international firm shares decision-making. The national partner may have preferences and/or experience with a national agency, which could be the decisive factor. In licensing agreements, advertising is largely in the hands of the licensee. Selling through distributors also reduces the control of the international company. Sometimes the firm may have a regenerative advertising programme with distributors but, generally, international marketers can choose only the agencies for the advertising paid for by their firms. Of course, when the firm has a 50–50 co-operative programme with its distributors, it may have some say in agency selection.

In stimulating demand, and ensuring impact in its advertising messages which takes account of cultural, social and other factors in key export markets, and brings about purchasing decisions, some short illustrations from actual campaigns may prove instructive:

(a) Rank Xerox office photocopiers. This was advertised widely in newspapers, but with different pictures to take account of national differences: in West Germany a photograph of a child to appeal to the executive secretary (usually female) who could make the decision to buy; in U.K. a group of footballers was used. In another series of advertisements, three office products, (including photocopier) were pictured together with a teapot (for U.K. customers) with the copy 'These three products solve all office problems: Rank Xerox make one of them'. Coffee pots were used in France and Benelux, but these were considered too flippant for the practical Swiss and German markets, so a telephone was substituted for the coffee pot.

(b) Coca Cola's international advertising is based on the premise that the product is used in the same way and meets the same needs, so the advertising message is standardized.

(c) General Electric's advertising is based on identifying buying motives for industrial as distinct from consumer products in its different overseas markets.

(d) Volvo, offering a standard, well-tried automobile uses similar visuals, but the copy concept and line is different to direct different appeals in its overseas markets; Volvo emphasizes economy, durability and safety both in Sweden and U.S.A.; status and leisure in France, performance in Germany, and unmatched safety features in Switzerland (scene of many fatal accidents).

(e) Martini Rossi use a common copy line '. . . the right one' in its T.V. advertising but very different visuals even within the E.E.C.: car racing scenes for Italy's obsessive car fans, straightforward, practical ski scenes showing how refreshing Martini is for West German viewers, but fantasy scenes (ballooning sequences over castles) and more complex visual images for its British viewers.

An analysis of travel advertisements over recent years in international weeklies of wide circulation, such as *Time* and the *Economist*, shows a number of themes stressed in the advertising copy (Table 5.6).

*Table 5.6*
*Selected International Advertising Themes*

| Advertiser Carrier | Themes Stressed | Concept |
|---|---|---|
| KLM | 'Brilliant tradition' (Father-to-son diamond polishing) Rembrandt Tax-free shopping Museum guide Windmill and water power Smiling welcome | Holland's standard attractions |

*Table 5.6 (continued)*

| Advertiser Carrier | Themes Stressed | Concept |
|---|---|---|
| Pan AM | 'The world's most exclusive place to dine . . .' (First class dining room upstairs in a 747) | Distinction |
| Kenya Airways | Africa's mountains Wildlife and game reserves Pearl-white beaches Fishing | Kenya's standard attractions |
| TWA | Food and drink (3 international entrees) 8 audio tracks Friendly service Contour seats Speed through customs | In-Flight's attractions |
| Jap Air Lines | 'Happi' coat (clothes less crumpled) Japanese or European cuisine 1000 year tradition of hospitality Hot towels | Exotic, millenial Orient |
| Singapore Airlines | Gentle hostess All-Boeing fleet 300 flights per week | Oriental charm Technical competence Wide coverage |
| KLM | 'More', 'Better' Extra fast check-in Special seat selection Quiet for businessman Special cabin service Special baggage handling Special office attention | Value for money Special treatment |
| Lufthansa | 'Flights made in Germany' 273 offices. On all continents | German quality Worldwide coverage |
| SAS | Arrival in Japan Sunday morning | Overcome 'Jet lag' |
| Pan Am | World's largest fleet of 747's Comfortable seats First-class dining room More space Films and music | Flight comfort |

*Table 5.6 (continued)*

| Advertiser Carrier | Themes Stressed | Concept |
|---|---|---|
| British Airways | Direct from London to 11 North American destinations Cool, calm and collected crew | Wide choice of destinations British character |
| Avianca | The people who know South America best Since 1919 | South American specialists |
| SAS | Fast Way West Polar experience Wide body jets | Go West in comfort |
| Thai Airways | 'Beyond Bangkok' 'Beautiful Thai' | The other Thailand Thai women |
| South African Airways | International coverage 'Where no one's a stranger' | Big-hearted growth |

## 5.7 Export Consortia

Exporting companies in particular sectors of manufacturing industry have for many years set up consortia to obtain large-scale capital and engineering orders overseas. There are, however, some organizational developments among major industrial competitors of the U.K. which need, and indeed repay, detailed study, particularly 'federated' marketing, and the role of the international 'trading house' favoured by Japanese industry. It is also a common misconception that export consortia are appropriate only for industrial conglomerates and large-scale engineering companies: in fact, consortia have been used effectively in many parts of the world by small-scale enterprises, as will be explained. But companies which have most often engaged in some form of large-scale joint venture, including manufacturing and/or sales are to found in the transport, weapons and weapons systems, chemicals, aerospace, other high-technology sectors and in construction where finance, management, contracting and equipment supply are combined. There are also (though less commonly) reciprocal agreements between firms manufacturing complementary products, whereby each markets the other's products in its own country. Some of the benefits to be derived from a consortium arrangement include:

(a) Stronger market position to develop long-term sales potential, particularly contracts and tenders;
(b) Sharing of financial and technical resources and risks, with better financing prospects and terms;
(c) Increased direct participation in market and more control of the sales operation;
(d) Strengthening of both technical and market competitiveness world-wide.

Much depends of course on the precise terms of the consortium: there must be technical complementarity, and a joint management task force (usually with a Project director) needs to be set up in the early stages. This is particularly so if the project is a large-scale capital or 'turnkey' project, requiring substantial manufacturing investment, export credit insurance, long-term negotiating etc; indeed, it is not uncommon at this level to have participation by the appropriate section of government foreign trade: in the U.K. the Projects and Export Policy Division of BOTB. Recently, a major power plant deal was signed between the Chinese People's Republic Government and a U.K. consortium headed by a senior official of the Deparment of Trade and Industry.

Many companies in the manufacturing industry (particularly in general engineering, paper, board and packaging machinery, food processing equipment, vehicle and vehicle parts, electronic testing and fire control equipment) develop licencing agreements as part of their overseas sales operations. This system works especially well in more distant export markets where the extra costs and logistics of shipping finished machines would make the products uncompetitive (or the exporting manufacturer may not have the required production capacity); it is a profitable approach to market entry and development; particularly, if there are high tariffs on finished imported manufacturers or plant, high costs of setting up wholly owned subsidiaries, and difficulties in the repatriation of profits or dividends. There is still a lot of scope for more and more profitable licensing agreements for British industry, where technical creativity, innovation and invention have been abundant, but where putting these ideas into production, commercialization and worldwide profitable sales has been sadly deficient (examples of recent new technical ideas in transportation make this point clearly e.g. linear and electric motors, hovercraft, jet-propelled sea transport, etc).

Two further instances of manufactured products illustrate these joint developments: General Motors and Chrysler promote models with standardized sub assemblies, castings and components which are manufactured in supply factories in different countries. Grundig and Phillips have major supply plants in various countries where land and labour are cheaper and more plentiful than in the metropolitan countries. Moreover, economies of scale in research and development as well as in production can be achieved only if there are worldwide sales operations over which to spread such costs, often to the point where the multi-national company is heavily dependent on worldwide sales revenues.

Some mention has been made of the role of government officers on the supply side: on the purchasing side, export consortium members are increasingly having to make presentations of tenders, to negotiate with and close the sale of major capital projects to government tender boards or centralized purchasing committees. Not only this, but many overseas governments, in awarding such major contracts, particularly in the Middle and Far East, stipulate some direct government participation, whether technical, managerial or financial. There can also be stipulations about plant capacity and location (for example, in France DATAR directs local and new plants), training of local management, and sometimes a 'buy back' condition, or one relating to a minimum percentage of the output which must be exported to earn foreign exchange.

One recent analysis[10] reports the operations and benefits of 'federated' marketing in overseas operations, where a group of three or four companies or divisions of companies offering complementary, non-competing products or services and selling broadly to the same customers, set up a joint overseas marketing facility with a co-ordinator company; the costs and risks are shared, and the whole range of products or services receives full-time sales coverage. Sales effectiveness can be improved, the grouping has a synergy and a sale by one company can open up sales opportunities for others. A grouping of this sort was set up successfully by three manufacturing companies to tackle the U.S.S.R. food market with the support of a leading commercial bank. A key role is played by the co-ordinator company which catalyses this joint venture and then provides the administrative and financial services and technical co-ordination which combined operations between independent manufacturing companies require. Note should be taken at this point of the well-documented success overseas of the Japanese trading houses such as Marubeni which combine operations between manufacturing, banking, contracting and trading. This is in some contrast to the normal structure of the European conglomerate, comprising large numbers of small subsidiary companies, each standing on its own. Indeed, these very diversification policies which extend product and service ranges, and which spread the product/market risk across many export markets, actually tend to weaken the group's ability to concentrate its efforts internationally, rather than re-inforce it. Above all, such a federated group collectively can deploy resources sufficient to set up a fully manned and effective sales presence overseas at costs which together the companies can afford and justify through the total sales revenue achievable.

This principle of collective effort and sales is growing in importance and applications: but there must be efforts to ensure equal opportunities for the products of all participating firms, particularly if assortments are heterogeneous, so that the same sales organization and the same channels of distribution can be used. The choice of markets is therefore dependent on the types of firms in the marketing group – and vice versa.

If potential group members have already been actively engaged in export marketing and have established sales, then the choice of market becomes more complex because these firms might want to:

(a) Have those markets included, hoping to strengthen their position with the help of the whole group even if this choice might prove disadvantageous for the rest; or

(b) Have those markets excluded, as they are already well established there and are more interested in new market areas, while their prospective partners are especially interested in profiting from the experience gained by these firms.

Again, only a market survey can serve as a basis for the final decision in order to ensure that the best possible market chances for the majority of member firms shall be exploited. Firms which cannot agree to such a decision should be left out. It seems better to limit the number this way than to start off with compromises, which will hamper the commercial success of the marketing group.

Some existing export groups – like the DELTA Group in Switzerland – have tried to solve this important problem by constituting subgroups for those member firms who are only interested in certain markets and regions or in certain specified outlets like the department stores or government buying. This certainly is a useful solution, but it seems doubtful whether such a choice is feasible at the beginning of the enterprise when too many complications may jeopardize the efficiency and success of the export activities. It should, therefore, be considered as a second stage when the spreading of activities to new markets is planned.

Export co-operation between smaller firms of different countries does not seem yet to be very common, but is obviously growing in importance. If the selection of partners is made carefully enough, not only is such co-operation as good as export marketing with firms of the same country, but it can bring even faster and more profitable results. The foreign partner already has his sales organization established, knows the trade outlets and market conditions well, and has established a reputation of his own which can be of great advantage to the manufacturer who enters into co-operation with the firm; but the risks involved are naturally greater than with manufacturers of their own country who are well known to the firm. A close look has to be taken, therefore, at the following points which could mean failure or success in co-operating with the foreign partner or partners.

(a) Position of firm in market (reputation, strength, channels used, market coverage);
(b) Production facilities and capacity of the firm;
(c) Liquidity, financial sources and management ability;
(d) Marketing policies;
(e) Assortment range.

The last item is especially important, as lack of harmonization in assortments can easily lead to misunderstanding, unwanted competition with partners, overlapping of efforts and failure of the co-operation.

It is easier for manufacturers to co-operate if their products are complementary to each other. If their production programmes overlap, they must endeavour to specialize in such a way that the individual product is manufactured in one factory only, with a resultant lowering of manufacturing costs. An Italian manufacturer of motor scooters may, for instance, enter into co-operation with a Dutch manufacturer of bicycles and bicycle trailers by selling the Dutch products through the same channels of distribution as the motor scooters. In this way the marketing costs are distributed over a larger number of products, and the Dutch manufacturer derives advantage from a well-established marketing organization on the Italian market. Similarly, the Dutch manufacturer includes the Italian motor scooters in his marketing organization and the Italian manufacturer derives a corresponding advantage in Holland.

This type of co-operation can be expanded to other countries in which two manufacturers wish to promote their export sales. By employing a joint marketing organization they will be able to reduce the cost of market research, sales promotion and actual distribution. Co-operating firms, of course, run the risk that one of the participants may take up the manufacture of the products of one of the others after sales in the product are rising. This risk is particularly serious in the case of international co-operation, as it may be difficult to take legal proceedings, but the risk may be reduced by arranging for the payment of substantial penalties in case the agreement is broken.

Firms in different countries may also work together in more restricted fields. A French, a German and a British shirt maker may, for instance, co-operate on advertising their cotton shirts in preference to shirts of synthetic fibres. Firms also frequently combine in arranging specialized international exhibitions. If co-operation is only to comprise a general publicity campaign, then it is of no consequence that the range of products is identical. Collective quotations for large contracts are also frequently submitted. Such contracts often comprise products that are not made by a single manufacturer alone, or are of a volume that exceeds the productive capacity of a single manufacturer. The Belgian GAMMA Group for textile machinery co-operate with manufacturers in other countries both as regards exhibitions and quotations for large contracts.

The fields of co-operation for export consortia are, therefore, considerable and are by no means confined to manufacturing and selling. An export group may be established for the sole purpose of procuring detailed market information, even though it is nowadays possible to obtain this from public institutions, trade organizations, chambers of commerce, etc. It is, however, necessary to adapt these data to the particular interests of the manufacturers in the group. Moreover, such desk research may be the beginning of more extensive co-operation in future. The advantages of co-operation become more apparent when a group undertakes field research on a joint basis. Such research is difficult and calls for larger investments which are easier to finance if undertaken jointly. Export market analyses are frequently supported financially by public authorities, provided a group of firms will benefit from them and itself contributes financially.

If co-operation includes sales promotion, the economic advantages become still more obvious. Advertising may well be undertaken collectively even though the participating firms continue individually to canvass their own customers.

If manufacturers do not want to restrict their co-operation to prestige advertising, but to extend it to the promotion of individual products, such products should be advertised under a common name of brand which should also be used by the individual firms in their own sales propaganda on the packages, etc. Collective advertising can only be fully efficient however when group exports are centralized. This may include a central export office and the use of joint channels of distribution on the export markets. In fact, export co-operation will be much more economic and successful if products are sold and distributed through a joint export office.

A thorough co-ordination and centralization of all export functions thus becomes possible and enables firms to get a better return for their marketing costs. It is usually advisable to locate the export office in the home market in order to facilitate the close co-operation between managers of member firms, but if a group concentrates on a single foreign market with a large turnover it may be expedient to establish the sales office in that market.

In order to derive full advantage from export co-operation, it is necessary to establish joint marketing channels in export markets as well. An export group is able to procure the best channels of distribution in the individual markets owing to the advantages presented by this type of co-operation to foreign distributors.

Normally, an export group should begin its life carefully with a selection of possible and, in the long run, desirable, functions. Desk research, collective advertising and sales promotion form the basis for marketing groups abroad. Field studies, branded goods policy and product development might follow later when the co-operation has proved successful. A full marketing service should always be the goal when looking ahead as export groups must offer their members collectively the same competitive weapons as are available to the larger firms individually. In later stages, of course, the group can and should include other fields like buying, harmonization of production and basic technical research, to name a few.

The International Trade Centre UNCTAD/GATT has reported some experience of 'joint export marketing groups' or 'consortia' in different parts of the developing world. They have not been characterized by multinational corporations or industrial conglomerates. These groups or 'consortia' can consist of private businesses, producers, co-operatives and manufacturing companies who jointly establish an export marketing venture, often with government help; the General Export Association of Sweden, for example, has for some years had experience in establishing export consortia based on the membership and efforts of diverse interested companies.

This ITC research[11] sets out the basis of exporting experience gained:

(a)  The benefits provided by joint export marketing groups both for the nation and for consortium participants;
(b)  The steps necessary to establish such groups;
(c)  Case histories illustrating successful export consortia ventures: These cover a diversity of trades: Argentinian Wine Growers; Indian Consortium for Power Projects Limited under which several factories for advanced electrical power plants producing complementary equipment using the services of a central design and marketing group: Clothing consortium in Colombia; Horticultural Co-operative Union in Kenya which exports a variety of produce to markets in Western Europe, and Consortia in Brazil for exporting automobile components and 'Imbuia' timber.

In Singapore, INTRACO LTD., a consortium financed by 200 manufacturers, trading companies and banks performed or participated on a commercial basis in a variety of export services, general trading, export financing, raw material processing, and agency functions on behalf of the business community of Singapore: particularly servicing an overseas agent for a Singapore manufacturer, or more typically, acting as principal in relation to a foreign buyer, purchasing goods from Singapore manufacturers on its own account, and reselling to exporters at a profit.

Joint export marketing, particularly the sharing of promotional costs, is by no means confined to the production and export sale of commodities. It is increasingly found in franchising and licensing operations to promote worldwide sales of consumer and industrial goods and in processing industries. The precise type of export licensing arrangement depends upon the particular circumstances of the industry concerned and can vary widely. Many trucks and buses are manufactured under licence, for example in South America, where there is a growing market to be served locally and where land and labour are cheaper than, for example, in Germany. Sometimes the processing technology is not available in the country which is the source of the raw materials, or the importing organization might offer the raw material exporter a licence to process or assemble the export product; this can then be sold to that firm or exported in their name on payment of a royalty for using their technology and trademark. Alternatively the licensee can become a subsidiary company, facilitating exports to overseas markets by

(a)  Avoiding tariff barriers;
(b)  Avoiding import quotas;
(c)  Gaining possible tax concessions;
(d)  Achieving more comprehensive representation and promotion;
(e)  Offering the finished product at a most competitive price in the local and nearby export markets.

In conclusion, in specific terms, the benefits to the company of joining an export consortium can be viewed as follows:

(a)  Penetration of new export markets. Firms that have never ventured further away than the home market or perhaps to a neighbouring country are able to sell more widely thanks to the increased know-how, finance and managerial expertise available.
(b)  Access to new types of buyers. A joint export marketing group is much better placed than an individual firm to research foreign markets and identify new types of prospective buyer. A consortium may be able to employ specialist designers to adapt the product, if necessary. A potential buyer may want a quantity or range of goods that can only be supplied by the combined efforts of a joint export marketing group.
(c)  Security through market diversification. The specialist staff of a consortium are able to service a wider range of export markets than an individual firm and yet can respond more flexibly and quickly to changes in any one market.
(d)  Turning seasonal fluctuations to advantage. Consortia can have the

size and the expertise to turn seasonal fluctuations in sales to advantage particularly by exporting to countries on the other side of the equator. For example, tropical growers can sell fresh vegetables, fruit and flowers to Western Europe during the European winter.

(e)  Making long-term planning possible. The increased business provided by a joint export marketing group can enable member companies to plan ahead with more confidence.

(f)  Reducing unit costs of production. When the selling effort of a joint marketing group leads to increased demand for a member company's products, that company can step up production. This enables it to spread its fixed costs over a larger number of products and so reduce its unit costs.

(g)  Better prices and profit margins. Goods tend to fetch a much higher price in export markets than in the home markets of the developing countries themselves. This can make export sales much more profitable than home sales – given the kind of marketing expertise that can be available through a joint export marketing group. For instance, some tropical fruits have a retail price in Europe, North America or Japan up to forty times their retail price at home.

(h)  Benefits of foreign currency earnings. Increased export sales through a joint export marketing group can have important foreign currency attraction for the individual member firm. For example, foreign currency contracts can be useful insurance against inflation at home. Governments may also give export incentives, including large foreign exchange allocations for the import of materials and machinery, favourable rates of exchange, and tax rebates on export earnings. The experienced management of consortium may also be able to secure such foreign exchange advantages as paying for transportation in local currency then charging the export customer in convertible currencies.

(i)  International marketing know-how. As a member of a joint export marketing group, a company can often gain more international marketing experience in a few months than it could hope to gain in several years on its own. This experience might cover not only selling, but credit and financial arrangements, documentation procedures, export and import regulations, foreign technical requirements, packaging techniques and methods of handling and transportation.

(j)  Improved company morale. Export selling success through a joint export marketing group has often had a beneficial effect on morale throughout a company. This can be particularly marked in small-and medium-size companies that have not previously exported their products.

(k)  Gaining a stronger voice for the industry. The improvement in government/industry communications produced by joint export marketing groups can be of considerable benefit to companies. Through consortia they are better placed to draw government attention to obstacles to exporting and to press the case for concessions or incentives.

(l) Spreading export selling overheads. Through a consortium there is a sharing or spreading of export selling overheads such as those incurred in running an export office or carrying out market research.

(m) Alternative to export agents. Many exporters have happy and profitable co-operation with their agents in export markets. However, membership of a consortium that has specialist selling staff means that a company can more easily sell through its own salesmen or rather the consortium's salesmen – if this would be a more easily controllable arrangement. Even if a company decides to continue having an agent, the consortium may be able to give valuable advice on selecting the right agent and then working effectively with him after he/she has been appointed.

# References

1. Central Policy Review Staff, *Review of Overseas Representation*, (H.M.S.O.: London, 1979).
2. Ellison, R. *Overseas Selling Methods of U.K. Exporters*, (University of Manchester; 1976).
3. Schmitthof, C. M. *Agency Agreements in the Export Trade* (Institute of Export: London, 1980).
4. Barclays Bank International 'Export Development in France, Germany and U.K. – Factors for International Success' *ITI Research*, London, 1979.
5. Baker, M. J., Parkinson, S. and Saren, M. *Off-shore Inspection and Maintenance – The Implications of North Sea Experience*, (Financial Times Business Publications: London, 1979).
6. Ricks, D. A. *Big Business Blunders: Mistakes in Multinational Marketing* (Don James – Irwin: New York, 1983) pp. 15–16.
7. Lavidge, R. and Steiner, G. 'A Model for Predictive Measurements of Advertising Effects' *Journal of Marketing*, **75**, October 1961.
8. Majaro, S. *International Marketing: A Strategic Approach to World Markets*, 2nd edn., (Allan & Unwin: London, 1983) (adapted).
9. Terpstra, V. *International Marketing Management*, 2nd edn., (Holt-Saunders International: New York, 1984) p. 398.
10. Claxton, C. 'Federated Marketing', *Marketing*, December 1979.
11. ITC/UNCTAD/GATT *Creation and Management of Joint Export Marketing Groups* (ITC/UNCTAD/GATT: Geneva, 1973).

# 6. OFFICIAL EXPORT SERVICES AND ADMINISTRATION

## 6.1 British Overseas Trade Board (BOTB)

Specifically for exporters in U.K. the organization and services of the British Overseas Trade Board (BOTB) require some detailed description and analysis. The Board itself draws members from both industry and Government, the President being the Secretary of State for Trade and Industry and the Chairman a leading businessman. BOTB has set out its official responsibilities as follows:

(a) To advise the Government on strategy for overseas trade;
(b) To direct and develop the Government export promotion services on behalf of the Secretary of State for Trade and Industry;
(c) To encourage and support industry and commerce in overseas trade with the aid of appropriate governmental and non-governmental organizations at home and overseas;
(d) To contribute to the exchange of views between Government and industry and commerce in the field of overseas trade and to search for solutions to problems.

In discharging these official responsibilities, BOTB works closely with the Foreign and Commonwealth Office (which is responsbile for Diplomatic posts overseas) and with the Export Credits Guarantee Department (which is responsible to the Secretary of State for Trade and Industry). BOTB provides a wide range of information, advice and services to help exporters. Specifically, BOTB provides, for exporters in the U.K. through its head office and regional offices in the U.K., the following assistance, information and advice:

(a) Preliminary Research and market information: Statistics and Market Intelligence Library (SMIL) and Product Data Store (PDS) provide the exporter with excellent facilities for desk-research.
(b) Advice on individual markets; this is a free service provided by the Market Branches of the Overseas Trade Divisions (see Chart on p. 178); it includes information on tariffs and import regulations.
(c) Market Advisory Services; this group of services (Market Prospects Service, Export Representative Service and Overseas Status Report Service) provides information about the prospects for particular goods and services in a chosen market including advice on how to exploit the market's opportunities and how to obtain effective local representation including reports on the status of potential agents.

172

(d) Export Marketing Research Scheme: Advice on and financial help with overseas market research are available for approved projects outside the European Community.

(e) Publicity Unit; in conjunction with Central Office of information (COI) and BBC External Services, BOTB can help exporters publicize their products and services abroad. BOTB keeps trade press in U.K. informed of important trade events overseas and helps alert British manufacturers to overseas promotional events.

(f) Technical Requirements of Export Markets: Technical Help to Exporters helps British exporters to comply with technical specifications in overseas markets and to avoid the pitfalls of technical requirements.

(g) Outward Mission Scheme: Support for groups of businessmen travelling to selected markets overseas to sell or promote British goods or to assess the prospects for exports.

(h) Inward Mission Scheme: Financial assistance is offered to groups of firms wishing to bring to Britain overseas businessmen or others who can influence exports.

(i) Joint Venture Scheme: BOTB's Fairs and Promotions Branch organizes group participation of British firms in overseas trade fairs and exhibitions, store promotions, seminars and symposia.

(j) Market Entry Guarantee Scheme: Designed to help smaller and medium-sized firms deal with the financial risk and problems associated with a venture to develop a new export market.

(k) Overseas Projects: The Projects and Export Policy Division of the Department of Trade and Industry is the focal point within Government to which consultants, contractors and manufacturers can look for official support in their pursuit of major contracts in large overseas projects, especially in difficult and complex cases. There is also information on projects financed by principal world lending agencies from World Aid Section (Projects and Export Policy Division).

(l) Small Firms Information Service: This provides assistance to many first-time 'exporting companies with limited resources'.

(m) Export Intelligence Service (EIS): This provides up-to-date information about overseas opportunities and other market intelligence.

The last of these, the Export Intelligence Service (EIS), is the most significant and the longest established. This is so because it provides actual and potential exporters with a comprehensive range of market intelligence. The operation is designed to provide a fast, reliable and specific service to subscribing firms, whose information requirements, self-selected from the EIS classification system, are computer-matched against market intelligence received from diplomatic posts overseas. Section 1 of the classification covers a range of intelligence types as follows:

(a) Specific Export Opportunities;
(b) Short market pointers to new trade opportunities;
(c) Market Reports;

(d)  Overseas agents seeking British principals;
(e)  Calls for tender (including invitations to pre-qualify);
(f)  Successful bidders and awards of contracts;
(g)  Overseas business visitors to U.K.;
(h)  Outward opportunities for co-operation with overseas firms;
(i)  Inward opportunities for co-operation with overseas firms;
(j)  Changes in overseas tariffs and import regulations;
(k)  Aid and loan agreements (International and U.K.) including major aid projects under consideration;
(l)  Trade Agreements;
(m) National and other development plans; general economic reports;
(n)  Lines of credit opened by Export Credits Guarantee Department (ECGD);
(o)  Notification of Overseas Trade Fairs, Exhibitions, Missions (inward and outward); store promotions;
(p)  World economic comments and quarterly overseas trading reports.

Selectivity is also provided in respect of geographical areas (Section 2) and commodity classifications (Section 3). Chapters 1–98 of this classification deal with individual products; (Chapter 99) covers consultancy services, projects, contracting services, plant and equipment, supplies, and components manufactured to overseas customers' specifications. This part of the EIS classification covers those products and services which cannot be identified in terms of the individual commodities in Chapters 1–98. A subscriber may have as many permutations as necessary to fulfil their declared interests.

It is not generally appreciated by many British companies that the EIS is continually researching ways and means of improving both the range of data and the speed of transmission. The possible improvements offered by the latest information technology are constantly under review.

With the present system, the information received from Britain's commercial officers in British Embassies and diplomatic posts around the world is keyed into an ICL 2966 computer using a Microdata Sovereign multiple processor keying system, although direct access via telex line is currently being introduced,whereby the posts will feed information directly to the computer. After the computer has identified subscribers' interests, the information is reproduced on continuous stationery by computer-linked high speed printers. This output, called 'notices', is then enveloped by a Kern mark-sensing on-line guillotine inserter ready for mailing to subscribers. The same computer also prints out the master copy of the *Daily Gazette*, a compendium of each day's information complete with an index for those subscribers who do not require selectivity. Using this master, copies of the *Daily Gazette* are reproduced on a Rank Xerox 9500.

Significantly, a number of other countries are now storing 'export opportunity' sales leads for their nationals, collecting from their embassies abroad on computer data bases but distribution, where it takes place, is to the Chamber of Commerce movement and similar bodies not, as in the EIS case, to specific companies. It is clear that British Embassies in important markets will soon need to have terminal facilities for the remote searching and updating of these data bases, available to any travelling national who has not his own terminal and password. And, more seriously, according to BOTB, 'British companies are losing export business because they do not subscribe to the Export Intelligence Service'. This, therefore, raises the question of just how much British management is as aware as it should be of the range of these services, and just how valuable they are perceived to be by users in trade and industry.

*Yearly Analysis of Most Frequently used Intelligence Types**

*Rank Order*

| | |
|---|---|
| 1 | Calls for Tender |
| 2 | Specific Export Opportunities |
| 3 | Finding Overseas Agents |
| 4 | Opportunities of co-operation with overseas manufacturers |
| 5 | Short market pointers to new trade opportunities |
| 6 | Successful bidders and awards of contract |

* BOTB Annual Report 1983

The Central Policy Review Staff, in the course of their somewhat critical study[1] of Overseas Representation, examined the value of EIS in a particular research study to find out from subscribers what use EIS notices are. This study has identified that only a minority – 30% – of the 'notices' received by the sample of subscribers interviewed were considered useful. The majority were seen as 'too late', 'inappropriate to the subscriber's business', etc. Of this 30% minority, only a third, or 10% of the notices received lead to some action being taken in terms of export development. The researchers regard this as a low success rate, although it compares quite favourably with the average response rate experienced in direct mail (about 2%).

The most interesting finding, however, is that the information contained in the 'notices' – whether actionable or not – is, in the view of the sample subscribers, available elsewhere only in a small minority (under 20%) of the cases. There seems clear evidence that whatever its quality, efficiency or cost-effectiveness, EIS can fairly be regarded as an irreplaceable intelligence medium, and is so regarded by its subscribers in respect of 80% of the 'notices' received.

How can the scope and impact of EIS be improved? Clearly, one essential step is to make the EIS Computer accessible to British companies by Telex or by Prestel, the new remote access teledata system operated in U.K. by the Post Office Telecommunications. Export sales leads and market opportunities can then not only be input directly into the computer from foreign posts but be accessible directly by subscribing companies in their offices. The technology for this, of course, exists; indeed, the U.S. Department of Commerce, through its Trade Opportunities Scheme

(TOP), and the Italian External Commerce Institute (ICE) are introducing just such a system for their exporters this year.

With modern data retrieval software, the subscriber can have far more flexible options for enquiry than the rigid 'pre-keyed' coding of 'notices' and 'subscriber profiles'. Also, with this software, the subscriber can communicate back directly to the overseas post which is the source of the original sales lead, requesting further information or other follow-up action on the spot, within minutes of identifying leads which do seem worth following up. A later survey, published early in 1982 by the City Research Associations (CRA) revealed the following:

(a) On average subscribers respond to 50% of relevant notices, 35% of subscribers respond to three quarters or more whilst 22% respond to all such notices.

(b) Nearly a quarter of EIS subscribers enter new export markets as a result of the EIS information, while 7% start exporting products or services not previously sold overseas. Perhaps most interesting of all, 5% have actually developed new products or services as a result of EIS information.

(c) Subscribers to EIS use the information not only as a primary source of new potential business but as a means of verifying other sources, including their local agents.

(d) Based on exporters' own estimates, the value of U.K. exports directly attributable to the EIS information was assessed at MORE THAN £1 BILLION per annum.

The Simplification of International Trade Procedures Board (SITPRO) works to simplify international trade procedures and documents and provide more cost-effective methods of trading. It is funded by the BOTB and from self-generated income.

Among other things, SITPRO has developed export documentation systems that utilize international standards and provide fast and accurate document production. These systems are used by more than 4000 companies and include 'Overlays' (for use with ordinary office copiers) 'Spex 2' (a microcomputer package that operates on over 40 different makes of machine) 'Postpacks' (one typing set for post exports) and 'Docspeed' (special system for freight forwarders). SITPRO has also developed data standards to allow exchange of data between otherwise incompatible computers and supporting software called 'Interbridge'. A range of publications and leaflets on simplified export procedures (e.g. Customs procedures, costing guidelines and effective export office routines, managing letters of credit etc.) and audio-visual training aids on key export subjects have also been produced.

The SITPRO Board and advisory groups are drawn from a wide range of interests including carriers, freight forwarders, bankers, exporters and government departments. Some 200 businessmen and officials offer their specialist advice. SITPRO maintains close contacts with similar bodies abroad, co-operates with the EEC Commission and the United Nations and with organizations such as the International Chamber of Commerce,

International Standards Organization, International Association of Ports and Harbours to assist the harmonization and simplification of trade procedures worldwide. SITPRO provides advice to U.K. companies via open days and network of approved distributors. Workshops and seminars are also held. Latest developments are published in a free quarterly bulletin *SITPRONEWS*.

In 1982 SITPRO launched an Export Consignment and Invoicing microcomputer software package, Spex. This has quickly become the market leader for export documentation applications. Now implemented on over 40 different microcomputers, Spex is a highly portable and flexible package which allows British exporters to take advantage of information technology. Operating from the stored details of regular customers, products, Declarations of Origin etc., it rapidly and accurately performs a wide range of the functions that are required to export goods. These include carrying out all of the calculations necessary to invoice in sterling or in foreign currency and to produce cube and weight information. It can generate either invoices and a master document for use with a SITPRO Overlay, or print over forty different export documents direct. During 1984 the Spex package has been considerably enhanced and a new, more powerful package, Spex 2 is currently being introduced. In addition to all of the facilities of its predecessor, many of which have been improved, Spex 2 has the ability to link to other computer systems, including mainframes, which either hold some of the information needed by the export department or which require information on export consignments. A future enhancement will be the automatic production of a computer message formatted according to the U.N. Syntax Rules which will contain all of the consignment information currently carried on documents from exporters to their freight forwarders and/or shipping companies.

*Trade Data Interchange*
If the information or data relating to the goods and payment flow in international trade could be provided to all of the participants both in U.K. and overseas rapidly and accurately by computer, many of the problems which confront traders would recede. However, two major technical problems have restricted this development. One is the current inability of different manufacturers to communicate with each other easily, and the other has been the need for an internationally accepted standard for formatting and exchanging computer data. Over the past five years progress in this latter area has been rapid, much of it inspired by SITPRO. The need for rules governing the interchange of data led to the development in 1978 of Sitpro Syntax Rules, the core of which was adopted by the United Nations in their guidelines. Data Interchange based on these Syntax Rules is now increasing quickly and, in many cases, this growth has been supported by SITPRO's software package, Interbridge.

This is two suites of programs, construction and translation, developed and marketed by Sitpro, which implement both the Syntax Rules for data interchange the equivalent U.N. guidelines. These portable programs are independent of the computers on which they operate, the applications in which they are used and of the users which use them. The Syntax Rules –and in many the Interbridge package – are in use in the U.K., Belgium, West Germany, Finland, Netherlands, Australia, and recently, in a test environment in Canada. The applications covered include official, administrative, domestic and international trade, transport, port and shipping requirements.

The Mercator project, is sponsored and financially supported by the European Commission and is designed to prove the acceptability and effectiveness of the data interchange formatting standards developed and published by the United Nations. Trade, transport and official data are interchanged between, in the U.K. Vauxhall Motors, H.M. Customs and Excise and SITPRO; in Belgium, General Continental, Belgian Customs, Sabena World Airlines, National Bank of Belgium and Ziegler Freight Forwarders and in West Germany, Standard Elektrik Lorenz, AEG, Telefunken, Bundesamt für Wehrtechnik und Beschaf (BWB) and DEUPRO.

### 6.11  BOTB Organization – Checklist

*Overseas Trade Divisions* (at 1 Victoria Street, London SW1H 0ET, U.K.)
The Overseas Trade Division 1 – Projects and Export Policy
Branches 1/4   Projects and Export Policy
Branch 3b     World Aid Section

Overseas Trade Division 2
Branch 1      North American Branch
Branch 2      Nort-East and South-East Asia and Australasia Branch
Branch 3      BOTB South-East Regional Office

Overseas Trade Division 3
Branch 1      Administration and Finance
Branch 2      Fairs and Promotions Branch
Branch 3      Exports to Europe Branch
Branch 4      Export Data Branch

Overseas Trade Division 4
Branch 1      East Europe Branch
Branch 2      China and South Asia Branch
Branch 3      Export Licensing Branch
              (this now comes under the Research and Technology Policy
              Division of the Department of Trade and Industry)

Overseas Trade Division 5
Branch 1      Middle East Market Branch
Branch 2      Latin America and Caribbean Branch
Branch 3      Sub-Saharan Africa Branch

## 6.12 BOTB Regional Offices

**South Eastern**
Ebury Bridge House
Ebury Bridge Road
London SW1W 8QD
Telephone
01-730 9678
Telex 297124

*Norfolk*
*Suffolk*
*Cambridgeshire*
*Bedfordshire*
*Buckinghamshire*
*Hertfordshire*
*Essex*
*Oxfordshire*
*Greater London*
*Middlesex*
*Berkshire*
*Surrey*
*Hampshire*
*Kent*
*East Sussex*
*West Sussex*
*Isle of Wight*

**North Eastern**
Stanegate House
2 Groat Market
Newcastle upon Tyne
NE 1 1YN
Telephone
Newcastle upon Tyne
(0632) 324722
Telex 53178

*Northumberland*
*Tyne and Wear*
*Durham*
*Cleveland*

**Yorkshire and**
**Humberside**
Priestley House
Park Row
Leeds LS1 5LF
Telephone Leeds
(0532) 443171
Telex 557925

*North Yorkshire*
*West Yorkshire*

*South Yorkshire*
*Humberside*

**West Midlands**
Ladywood House
Stephenson Street
Birmingham B2 4DT
Telephone Birmingham
(021) 632 4111
Telex 337919

*Staffordshire*
*Shropshire*
*West Midlands*
*Warwickshire*
*Hereford and Worcester*

**North Western**
Sunley Building
Piccadilly Plaza
Manchester M1 4BA
Telephone Manchester
(061) 236 2171
Telex 667104

*Cumbria*
*Lancashire*
*Merseyside*
*Greater Manchester*
*Cheshire*
*Derbyshire (High*
*Peak District)*

**East Midlands**
Severns House
20 Middle Pavement
Nottingham
NG1 7DW
Telephone
Nottingham (0602)
506181
Telex 37143

*Derbyshire (except*
*High Peak District)*
*Nottinghamshire*
*Lincolnshire*
*Leicestershire*
*Northamptonshire*

**South Western**
The Pithay
Bristol BS1 2PB
Telephone Bristol
(0272) 291071
Telex 44214

*Gloucestershire*
*Avon*
*Wiltshire*
*Somerset*
*Dorset*
*Devon*
*Cornwall*
*(including*
*Isles of Scilly)*

**The following also**
**act as BOTB**
**Regional Offices:**

**Welsh Office**
New Crown Building
Industry Department
Cathays Park
Cardiff CF1 3NQ
Telephone Cardiff
(0222) 824171
Telex 498228

**Scottish Export**
**Office**
Industry Department
for Scotland
Alhambra House
45 Waterloo Street
Glasgow G2 6AT
Telephone Glasgow
(041) 248 2855
Telex 777883

**Industrial**
**Development**
**Board for Northern**
**Ireland**
IDB House
64 Chichester Street
Belfast BT1 4JX
Telephone Belfast
(0232) 233233
Telex 747025

## 6.2 Use of Trade Terms (INCOTERMS)

Trade terms used in export sales contracts stand for specific obligations of buyer and seller. Ignorance of their implications can turn an expected profit into a serious loss. International traders use a number of terms that cover both the conditions of payment and the conditions of delivery.

Varying conditions are reflected in the coming into common use of these trade terms. For example, goods often have to be transported over long distances on land and sea before they reach the customer. The cost of transporting them is an important element in their value. It is therefore important that both the buyer and the seller understand clearly at all times who is to pay for each segment of the transportation.

Every commercial transaction is based upon a contract of sale and the trade terms used in that contract have the important function of naming the exact point at which the ownership of the merchandise is transferred from the seller to the buyer. The contract also defines the responsibilities and expenses of the seller up to that point and those of the buyer at that point. In using these trade terms, it is important to remember that the rights of each party correspond to the duties of the other. Trade terms are accepted in broad outline by the principal trading countries, but they are not accepted in all details by all countries. The exporter must therefore watch out for variations in certain countries and in certain trades.

Where there were major differences in current practice, ICC has adopted the principle that a contract price settled on the basis of INCOTERMS provides for minimum liabilities on the part of the seller, leaving it to the parties to provide in their contracts for greater liabilities than those in the set of rules, if they wished to do so.

The simplest type of sale for the seller is 'as is, where is'. This type is common at auctions, in sales of surplus goods by government agencies, and so on. When the sale is for export, the seller must guarantee that the buyer will receive an export permit, but there his responsibility ends.

The easiest terms of sale for the buyer is 'Franco Delivered', including duty and local cartage, to his warehouse. He has only the responsibility of obtaining an import permit, if one is needed, and passing the customs entry – at the seller's expense.

Between these two terms – 'as is, where is' and 'Franco Delivered' – there are many expenses that accrue to the goods in the country of export, and this is why the buyer normally appoints an agent, such as a freight forwarder, in the country of export to look after the shipment. The following are some of the steps involved in moving goods from the factory to the ship at the port of departure:

(a)  Getting an export permit, if one is required;
(b)  Obtaining a currency permit, if required;
(c)  Packing the goods for export;
(d)  Cartage to place of departure;
(e)  Carriage of the goods to the docks, including preparation of a bill of lading and payment of carriage;
(f)  Paying for wharfage and/or storage in a shed;

(g) Weighing and sampling, if required;
(h) Completing any necessary customs export formalities;
(i) Preparation of customs or consular invoices as required in the country of destination;
(j) Preparation and submission of ocean bills of lading;
(k) Prepaying of the ocean freight, if necessary;
(l) Obtaining marine insurance certificate or policy, as required.

Who pays for any or all of these? The answer depends on the terms of sale. In the following paragraphs, some of the major trade terms are defined and discussed.

*Ex Works (or ex factory, ex mill, ex plantation, ex warehouse)*
In this contract, the seller must place the goods at the disposal of the buyer at all times specified in the contract. When these goods have been clearly set aside or otherwise identified as the contract goods, the buyer takes delivery at the premises of the seller and bears all the risks and expenses from then on.

This type of contract is mainly used when specialized exporters purchase such plantation-grown commodities as coffee, tea, cocoa or even an entire crop. Or large importers may decide to select the products they want on the plantation and to arrange for the transportation themselves.

*Ex warehouse*
'Ex warehouse' is sometimes the term used by sellers whose products are often stored for long periods. An example is carpets, sent to a country and stored in a bonded warehouse until the buyer is ready to come and make his choice. Complicated machinery made to the order of a particular client and high in value is also sometimes sold under an ex-works contract.

*FOB*
In an FOB (Free on Board) contract, the responsibility and liability of the seller do not end until the goods have actually passed the ship's rail. The term should preferably be 'FOB ship (named port)'. In an FOB contract, the seller must:

(a) Deliver the goods on board the vessel named by the buyer at the named port of shipment, in the manner customary at that port, and on the date or within the period that is stipulated;
(b) Provide at his expense for the customary preparation and packing suitable to the nature of the goods and to their carriage by sea;
(c) Bear all costs payable on or for the goods until they have effectively passed ship's rail at the port of shipment;
(d) Give the buyer (at his own expense) such notice of shipment of the goods as may enable him to insure them;
(e) Provide at his expense the customary 'clean' document in proof of delivery of goods aboard the vessel. A 'clean' document means that the bill of lading (or mate's receipt) does not bear any superimposed

clauses stating that either the goods or the packaging are defective in some way;

(f) Bear the costs of checking operations (such as checking the quality, measure, weight or quantity) necessary for the purpose of loading the goods on board at the port of shipment;

(g) Bear the cost of all dues and taxes payable on the goods for the purpose of loading them on board;

(h) Bear all risks of the goods until such time as they shall have effectively passed ship's rail;

(i) Provide the buyer, at his request and expense, with the certificate of origin and the consular invoice;

(j) Render the buyer, at the latter's request, risk and expense, every assistance in obtaining a bill of lading and any documents, other than in (i) above, issued in the country of shipment and/or of origin and which the buyer may require to import the goods into the country of destination (and, where necessary, for their passage in transit through another country).

In turn, under an FOB contract, the buyer must:

(a) At his own expense, charter a vessel or reserve the necessary space on board a vessel and give the seller due notice of the name, loading berth of, and delivery dates to the vessel;

(b) Bear all costs and risks of the goods from the time when they shall have passed the ship's rail effectively at the named port of shipment, and pay the price as provided in the contract;

(c) Bear any additional costs incurred because the vessel he named has failed to arrive on the stipulated date or the end of the period specified, and all the risks of the goods from the date of expiration of the period specified. This is provided, however, that the goods were duly appropriated to the contract – that is, clearly set aside or otherwise identified as the contract goods;

(d) Should he fail to name the vessel in time, or if he has reserved to himself a period within which to take delivery of the goods and/or the right to choose the port of shipment, should he fail to give detailed instructions in time, he shall bear all the additional costs incurred because of such failure and all the risks of the goods from the date of expiration of the period stipulated for delivery – provided, however, that the goods shall have been duly appropriated to the contract – that is to say, clearly set aside or otherwise identified as the contract goods;

(e) Pay any costs and charges for obtaining a bill of lading if incurred under article (j) above;

(f) Pay all costs and charges incurred in obtaining the documents mentioned in articles (i) and (j) above, including the cost of certificates of origin and consular documents.

*FOR and FOT (Free on Rail and Free on Truck)*
These two terms are used for land transport and mean that the seller has the liability of delivering the goods on board a freight car or a truck at the

place of departure of the land transport. The term 'FOR' should be followed by the name of the railway station nearest to the seller's factory plantation, or warehouse. If the name is not given in the contract, the seller may choose the station that suits him best. If there has been no other agreement, the seller has to get in touch with the railway officials or a forwarding agent to provide the proper means of transport for which the buyer pays.

## FAS (Free Alongside Ship) (named port of shipment)

This term is quite widely used and its meaning is clear. The seller must place the goods alongside the vessel during its loading period and pay all charges up to that point. Although the seller's legal responsibility finishes once he has obtained a clean receipt, actually, as in other terms, he must assist the buyer (at the latter's expense) to obtain any other documents that the buyer requires to complete export and carriage, plus those needed for clearance at destination. (This term of sale is particularly convenient when dealing in heavy commodities such as locomotives, etc.) In some ports, it may not be possible to deliver the goods to the port authorities at a certain place, and the latter are responsible for transporting the goods alongside. The expense may be added to the freight charge.

## CIF (Cost, Insurance, Freight) (named port of destination)

Under this term and also C & F (cost and freight), as in the FOB clause, the risk of the goods is transferred to the buyer once these have been loaded on board ship, freight car, or truck. But the seller has to pay the expense of transportation for the goods up to the port of destination. The exporter often prefers these terms because he can channel all his exports through the freight forwarder of his choice to the port of export, and ship by the vessel that he selects. For the importer, these terms mean fewer responsibilities because (unless there is a suitable clause in the contract) it is the exporter who has to gamble on fluctuations in the freight and insurance rates. Because CIF includes a transfer of documents, it is necessary for the importer to take up the documents at his bank even if the ship does not reach its destination.

If the terms are C & F, the buyer is responsible for taking out the marine insurance, as opposed to the CIF contract, where the seller must obtain an insurance policy that covers the CIF price plus 10%. If the seller is willing to assume the risk of the exchange rate fluctuating between the time that the contract is accepted and the date of payment, the terms are CIF & E (or they can be FOB & E). 'CIF & C' means that the commission charged by the middleman is included in the price, and also the interest charges that accumulate in indent transactions.

## Duty Paid Delivery

One other term ought to be mentioned; 'Duty Paid Delivery'. This is the easiest of all possible terms for the buyer, because under it, the seller undertakes to deliver the goods to him at the place he names in the country of import, with all costs, including duties, paid. The seller even gets the import licence if one is required, though the buyer is bound to offer a reasonable amount of help in obtaining the documents needed in the country of import.

In markets where competition is particularly keen, quoting a delivered duty-paid price may mean the difference between making or losing a sale. The seller, however, must work out his export price very carefully, making sure that expenses of every kind are included, or he may lose on the transaction. The new exporter, if he wishes to quote these terms, would be well advised to seek the help of an experienced freight forwarder in calculating his costs.

If a dispute arises with the buyer over whether the terms of the contract have been properly carried out, it is vital to know what law of what country applies. ICC Guide to Commercial Arbitration suggests that the following clause be included in foreign contracts to take care of all necessary commercial arbitration:

All disputes arising in connection with the present contract shall be finally settled under the rules of conciliation and arbitration of the International Chamber of Commerce by one or more arbitrators appointed in accordance with the rules.

In many countries (such as France, Britain, Italy, Norway, Belgium and the Netherlands) there are special commercial courts. These are composed of businessmen who can, by reason of their powers and their knowledge of various trades, quickly arbitrate all disputes. In the U.S.A., the American Arbitration Association sets out the rules for arbitrating disputes. Canada has a number of Boards of Arbitration which perform functions similar to those of the courts in other countries.

Also, when the contract is CIF, the buyer should make sure that the seller has adequate insurance against marine risks. When the terms are FOB (named port of export), the buyer usually takes out full coverage warehouse to warehouse. If, however, the seller's business is not located in the port of export, he should take out his own insurance to the FOB point, because although the buyer has warehouse-to-warehouse coverage, his insurable interest does not begin until the goods reach the FOB point.

In 1980, ICC published a new edition of INCOTERMS which has two new terms to meet the needs of container shipments. The term 'free carrier' (named point) is now in use for multi-modal transportation – such as containers, trailers and 'roll on/roll off' ferries. It is based on the same principles as FOB except that the seller fulfills his obligations when he delivers the goods into the custody of the carrier at the named point. The term 'freight or carriage and insurance paid to' (named point) is the same, but with the addition that the seller has to obtain transport insurance against the risk of loss or damage during the carriage. This is the multi-modal delivery equivalent of CIF. Freight or carriage paid to (named point of destination) has also been revised. Like C & F this term means that the seller pays the freight for transport of the goods to the named destination. However, the risk of loss or damage, as well as any cost increase, is transferred from the seller to buyer when the goods have been delivered into the custody of the first carrier, not at the ship's rail.

## 6.3 Documentary Credits

In payment for export sales, Bills of Exchange, Letters of Credit, Promissory Notes and Open Accounts are used. The documentary credit is the most important mechanism for payment in international sales transactions and it is used in innumerable export transactions. It has been judicially described as follows:

> 'The general course of international commerce involves the practice of raising money on the documents so as to bridge the period between the shipment and the time of obtaining payment against documents.'

The law relating to documentary credits is fairly well settled. Moreover, the International Chamber of Commerce has published its *Uniform Customs and Practice for Documentary Credits*, which are used by banks all over the world and have become virtually world law. The Uniform Customs and Practice apply only if they are adopted by the parties, which is done almost universally. Most documentary credits contain a statement that they are operated under the Uniform Customs and Practice. The present revision of the Uniform Customs and Practice is that of 1974, but the first issue of this code was published in 1933, the code was then revised in 1951, and later in 1962; a revision of the 1974 issue was published in 1980. The Code has thus been in operation for over 50 years.

Although practice relating to documentary credits is fairly well settled, it is not surprising that new problems arise from time to time. A few reach the courts but most problems are settled in the offices of international banks or reach the chambers of barristers practising in this field, without ever being taken to court. All this, as observed, is not surprising, in view of the regular use made by this means of payment in international trade. This section, therefore, reviews some of the more important aspects of Documentary Credits likely to be encountered by the exporter.

### 6.31 Transhipment Clauses

In one case, instructions by the buyer to the issuing bank stated that transhipment was prohibited. These instructions were duly transmitted by the issuing bank to the correspondent bank. The seller was informed of this stipulation. But the bill of lading which he tendered to the bank had imprinted on its face the words 'transhipment permitted'. The question arose whether the bank should accept that bill of lading or reject it. In Uniform Customs and Practice, article 21 states:

(a) Unless transhipment is prohibited by the terms of the credit, bills of lading will be accepted which indicate that the goods will be transhipped en route, provided the entire voyage is covered by one and the same bill of lading

(b) Bills of lading incorporating printed clauses stating that the carriers have the right to tranship will be accepted notwithstanding the fact that the credits prohibits transhipment.

This bill of lading tendered to the bank is unusual. Printed clauses allowing transhipment are found regularly in the 'small print' on the reverse of the bill of lading. The meaning of paragraph (b) of article 21 is obviously that the bank may disregard such clauses in the small print, even if the instructions provide that transhipment is prohibited.

### 6.32 Confirmed Documentary Credits

Another question which sometimes arises is whether a correspondent bank which is asked to advise a credit, but which has not been instructed to confirm the credit, is entitled to add its own confirmation to it. In one case, a seller wished the credit to be confirmed by the correspondent bank or the buyer.

The answer to this question is that the correspondent bank should not add its confirmation. It should refuse to do so. The issuing bank and the correspondent bank are agents of the buyer and not the seller. They should act on his instructions and not on the instructions of the seller. If there are no instructions from the buyer to confirm, the bank would exceed its authority if it confirmed. The proper course to resolve this difficulty is for the correspondent bank to inform the seller that it cannot confirm the credit on his instructions and that the seller should request the buyer to amend the original instructions asking that the credit should be confirmed.

In the case of a confirmed credit, the correspondent bank will naturally charge for the confirmation.

### 6.33 Transferable Documentary Credits

The question of confirmation has also arisen in connection with transferable documentary credits. According to article 46 of the Uniform Customs and Practice, such a credit must be designated from the beginning as a transferable credit. In other words, it is the buyer, or more precisely the issuing bank on the buyer's instructions, which makes the credit transferable. Here again, the issuing and correspondent banks are the agents of the buyer, but the authority which he has given the banks is different in that the correspondent bank is authorized to honour the credit if it has been transferred. Under a transferable credit there are two beneficiaries: the 'first beneficiary', who is the seller and potential transferor of the credit; and the 'second beneficiary', who is the seller's supplier and potential transferee. According to article 46(e), 'A transferable credit can be transferred once only . . .

'The credit can be transferred only on the terms and conditions specified in the original credit, with the exception of the amount of the credit, of any unit prices states therein, and of the period of validity or period for shipment, any or all of which may be reduced or curtailed.

Additionally, the name of the first beneficiary can be substituted for that of the applicant for the credit, but if the name of the applicant for the credit is specifically required by the original credit to appear in any document other than the invoice, such requirement must be fulfilled.'

How then, can this situation be dealt with in practice? One answer is to use the mechanism of a back-to-back credit rather than that of the transfer of the transferable credit. The seller who is obliged to open a confirmed credit to his supplier but who has only received – in accordance with his contract with the buyer – an unconfirmed (but transferable) credit, should use the latter as a security when requesting the correspondence bank to open a confirmed credit in favour of his, the seller's, supplier. The correspondence bank should, and probably will, comply with this request. The net result would be that the first credit – that between the buyer and the seller – is unconfirmed but the second credit – that between the seller and his supplier – is confirmed. There is no legal or practical difficulty in proceeding in this manner.

## 6.34 Minor Shipping Documents

Cases are increasingly frequent in which the parties to the contract sale agree that the credit may be drawn upon by the seller on production of shipping documents which do not include a formal bill of lading but which are of more minor legal importance than a document of title, such as a forwarder's bill of lading, a waybill or even a postal receipt. Such minor documents are perfectly acceptable to the correspondent bank, provided that it is expressly instructed to make the credit available on production of such a document and that the document itself is in the proper form and presented before the expiry of the credit. It may be recalled that article 24 of the Uniform Customs and Practice provide:

'Banks will consider a railway or inland waterway bill of lading or consignment note, counterfoil waybill, postal receipt, certificate of mailing, air mail receipt, air waybill, air consignment note or air receipt, trucking company bill of lading, or any other similar document as regular when such document bears the reception stamp of the carrier or his agent or when it bears a signature purporting to be that of the carrier or his agent.'

As regards forwarders' bills of lading, a word has to be added. Such documents, although described as 'bills of lading,' are not bills of lading in law. They are in the nature of receipts for the goods. They are not, as such and by virtue of the law, documents of title. But a forwarder's house bill of lading, without being a document of title, may be endowed with the surrender quantity by express stipulation in the contract between the carrier and the consignor.

A credit under which the bank is instructed to make finance available against minor documents, i.e. documents other than a true bill of lading is known in law as a 'packing credit'.

## 6.35 The Claused Bill of Lading

Banks must exercise special care. It has been judicially established that in principle, a bill of lading is to be considered 'clean' if it states without qualification that the goods are in apparent good order and condition at the time when they were loaded and that any annotation on the bill which refers to an event subsequent to the loading does not make the bill a 'claused' bill.

A correspondent bank which is instructed to make finance available on tender, inter alia, of a clean bill of lading cannot refuse on the ground that something is scribbled in the empty space of the bill. Not every annotation is a 'clausing'. The annotation has to be read and analysed. Only if it qualifies the proper receipt of the goods when the carrier takes delivery, is it a 'clausing' in law and the bill should then be rejected by the bank.

In summary, therefore, the following documentary credits and methods of payment are available to the exporting company:

(a) Letter of Credit. A written undertaking issued by the buyer's bank agreeing to pay a certain sum of money within a stipulated period against a specified set of documents.

(b) Documentary Bill. Documents such as Bills of Exchange requiring payment on acceptance or presentation (payment on sight) or 'usance' (maturity of 30, 60, 90 days) with (a) documentary bill is paid for and accepted by consignee, but with (a) it is accepted by the bank.

(c) Acceptance Finance. Pre- and post-shipment finance; the bank is not required to commit funds, but to lend its name and creditworthiness by accepting bills.

(d) Open Account. Exporter ships goods and sends document direct to importer who then takes delivery as soon as goods reach the port; accounts settled periodically by remitting balance by demand draft or cheque.

The International Chamber of Commerce (ICC) has recently published a new edition (effective October 1984) of the Uniform Customs and Practice for Documentary Credits (UCP). This restates the basic principles of UCP, namely:

(a) That the buyer is responsible for stipulating clearly and precisely, the documents required and the conditions to be complied with;

(b) The increasing interest and influence in international trade of developing nations less experienced in this area.

This edition also takes account of new developments in international payments, as follows:

(a) Continuing revolution in transport technology and the geographical extension of containerization and combined transport;

(b) Increasing influence of trade facilitation activities on development of new documentation;

(c) Communications revolution, replacing paper as a means of transmitting trade data by automatic or electronic data processing (ADD/EDP);

(d) Development of new types of documentary credits, such as the 'deferred payment credit' and the 'stand-by credit'.

**6.4 Export Credits Guarantee Department (ECGD)**

Many exporters are obliged to sell overseas on credit, for in the highly competitive conditions of international trade the terms and length of credit are often crucial to getting the business. Giving credit for exports makes additional calls on an exporter's liquidity and is more hazardous than credit risks in home trade transactions. The exporter consequently needs to be certain that he will have access to finance adequate for his requirements over the often lengthy period from beginning production for an export order to receipt of final payment, and to insure against all the risks involved at the several stages of handling export business. Credit insurance and finance for exports are generally inter-dependent features; the facilities and service available to exporters are summarized here.

Cover against overseas buyer risks is available from some insurers in the commercial market, and for buyer and country risks (such as exchange transfer difficulties and civil strife) from the Export Credits Guarantee Department (ECGD), and from the commercial insurance market.

ECGD is a government department whose statutory aim is to encourage exports by providing insurance for exporters against a wide range of risks in overseas trade which may not ordinarily be insurable in the commercial market. It also gives guarantee direct to banks in the U.K. to enable exporters to have access to finance at preferential fixed rates of interest for export credit. The insurance business is operated on a commercial basis with the aim of involving no cost to the taxpayer. Normal insurance principles apply to the proportion of an exporter's overseas business which is required to be covered and the percentage of any loss borne by the policy holder. ECGD normally insures the whole of a firms export turnover, but may accept business on a range of markets if it represents a substantial part of total export sales and a reasonable spread of risk. Cover under the ECGD policy is limited to 90% of loss from buyer risks and 95% loss from political risks. Insurance is afforded for the following risks in the export of goods and services sold on terms of up to six months credit:

(a) Insolvency of the buyer;
(b) The buyer's failure to pay within six months of due date for goods which he has accepted;
(c) The buyer's failure to take up goods which have been despatched to him where the failure is not attributable to any action of the policy holder and where ECGD decides that the institution or continuation of legal proceedings against the buyer would serve no useful purpose;
(d) A general moratorium on external debt decreed by the government of the buyer's country or of a third country through which payment must be made;
(e) Any other action by the government of the buyer's country which prevents peformance of the contract in whole or in part;
(f) Political events, economic difficulties, legislative or administrative measures arising outside the U.K. which prevent or delay the transfer of payments or deposits made in respect of the contract;

(g) Legal discharge of the debt (not being legal discharge under the proper law of the contract) in a foreign currency, which results in a shortfall at the date of transfer;

(h) War and certain other events preventing performance of the contract provided that the event is not one normally insured with commercial insurers;

(i) Cancellation or non-renewal of a U.K. export licence, or the prohibition or restriction on export of goods from the U.K. by law;

(j) The failure or refusal by a public buyer to fulfil the contract for reasons not arising from any fault of the policy holder.

*Comprehensive Short-Term Guarantee*

This covers sales on credit terms not exceeding six months and is available to all exporters, including merchants and confirmers. Policies are continuous and renewable annually. Cover is effective from date of shipment; in addition pre-shipment cover, effective from the date of the contact of sale, is available for an extra flat-rate premium. Cover is limited to contracts for goods to be shipped within 12 months of the date of contract.

Policy holders may be able to obtain a direct guarantee from ECGD to a bank for finance made available under this guarantee.

*Supplemental Extended-Terms Guarantee*

This is a separate policy, available to holders of Comprehensive Short-Term Guarantees, which covers business where credit terms of between six months and five years are frequently necessary and considered normal international trading practice. Cover is normally given only on a whole turnover basis, the exporter offering all his business on six-month to five-year terms for cover. The risks covered and the form of the insurance are similar to that provided for short-term cover, but ECGD approval of contracts and payment for premium follow rather different procedures. Applications for extended-terms cover must be made for each individual contract at an early stage and before a commitment has been made to any contractual obligations. The premium for this form of cover is determined according to the period for which ECGD is at risk and the politico-economic conditions of the buyer's country. Policy holders may obtain a direct guarantee from ECGD to a bank for finance made available under this guarantee.

*External Trade Guarantee*

This is available to U.K. merchants and confirmers and covers transactions where goods are shipped direct from an overseas supplier to a buyer in another overseas country on credit terms not exceeding six months. The conditions of the policy and the risks covered are broadly the same as for the Comprehensive Short-Term Guarantee, but cover is not given against the failure of the buyer to take up goods or against the imposition of either export or import licencing or the cancellation or non-renewal of licences previously issued. No cover is available for extended-terms business. Special arrangements apply to the annual premiums and to credit limits where the policy holder holds a Comprehensive Short-Term Guarantee and an External Trade Guarantee. ECGD guarantees to financing banks are not available in connection with external trade transactions.

*Specific Guarantee*
This provides cover for transactions on credit up to five years – no longer – involving capital goods or projects which are unsuitable for ECGD comprehensive policies. Cover is restricted to 90% of loss. ECGD guarantees to financing banks are available for finance provided at preferential interest rates varying according to the buyer's country and length of credit; the preferential rates do not apply to business with E.E.C. countries.

*Services Guarantees*
This provides cover (broadly on the lines of ECGD insurance for sales of goods) for earnings from technical or professional services for overseas clients provided that the services are performed overseas, or that the benefit of the services performed in the U.K. is enjoyed overseas by the client. Comprehensive whole turnover cover is available where there is a recurrent pattern of business and cover is provided on a specific basis where only one service is to be carried out.

*Cost Escalation Scheme*
This provides partial protection against certain U.K. cost increases for firms with capital goods contracts worth over £5m with a manufacturing period of at least two years.

*Foreign Currency Contracts Endorsement*
Policy holders who invoice in foreign currencies can be protected under foreign currency contracts endorsements to their credit insurance policies against extra losses through participation in the forward exchange market or foreign borrowing.

*Subsidiaries Guarantee*
Sales by an overseas subsidiary of a policy holder of goods sold to it by its parent or associated companies in the U.K. may be acceptable for credit insurance cover under a separate guarantee.

*Supplementary Stocks Guarantee*
In addition to the cover provided under the Comprehensive Short-Term Guarantee for sale from stock held overseas, ECGD will cover goods held in stock against loss before sale arising from war, confiscation or measures preventing re-export.

*Overseas Investment Insurance Scheme*
This provides British investors with insurance for up to 15 years against political risks in respect of new investment overseas. The investor must be a company carrying on business in the U.K. or a subsidiary of such a company.

*ECGD Buyer Credit Financing*

Exporters concerned with large contracts may find it more convenient to arrange for a loan to be made available to the overseas buyer by a bank or consortium of banks, enabling the overseas buyer to settle with the exporter on cash terms which may include progress payments during the construction period and prior to shipment. These loans are at a favourable rate of interest assessed according to the length of credit and the per capita income of the buyer's country. The overseas buyer is normally required to pay not less than 15% of the contract price direct to the exporter from his own resources. The buyer credit guarantee covers the whole of the bank loan which would normally only be for goods manufactured in, or services from, the U.K. but other items may be included at the discretion of ECGD.

A U.K. supplier must approach ECGD at an early stage. As soon as discussions have begun with the buyer on the basis of buyer credit and a financial institution ready to finance the borrowers has been found, the supplier and the lender should jointly approach ECGD to discuss the terms of its guarantee.

### 6.5  Coping with International Trade Regulations

NTMs or Non-Tariff Barriers (NTBs) are brought about by the absence of harmonization, whether deliberate or historical, between national markets. Like the barriers created by cultural differences (see Section 4.1) or those deriving from management policy, many of these barriers due to administrative and technical regulations can be surmounted by the exporter, albeit at some time in cost and money.

Reference has been made in Section 1.2 to GATT and the Tokyo Round; there are three Articles of GATT which permit countries to impose controls. Article 6 states that, in cases of unfair international competition, when a country is subsiding its exports or dumping its products on the international market, the importing country may impose a countervailing or a dumping duty – that is a duty to counteract the export subsidy, to bring the price up to the price the product is sold at in the home market.

Article 19 of GATT states that if a sector of industry is suffering injury or needs protection in order to survive, a country may introduce tariffs or other controls as a temporary protection, but the country must offer its trading partners a trade advantage somewhere else to balance the trade restriction caused by the tariff. If this advantage is not offered, exporting countries are free to retaliate. Under Article 12 a developed country may also impose import controls for severe balance of payment reasons – the UK had an import deposit scheme between 1968 and 1970 and Italy has twice recently imposed import deposits. Developing countries may also impose import controls to protect growing industries, and, under Article 18, for balance of payment reasons.

The countries against whom many complaints are made are U.S.A. and Japan; together with the E.E.C. these are the biggest trading nations in the world. Thus, manufacturers doing business with U.S.A. must cope with the Buy American Act (1933), the U.S. Merchant Marine Act (1936), the

American Selling Price, Domestic and Foreign International Sales Corporations (DISC and FISC) and U.S. Trade Act (1974).

Under this last Act, the U.S.A. reserves the right to start investigations into allegations of dumping and of export subsidies before there is any evidence of this injury being caused to U.S. firms by the alleged practices. This question of injury is important, as the U.K., in line with many other countries, will not investigate a dumping allegation until there is evidence of some material injury to U.K. industry. The exporting company should also note that, although CCCN is the generally accepted method of listing products, U.S.A. uses its own classification system.

DISC and FISC are also legislated NTMs which exporters to U.S.A. must cope with. DISC is a separate organization set up by U.S. companies to deal with their exports; through it they are permitted to defer payment of up to 50% of their tax liability almost indefinitely. A similar organization is Foreign International Sales Corporation, based outside U.S.A., which can also defer its U.S. tax liability.

Substantial facts about Japanese NTBs are very difficult to find, and the Japanese themselves do not admit that these standards differences amounts to barriers to trade. They merely point to their own success in countries all over the world which have different standards from their own. The strong implication is that they consider that British businessmen to not try hard enough. One Japanese exporter has recently spent two years in this country, learning the language, the regulations and the markets before even starting to do business here.

Inside the E.E.C. there are moves towards harmonization of standards and the elimination of NTBs; but the problem is far from straightforward. The French, for example, insist on the local manufacture of pharmaceuticals and what is more, the production must be under the control of a French pharmacist. The French market for lamb is also a problem to the exporters as it is sometimes open to foreigners, and sometimes closed. And even when it is open, matters are complicated by the imposition of a variable levy. There are also varying internal taxes inside the E.E.C. on sugar and chocolate products, and at present, there are no immediate plans to phase these out. On packaging, there is already agreement on the weights in which products must be sold but disagreement on the declaration of ingredients – particularly those bought in from other suppliers by the main manufacturer.

Of course, the degree of standardization, and therefore, by implication, the extent to which NTBs can be used by government agencies to keep out imported products, must depend – also on the type of product, and this is an important point for the exporter:

(a) Consumer non-durables. Due to the fact that most of these products appeal to taste, habits, and customs which still differ among nations, central co-ordination with adaptation to local conditions will remain significant. Food products will be least standardized in this category.

(b) Consumer durables. Since most of these products have been introduced simultaneously in all Common Market countries, and

are relatively uniform throughout the area, standardization of the marketing mix will be fairly complete in the near future.
(c) Industrial goods. Because national differences have a less impact, standardization will soon be largely complete.

From a purely theoretical economic point of view, increased pressure towards standardization within E.E.C. should lead to the re-allocation of productive resources towards more standardization or production in centralized plants serving the whole Community. In the wake of this, export marketing functions would be more standardized in order to achieve greater effectiveness at lower costs. The realities, however, are that some NTBs will persist, and these can be classified into five categories:

(a) General economic policies (e.g. fiscal and monetary) at the national level;
(b) National government regulations and restrictions enforced by national bureaucracies outside the jurisdiction of the E.E.C.;
(c) A lack of international standardization relating to technical matters (e.g. each country has its own size of couplings for welding gas cylinders);
(d) Differences in market size and economic development (i.e. a country with a lower level of economic development requires different products and technologies from a highly developed economy). E.E.C. countries are not at present completely equalized as to economic development
(e) Differences based on culture (i.e. language, habits, tastes, way of life, personal priorities, beliefs, etc.) which remain very important.

Indeed NTBs are themselves further re-inforced by the inability of the European Commission to eradicate differences and to establish all the common policies, rules and regulations specified in the Treaty of Rome. On the other hand, there are definite indications that progress has been made in creating a common market for goods, in aligning the economic policies of the members' countries, and in reducing non-tariff barriers.

Recent research[2] by Arthur D. Little and Co has shown up some interesting differences in the approaches of British and West German exporting companies to meeting international standards. For example, many British companies still face genuine problems of adaptation to European standards, either because the product standards themselves had not yet been fully harmonized or because of the inconsistencies of type testing or the long formalities of patent and licence approval. To some degree, these problems are attributable to the U.K.'s later accession to the E.E.C. and can therefore be expected to diminish as companies adapt and as the E.E.C. and trade associations complete their harmonization measures.

Even allowing for the incomplete progress of European institutions towards the harmonization of established standards, and for deficiencies of management effort in some cases, there remain a category of significant barriers to trade that affected a minority of firms in this research.

This includes regulatory or administrative measures or policy decisions which seriously delay or impede companies seeking to develop their business in the E.E.C. Here are some examples:

(a) Standards: unilateral introduction of fresh national standards, with an innocent declared purpose – e.g. safety or environmental benefit – but with a high degree of protectionist intent;

(b) Type-testing, patent and trademark applications and other procedures: delays for non-national products are longer and the criteria apparently more rigorously applied than for national products;

(c) Public authority purchase policy: discrimination in favour of locally produced goods;

(d) Policy of other national governments: hostility to acquisitions and requirement that local capacity be established to support sales.

British companies, according to the research study cited, generally experience greater difficulties in meeting standards for other countries than German companies. There are two probable explanations for this.

(a) German standards generally do tend to be more stringent so that goods produced domestically to meet local specifications automatically meet those set by other countries. A British electrical company substantiated this, quoting its own experience of dealing with the Verband Deutsche Elektronik (VDE). The process of getting VDE approval has been arduous and had taken two years; German goods (or any other foreign goods) for sale in the United Kingdom did not need to have the corresponding BEAB approval, and could get in without difficulty. A building materials company also commented on U.K.'s relatively lenient standards, describing the Federal Republic as 'DINland' and considering its policy 'straightforward protectionism'. Another, however, suggested that there is a difference in basic philosophy: the German philosophy stresses a tight product specification (and hence product standard) and offers a fairly routine guarantee to the customer; British consumer pressures mean that the guarantee is relatively strong while specifications tend to be looser.

(b) This research also reported that there may well be a fundamental difference in expectations about quality. German companies found that their normal product features and product quality were readily acceptable in the United Kingdom whilst some British companies had initial problems in West Germany. One British company explained that at first, the procedures for obtaining German type-approvals raised so many problems that they seemed to be simply non-tariff barriers, but once the company studied them carefully and adapted general product quality and concept to fit them, they had no problem in obtaining approval. Another gave most attention to the requirements of the Federal Republic judging that if he could satisfy the German market, he was well set to compete everywhere. Thus different nominal standards may reflect different and higher real standards that set a higher competition hurdle for the expanded market.

In fact, the E.E.C. Commission had made some visible progress under Article 100. Representatives of Trade and Industry associations also play an important role at the working group stage of discussions about harmonization: concerned companies should therefore ensure that their views on product development are made known in Brussels whether or not they are trying to penetrate other markets.

For some products, however, other institutions with broader membership are concerned with standards harmonization. These include:

(a) CEN (Comité European de Normalisation) of which the E.E.C., E.F.T.A., and Spain are members;
(b) The International Standards Organization (ISO), the ultimate international harmonizing body;
(c) CENELEC, which specializes in electrotechnical standards;
(d) The United Nations Economic Commission for Europe (ECE) which has been involved in some work on harmonizing standards, including standards for vehicles;
(e) The Union of Agreement Boards – covering construction materials.

Although the speed of progress of any of these bodies risks being inverse to the size of its membership, some British companies prefer standards to be agreed upon through one of the bodies of wider scope (but, of course, including the E.E.C.) because this provides a basis for access to wider markets.

There are some important technical services available to British industry relating to technical standards, and specifications.

British Standards Institution (BSI) is the authorized body for the preparation of national standards in the U.K. It co-operates with counterpart bodies in other countries in drawing up international standards, and seeks to ensure that British standards are technically in line with them. The *British Standards Year Book* lists current British standards, and also gives the location of reference sets of British standards which can be consulted in many public libraries and other reference centres in the U.K. and overseas. Up-to-date information on British standards and international recommendations is published in the monthly journal *BSI News*.

Technical Help to Exporters (THE) is a department of the BSI, sponsored by the British Overseas Trade Board, established expressly to help British exporters to comply with the standard or other technical specifications necessary for the admission of products to overseas markets. It provides the following services:

(a) A technical enquiry service to deal with day-to-day problems;
(b) A consultancy service including examination of equipment or products;
(c) To determine whether or not they comply with the relevant foreign requirements;
(d) A range of publications and reports;

(e) Technical research when detailed information about a particular product or type of equipment is needed;
(f) English translations of a wide range of important overseas standards and codes of practice;
(g) Specialized services involving regular and continuing updating of requirements for a particular industry;
(h) An extensive library with a unique collection of documents of more than 160 countries.

THE provides services for members and non-members and any manufacturing company in the U.K. is eligible for membership.

Overseas purchasers of measuring instruments and gauges will generally be influenced by evidence of accuracy. Certificates can be provided by approved laboratories within the British Callibration Service (BCS) – a service of the National Physical Laboratory. These certificates bear the BCS badge and guarantee traceability of measurement to national and international standards. Further guidance on dealing with international trade regulations is available from commercial officers overseas, chambers of commerce and trade associations.

The third and last aspect of coping with trade regulations concerns Rules of Origin. The object of defining origin for preferential purposes is to ensure that preference is enjoyed only by goods genuinely coming from that beneficiary country. Clearly, we do not want goods from Country X with whom one has no relationship, to enter Country Y, to whom we have granted a preferential agreement and then to come in to our country without paying duty as the goods of Country Y. The important thing to understand is that there is not just one system of origin and origin is not a finite thing. What matters is why we want to know the origin of the goods and the first question that should be asked if we are requested to provide evidence of origin is 'why is this required, what are the people at the other end going to do with it?' It is vital to be quite clear that the origin of the same goods can be different in different circumstances.

The E.E.C. being a Customs Union, does not need a complicated origin system to govern its internal trade. Any foreign material, wherever it has entered the Community, has had the CCT paid on entry and there can thus be no deflection of trade; so foreign goods can move about freely once they have surmounted the tariff barrier. The Community Transit System has been devised to govern the internal trade in the Community and this is based on the concept of 'free circulation'. This term often puzzles people but all it means is that if goods have not been wholly produced in the Community, any imported goods used have paid duty. The documentation used in the Community Transit system is thus not a declaration of origin at all, but a Community Transit document which indicates whether the goods are in free circulation or not.

However, in the case of goods which are exported from the Community, then it may be necessary to make a declaration of origin since this may be required for various purposes in the country of destination. This does mean involvement in origin rules.

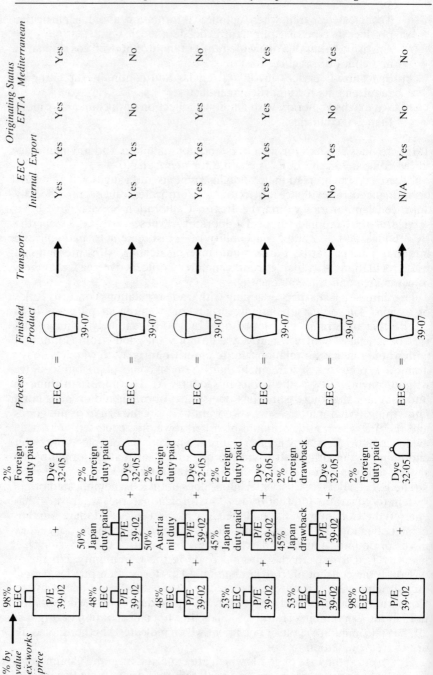

Figure 6.1  Operation of Origin rules
Source: Trade Affairs Department. ICI plc Ref. PMB/R/C 1977

All origin systems distinguish between two classes of goods, firstly those which are wholly produced in a country over which there is usually not much argument, since this means mostly animal, vegetable and mineral products and goods derived from them. In practice, this category is rarely used because there are few products which are truly wholly originating. The second class of goods presents more problems. These are goods which contain imported products. It is essential to devise some means of controlling products which contain imported goods.

The method of control looked at here is known as 'substantial transformation'. In other words, if imported goods are used they must be changed fairly radically in the beneficiary country. What distinguishes the various origin systems is the method they choose to define their substantial transformation. It may be expressed firstly by a rule requiring a change of tariff heading, secondly by a list of manufacturing processing operations which confer, or do not confer, origin on the goods, or thirdly by an ad valorem percentage rule where any non-originating materials used must not exceed a specified level.

In considering the origin of E.E.C. goods, where this is required to be known for export purposes, other than under preferential agreements, the rule used is that stated in E.E.C. Regulation 802/68 which defines the country of origin as being 'the country in which the last substantial process or operation that is economically justified took place in an undertaking equipped for the purpose, and which resulted in the manufacture of a new product or represented an important stage in manufacture' – and this is the rule used when issuing Certificates of Origin for exports to other countries for purposes other than preferences. The system used is a mixture of the possible alternatives that are listed above. Substantial transformation means that the tariff heading of any non-originating material must be changed. The main outline of the origin rule governing the preferential trade agreements is, therefore, that originating products are firstly goods which are wholly produced in that country. Any goods which incorporate material not wholly produced in that country are counted as non-originating, unless that material has changed its tariff heading (see Figure 6.1).

### References

1. Central Policy Review Staff *Review of Overseas Representation* (H.M.S.O.: London, 1982).
2. Arthur D. Little & Co, *Trading in the European Economic Community*, Research Report (Arthur D. Little & Co: London, 1980).

# READING LIST

BOTB *International Directory of Published Market Research.* (7th Edition), London, 1982.

*Blytmann's International Directory of Importers.*

Branch: *Elements of Export Practice.* Chapman & Hall. London.

*Croner's Reference Book for Exporters,* London.

Crouch, S.: *Marketing Research for Managers.* Heinemann. London. 1984.

Davies, G.: *Managing Export Distribution.* Heinemann. London. 1984.

*Dun & Bradstreet's Export Directory,* (Volumes 1 and 2). London.

*Directory of European Business Information,* Centre for Business Information, Paris.

Export Handbook: *Services for British Exporters.* BOTB. London.

Helleiner, G. K.: *International Trade & Economic Development.* Penguin. London. 1972.

*Kluwer's Handbook of International Trade.*

Majaro, Simon: *International Marketing: A Strategic Approach to World Markets.* Allen and Unwin, (2nd Edition), 1983.

McDonald, M. H. B.: *Marketing Plans.* Heinemann. London. 1984.

*Oxford Economic Atlas of the World.* OUP. Oxford.

Piercy, Nigel: *Export Strategy: Markets and Competition.* Allen and Unwin. London. 1982.

Schmitthoff, C.: *Agency Agreements in Export Trade* – Institute of Export. (3rd Edition). London.

Schmitthof, C.: *The Export Trade.* Institute of Export. London.

Sharman: *Thinking Managerially about Exports.* Institute of Export. London.

Terpstra, Vern: *International Marketing Management.* Holt Saunders International (Third Edition). New York. 1983.

Tookey, D.: *Export Marketing Decisions.* Trade Research Publications.

Watson: *Finance of International Trade.* (2nd Edition). Institute of Bankers. London.

Walsh, L.: *International Marketing.* Macdonald & Evans. Plymouth. 1976.

Ward, John: *Profitable Product Management.* Heinemann. London. 1983.

Whitehead, G.: *Elements of International Trade and Payments.* Woodhead-Faulkner. Cambridge. 1983.

Whiting: *International Trade and Payments.* Macdonald & Evans. Plymouth. 1978.

Wilmshurt, J.: *The Fundamentals and Practice of Marketing.* Heinemann. London. 1983.

# ORGANIZATIONS AND PUBLICATIONS PROVIDING EXPORT INFORMATION

1. British Overseas Trade Board, Export Intelligence Service, Department of Trade, 1 Victoria Street, London SW1H 0E7, U.K.
2. International Trade Centre UNCTAD/GATT, United Nations, CH1211, GENEVA 10, Switzerland; *The Creation and Management of Joint Export Marketing Groups*; *Getting Started in Export Trade*, and *Private Sector Organizations in Export Promotion*.
3. International Chamber of Commerce, 38 Cours Albertler 75008 PARIS in Report No. 246 *Export Marketing Research*. *Uniform Customs and Practice for Documentary Credits* No. 400.
4. Economist Intelligence Unit, *Quarterly Economic Review*, Special No. 27; *The Potential of New Commodity Cartels – copying OPEC or improved international agreements*: A. Edwards.
5. Export Credits Guarantee Department, Aldermanbury House, Aldermanbury, London EC2P 2EL, U.K.
6. Simplification of International Trade Procedures Board, SITPRO Almack House, 26/28 King Street, London SW1Y 6QW, U.K.
7. Institute of Export, World Trade Centre, St Katherine by the Tower, London E1 9AA, U.K.
8. London Chamber of Commerce and Industry, 69 Cannon Street, London EC4N 5AB, U.K.
9. Small Firms Information Service; No. 15; *How to Start Exporting*: *Guide for Small Firms*. Small Firms Division, Department of Industry, Abell House, John Islip Street, London SW1P 4LN, U.K.
10. Technical Help to Exporters, British Standards Institution, Marylands Avenue, Hemel Hempstead, Herts HP2 4SQ, U.K.
11. Central Office of Information, Hercules Road, London SE1, U.K.; The Publicity Unit operates jointly with BOTB to help British Exporters to publicize their products and services abroad.
12. E.E.C. Information Unit, Department of Industry, 1 Victoria Street, London SW1H 0ET, U.K.
13. International Directory of Published Market Research; British Overseas Trade Board in association with Research and Finance Management (International) Limited.
14. *The E.E.C. and the Council of Europe. A Summary of Issues affecting Advertising and Marketing*: Institute of Practitioners in Advertising.
15. *Concentration on Key Markets – A Development Plan for Exports*,

A. Tessler; I.T.I. Research in association with the BETRO Trust and the Royal Society of Arts.

16. *International Price Competitiveness, Non-Price Factors and Export Performance*; National Economic Development Office (NEDO) London, U.K.

17. *Managing the Export Function*, N. Philpot; British Institute of Management.

18. European Communities Commission, 30 Kensington Palace Gardens, London W8 4OQ, U.K.; Official Journal of the European Communities *Nomenclature of Goods for the External Trade Statistics of the Community and Statistics of Trade between Member States*, NIMEXE (21 Sections).

19. Customs Co-operation Council Nomenclature; 40 Rue Washington, B-1050 Bruxelles, Belgium.

20. *Import and Export Statistics of U.K.* H.M. Customs and Excise Bill of Entry Section, Statistical Office; Portcullis House, 27 Victoria Avenue, Southend-on-Sea SS2 6AL, U.K.

21. Organisation for Economic Co-operation and Development (OECD): 2 Rue Andre-Pascal, 75775 Paris 16, France.

22. *The Role of Physical Distribution Management in International Marketing, International Trade Data* and other Professional Papers: Institute of Marketing, Moor Hall, Cookham, Maidenhead, Berkshire SL6 9QM, U.K.

23. *Factors for International Success: Industrial and Export Performances of France, U.K. and West Germany*. ITI Research, 1979. Barclays Bank International, London.

# GLOSSARY OF INTERNATIONAL TRADE ORGANIZATIONS

| | | |
|---|---|---|
| ABCC | = | Association of British Chambers of Commerce |
| ACC | = | Asian Coconut Community |
| ACE | = | Association of Conference Executives |
| AGC | = | African Groundnut Council |
| AIB | = | Academy of International Business |
| AMA | = | American Marketing Association |
| ANDEAN | = | Andean Community |
| ASEAN | = | Association of South East Asian Nations |
| BECU | = | Banana Exporting Countries Union |
| BEHA | = | British Export Houses Association |
| BMTEA | = | British Machine Tool Exporters' Association |
| BOTB | = | British Overseas Trade Board |
| BSI | = | British Standards Institution |
| CAM | = | Communications, Advertising and Marketing Education Foundation |
| CARICOM | = | Caribbean Community |
| CCC | = | Customs Co-operative Council |
| COI | = | Central Office of Information |
| COMECON | = | Community for Mutual Economic Co-operation |
| DISC | = | U.S. Domestic and International Sales Corporation |
| EAIMR | = | European Association of Industrial Market Research |
| EBU | = | European Broadcasting Union |
| ECA | = | U.N. Economic Commission for Africa |
| ECAP | = | U.N. Economic Commission for Asia and the Pacific |
| ECE | = | U.N. Economic Commission for Europe |
| ECGD | = | Export Credits Guarantee Department |
| ECLA | = | U.N. Economic Commission for Latin America |
| ECOSOC | = | United Nations Economic and Social Council |
| ECOWAS | = | Economic Community of West African States |
| E.E.C. | = | European Economic Community |
| E.F.T.A. | = | European Free Trade Area |
| EMC | = | European Marketing Council |
| ESOMAR | = | European Society for Opinion and Market Research |
| FTA | = | U.S. Federal Trade Administration |
| GATT | = | General Agreement on Tariffs and Trade |
| GCBS | = | International Freight Forwarders' Association |
| IAA | = | International Advertising Association |
| IAPH | = | International Association of Ports and Harbours |

| | | |
|---|---|---|
| IATA | = | International Air Transport Association |
| IBA | = | International Bauxite Association |
| IBRD | = | International Bank for Reconstruction and Development |
| ICA | = | International Coffee Agreement |
| ICA | = | International Co-operative Alliance |
| ICAO | = | International Civil Aviation Organization |
| ICC | = | International Chamber of Commerce |
| ICCEC | = | International Council for Copper Exporting Countries |
| IE | = | Institute of Export |
| IFFAA | = | International Federation of Forwarding Agents' Associations |
| IIC | = | International Institute for Cotton |
| ILO | = | International Labour Organization |
| IM | = | Institute of Marketing |
| IMC | = | Institute of Management Consultants |
| IMCO | = | International Maritime Consultative Organization |
| IMF | = | International Monetary Fund |
| IOOC | = | International Olive Oil Council |
| IPA | = | Institute of Practitioners in Advertising |
| IPDC | = | International Patent Documentation Centre |
| IPRA | = | International Public Relations Association |
| IPU | = | International Postal Union |
| IRTC | = | International Railway Transport Committee |
| IRTU | = | International Road Transport Union |
| ISO | = | International Standards Organization |
| ITC | = | International Tea Council |
| ITC | = | International Trade Centre UNCTAD/GATT |
| IUTF | = | International Union of Trade Fairs |
| IWS | = | International Wool Secretariat |
| LAFTA | = | Latin American Free Trade Area |
| LCCI | = | London Chamber of Commerce and Industry |
| NEDO | = | National Economic Development Office |
| OECD | = | Organization for Economic Development and Co-operation |
| OPEC | = | Organization of Petroleum-Exporting Countries |
| OPMA | = | Overseas Press and Media Association |
| UDEAC | = | Economic Community of Francophone African Countries |
| UKTA | = | U.K. Trade Agency for Developing Countries |
| UNCTAD | = | United Nations Conference on Trade and Development |
| UNDP | = | United Nations Development Programme |
| UNESCO | = | United Nations Educational, Scientific and Cultural Organization |
| UNIDO | = | United Nations Industrial Development Organization |
| UNITAR | = | United Nations Institute for Training and Research |
| WIP | = | World Institute of Phosphates |

# GLOSSARY OF INTERNATIONAL TRADE TERMS

| | | |
|---|---|---|
| BTN | = | Brussels Tariff Nomenclature |
| CAD | = | Cash Against Documents |
| CAN | = | Customs Assigned Number |
| CAP | = | Common Agricultural Policy |
| CCT | = | Common Customs Tariff |
| C & F | = | Cost and Freight |
| CI | = | Consular Invoice |
| CIF | = | Cost, Insurance and Freight |
| CIP | = | Freight or Carriage and Insurance Paid to |
| CO | = | Certificate of Origin |
| COC | = | Cash on Collection |
| COD | = | Cash on Delivery |
| COP | = | Cash on Presentation |
| CTC | = | Combined Transport Convention |
| CWO | = | Cash with Order |
| DAF | = | Delivered at Frontier |
| DCP | = | Freight or Carriage Paid to |
| EDF | = | European Development Fund |
| EL | = | Export Licence |
| EXQ | = | Ex Quay |
| EXS | = | Ex Ship |
| EXW | = | Ex Works |
| FAQ | = | Fair Average Quality |
| FAS | = | Free Alongside |
| FOA | = | FOB Airport |
| FOB | = | Free on Board |
| FOR | = | Free on Rail |
| FOT | = | Free on Truck |
| FRANCO | = | Delivered to Customer's Premises Duty Paid |
| FRC | = | Free Carrier (named Port) |
| GSP | = | Generalized System of Preferences |
| ICLC | = | Irrevocable, Confirmed Letters of Credit |
| ICTC | = | International Customs Transit Convention |
| IRLC | = | Irrevocable Letter of Credit |
| MFA | = | Multi-Fibres Arrangement |
| MFN | = | Most Favoured Nation |
| NES | = | Not Elsewhere (Customs) Specified |
| OGL | = | Open General (Import) Licence |
| SDR | = | Special Drawing Rights |
| SITC | = | Standard International Trade Classification |
| TIR | = | Transports Internationales Routiers |
| UNCC | = | U.N. Country Code |
| VER | = | Voluntary Export Restraint |

# STANDARD INTERNATIONAL TRADE CLASSIFICATION (SITC) REVISED

SITC is a 5-digit code; thus the code for the Divisional heading, BEVERAGES, (SITC 11), would appear as 11000. Some additions and changes are described as follows to identify certain data sources which are not otherwise identifiable under SITC system.

| New Code Number | Description |
|---|---|
| 00000 | Used to identify information sources which include data on all commodities or those sources for which the Commodity Code is not relevant. |
| 00001 | Used to identify the section heading FOOD AND LIVE ANIMALS (SITC 0) |
| 89310 | Household articles (including indoor ornaments) or artificial plastic materials |
| 89320 | Articles of artificial plastic materials used in machinery or plant, n.e.s. |
| 89330 | Office and stationery supplies of artificial plastic materials |
| 89340 | Plastic shipping and packaging containers (except household), or artificial plastic materials. |
| 89390 | Miscellaneous articles of artificial plastic materials, n.e.s. |

n.e.s. = not elsewhere specified

## COMMODITY CODE

| 0001 | FOOD AND LIVE ANIMALS |
|---|---|
| 00100 | Live animals |
| 01000 | Meat and meat preparations |
| 02000 | Dairy products and eggs |
| 03000 | Fish and fish preparations |
| 04000 | Cereals and cereal preparations |
| 05000 | Fruit and vegetables |
| 06000 | Sugar, sugar preparations and honey |
| 07000 | Coffee, tea, cocoa, spices and manufactures thereof |
| 08000 | Feeding stuff for animals (not including unmilled cereals) |
| 09000 | Miscellaneous food preparations |
| 10000 | BEVERAGES AND TOBACCO |
| 11000 | Beverages |
| 12000 | Tobacco and tobacco manufactures |

| | |
|---|---|
| 20000 | CRUDE MATERIALS, INEDIBLE, EXCEPT FUELS |
| 21000 | Hides, skins and furskins, undressed |
| 22000 | Oil-seeds, oil nuts and oil kernels |
| 23000 | Crude rubber (including synthetic and reclaimed) |
| 24000 | Wood, lumber and cork |
| 25000 | Pulp and waste paper |
| 26000 | Textile fibres (not manufactured into year, threat or fabrics) and their waste |
| 27000 | Crude fertilizers and crude minerals (excluding coal, petroleum and precious stones) |
| 28000 | Metalliferous ores and metal scrap |
| 29000 | Crude animal and vegetable materials, n.e.s. |
| | |
| 40000 | ANIMAL AND VEGETABLE OILS AND FATS |
| 41000 | Animal oils and fats |
| 42000 | Fixed vegetables oils and fats |
| 43000 | Animal and vegetable oils and fats processed, and waxes of animal or vegetable origin |
| | |
| 50000 | CHEMICALS |
| 51000 | Chemical elements and compounds |
| 52000 | Mineral tar and crude chemicals from coal, petroleum and natural gas |
| 53000 | Dyeing, tanning and colouring materials |
| 54000 | Medicinal and pharmaceutical products |
| 55000 | Essential oils and perfume materials; toilet, polishing and cleansing preparations |
| 56000 | Fertilizers, manufactured |
| 57000 | Explosives and pyrotechnic products |
| 58000 | Plastic materials, regenerated cellulose and artificial resins |
| 59000 | Chemical materials and products, n.e.s. |
| | |
| 60000 | MANUFACTURED GOODS CLASSIFIED CHIEFLY BY MATERIAL |
| 61000 | Leather, leather manufactures, n.e.s. and dressed furskins |
| 62000 | Rubber manufactures, n.e.s. |
| 63000 | Wood and cork manufactures (excluding furniture) |
| 64000 | Paper, paperboard and manufactures thereof |
| 65000 | Textile yarn, fabrics, made-up articles and related products |
| 66000 | Non-metallic mineral manufactures, n.e.s. |
| 67000 | Iron and steel |
| 68000 | Non ferrous metals |
| 69000 | Manufactures of metal, n.e.s. |
| | |
| 70000 | MACHINERY AND TRANSPORT EQUIPMENT |
| 71000 | Machinery, other than electric |
| 72000 | Electrical machinery, apparatus and appliances |
| 73000 | Transport equipment |
| | |
| 80000 | MISCELLANEOUS MANUFACTURED ARTICLES |
| 81000 | Sanitary, plumbing, heating and lighting fixtures and fittings |
| 82000 | Furniture |

| | |
|---|---|
| 83000 | Travel goods, handbags and similar articles |
| 84000 | Clothing |
| 85000 | Footwear |
| 86000 | Professional, scientific and controlling instruments; photographic and optical goods, watches and clocks |
| 89000 | Miscellaneous manufactured articles, n.e.s. |
| | |
| 90000 | COMMODITIES AND TRANSACTIONS NOT CLASSIFIED ACCORDING TO KIND |
| 99988 | Industrial products |
| 99999 | Agricultural products |
| 97000 | Service Industries and Equipment |
| 97100 | Restaurant and Food Services; Catering Services |
| 97110 | Restaurant and Food Service Equipment |
| 97200 | Hotel and Lodging Services |
| 97210 | Hotel and Lodging Equipment |
| 97300 | Medical and Health Services; Safety and Security |
| 97310 | Medical and Health Equipment; Safety and Security Equipment |
| 97400 | Educational and Training Services |
| 97410 | Educational and Training Equipment |
| 97500 | Hairdressing, Barbering and Beauty Services |
| 97510 | Hairdressing, Barbering and Beauty Equipment |
| 97600 | Amusement and Recreation Services; Entertainment Industry, Booking Agents, Concert Managers |
| 97610 | Entertainment Industry and Recreation Equipment |
| 97700 | Art Galleries; Auctions; Art Shows; Museums: Botanical and Zoological Gardens |
| 97710 | Art Supplies and Equipment |
| 97800 | Automotive Repair Services; Service Stations |
| 97810 | Automotive Repair Equipment |
| 97900 | Communication Services and Equipment |
| 97910 | Computer Programming and Software |
| 97920 | Cable Television (CATV) Services |
| 97930 | Facsimile; Electrical Mail and Similar Services |
| 97999 | Service Industries and Equipment, n.e.s. |
| 98000 | Industrial Equipment and Services |
| 98100 | Pollution Control Equipment; Ecological and Environmental Equipment |
| 98110 | Air Pollution Control Equipment |
| 98120 | Water Pollution Control Equipment |
| 98130 | Noise Pollution Control Equipment |
| 98140 | Solid Waste Control Equipment |
| 98200 | Second-Hand Materials: Scrap and Waste Materials |
| 98300 | Building and Construction; Engineering Services |
| 98310 | Building and Construction Equipment |
| 98400 | Mining Industry and Equipment |
| 99988 | Used to identify sources concerned with all industrial products |
| 99999 | Used to identify sources concerned with all agricultural products. |

# U.N. COUNTRY CODE

This is a 5-digit code. The first two digits identify geographical area economic groupings or trade blocs and the final three digits identify individual countries (the three-digit country codes can be arranged alphabetically, providing for quick identification). One example only of a Country Code is given under each main heading.

| | |
|---|---|
| 01000 | Developed/Industrial Market Economies |
| 02000 | Developing Market Economies |
| | |
| 10000 | AFRICA |
| 11710 | South Africa |
| 13000 | North Africa |
| 13736 | Sudan |
| 14000 | Customs and Economic Union of Central Africa |
| 16000 | West African Customs Union |
| 16566 | Nigeria |
| 17000 | Other Africa |
| | |
| 20000 | AMERICA (NORTH) |
| 21840 | U.S.A. |
| 21843 | Great Lakes Region and Midwest (U.S.A.) |
| | |
| 30000 | AMERICA (LATIN or SOUTH) |
| 33000 | Latin American Free Trade Association (LAFTA) |
| 33032 | Argentina |
| 34000 | Central American Common Market |
| | |
| 35000 | Caribbean Community (CARICOM) |
| 35328 | Guyana |
| | |
| 36000 | Other South America |
| 36192 | Cuba |
| | |
| 40000 | ASIA |
| 41392 | Japan |
| | |
| 44000 | Middle East |
| 44368 | Iraq |
| 44784 | United Arab Emirates (U.A.E.) |
| 45000 | Other Asia |
| 45104 | Burma |
| | |
| 48000 | Centrally Planned Economies |
| 48156 | People's Republic of China (Mainland) |

| | |
|---|---|
| 50000 | EUROPE |
| 53000 | European Economic Community (E.E.C.) |
| 53286 | United Kingdom |
| | |
| 55000 | Euopean Free Trade Association (E.F.T.A.) |
| 55752 | Sweden |
| | |
| 56000 | Council of Mutual Assistance (COMECON) |
| 56810 | Union of Soviet Socialist Republics (U.S.S.R.) |
| | |
| 57000 | Other Europe |
| 57724 | Spain |
| | |
| 70000 | OCEANIA |
| 71036 | Australia |
| | |
| 90000 | OTHER ECONOMIC OR REGIONAL GROUPS |
| 90004 | Commonwealth of Nations |
| 90008 | Organization for Economic Co-operation and Development (O.E.C.D.) |
| 90012 | Arab Economic Unity Agreement |
| 90016 | Middle East Regional Co-operation for Development (RCD) |

# MARKET RESEARCH ORGANIZATIONS OVERSEAS

| | |
|---|---|
| AUSTRALIA | Market Research Society of Australia, P.O. Box 334, North Sydney, 2060 |
| AUSTRIA | Verband der Markforscher Österreichs-VMO, C/o Henkel Austria, A.1030, Wien, Erdbergstrasse 29 |
| BELGIUM | Belgian Market Research Association, Chaussee de Wavre 16, 1050, Brussels |
| CANADA | Professional Marketing Research Association, Mr R Thorneycroft, Procter & Gamble, 2 St Clair Ave West, Toronto 7 |
| DENMARK | The Danish Market Research Association, C/o Masius Reklame-bureau A/S, Halmtorvet 20, 1700, Copenhagen V |
| FINLAND | Finnish Marketing Research Society, Suomen BP Oy, Mikonkaku 8, 00100 Helsinki 10 |
| FRANCE | ADETEM Association Nationale pour le Development des Techniques de Marketing, 30 Rue d'Astorg 75, Paris 8 |
| GERMANY | ADM – Arbeitskreis Deutscher Marktforschungsinstitute e.V., 6231 Schwalbach am Taunus, Altkonisgstrasse 2 |
| GREECE | Institute of Marketing GMS, 6 Philellinon Street, Athens |
| HUNGARY | Hungarian Committee for Marketing, V Kossuth Lajos ter 6–8 Budapest |
| INDIA | Indian Marketing Association, Post Office Box 5560 Bombay 14 |
| IRELAND | The Marketing Society of Ireland, 19/20 Upper Pembroke Street, Dublin 2 |
| ITALY | Associazione Italiana per gli Studi di Marketing, Via Olmetto 3, Milana |
| JAPAN | Mr Eiji Hirutu, Ginza Studio Building, No. 13-2-Chome, Ginza-Higashim Chuo-ku, Tokyo |

211

NETHERLANDS    Nederlands Institut Voor Marketing, Parkstraat 18, Den Haag

Nederlandse Vereniging van Marktonderzoekers (NVM) Organisat ie-Bureau Wissenraet NV, Van Eeghenstraat 86, Amsterdam 1007

NEW ZEALAND    Market Research Society of New Zealand, Mr D Butler, Survey Research Company, P.O. Box 3685, Wellington

NORWAY    Norsk Markedsforskningsforening/M-Gruppen, C/o Marketing Assistanse A/S, Trondheimsveien 135, Oslo 5

PORTUGAL    Sociedade Portuguesa de Comercializacao (Marketing) Avenida Elias Garcia 172–2, Esq, Lisboa 1

SOUTH AFRICA    Market Research Africa, P.O. Box 10483, Johannesbury 2000

SPAIN    Asociacion Espanola de Estudios de Mercade y de Opinion, Mrs Isabel, Apartado 12, 170, Barcelona 6

SWEDEN    The Swedish M-Group M-Gruppen, Mrs Katrine Stenbach, Fladerstigen 7, 13671 Handen

SWITZERLAND    Verband Schweizerischer Markforscher (VSMF), C/o IHA, 6052, Hergiswil, Switzerland

U.S.A.    American Marketing Assocation, 222 S Riverside Plaza, Chicago, Illinois 60606;
Advertising Research Foundation Inc., 3 East 54th Street, New York, NY 10022

YUGOSLAVIA    Jugoslavensko Udruzenje za Marketing Makanceva 16, 4100 Zagreb

# APPENDICES

# APPENDIX 1 BALANCE OF PAYMENTS AUDIT

| Possible action to reduce outflows | OUTFLOWS | INFLOWS | Possible action to increase inflows |
|---|---|---|---|
| | *SERVICES* | | |
| Reduce expenditure on shipping owned by others *BUT we need to use shipping for our exports* | Shipping and insurance | Use of shipping/insurance | Increase the hiring out of our shipping space to other countries *BUT do we have enough shipping to do that?* |
| Reduce expenditure on tourism/visits abroad *BUT restrictions on travel could hit exports* | Tourism/visits abroad | Tourists to our country | Promote tourism to our country *BUT this requires tourist facilities at home and publicity abroad, and may be socially harmful* |
| | Payments for foreign know-how | Receipts from our know-how | Increase income from know-how sold abroad *BUT do we have enough expertise to do this and can we spare it?* |
| | *CAPITAL FLOWS* | | |
| Limit our investments and loans abroad *BUT are these significant?* | Our investments abroad | Foreign investments here | Encourage more foreign investment here *BUT interest will be needed (an outflow)* |
| | Our loans abroad | Loans made to us | Seek more loans *BUT we shall have to pay interest (an outflow) and to repay the loan eventually.* |
| Make repatriation of capital more difficult *BUT will this discourage investment and encourage illegal methods?* | Repatriation of capital | Repatriation of capital | Encourage more repatriation of our capital from abroad for investment at home *BUT remember this might provoke retaliation* |

## OTHER FLOWS

| | OUTFLOWS | INFLOWS | |
|---|---|---|---|
| Limit amount of pay that foreign workers in our country can send home. *BUT will this make it more difficult to get foreign labour?* | Remittances sent home by foreigners working here | Remittances from our people working abroad | Encourage our people abroad to remit more of their earnings to our country *BUT how? And with what effect?* |
| Only get loans we really need, at lowest interest rates *BUT we need loans for currency support and to finance our deficits* | Interest on loans made to us | Interest on our loans abroad | |
| Reduce payment of dividends on foreign investments in our country *BUT can we do this without reducing essential foreign investment?* | Dividends on investments here by foreigners | Dividends on our investments abroad | Invest more abroad *But this is an outflow* |
| | **VISIBLES** | | |
| Reduce our imports of goods *BUT what about goods vital for our industrial development? And HOW do we do this without damaging our own export trade?* | Visible imports | VISIBLE EXPORTS | Encourage our exports of goods *HOW?* |
| | **TOTALS** | | |
| | **DEFICIT OR SURPLUS** | | |

# APPENDIX 2
# MARKET ENTRY AND PENETRATION CHECKLIST

(1) *Transport*
   (a) Freight rates;
   (b) Speed and frequency;
   (c) Reliability;
   (d) Risks;
   (e) Packing requirements.

(2) *Sales and Distribution Channels*
   (a) Normal channels for the product (for each element: function, share of sales, changes in importance);
   (b) Alternative channels;
   (c) Advantages, disadvantages and feasibility of using normal or alternative channels;
   (d) Support functions performed by each element in the distribution channel (technical services, advertising and promotion, financial);
   (e) Stock levels held by each element;
   (f) Delivery time requirements;
   (g) Mark-ups and discounts at each level;
   (h) Credit facilities and terms of sale expected;
   (i) Major distributors (profiles of the most important ones and those most suitable to handle your product: size of the firm, sales growth, product line, sales force, type of customers, geographical coverage, service facilities, position in the market, regulations, possible conflicts of interest and so on).

(3) *Pricing Strategy Factors*
   (a) Practical limits;
   (b) Supply of competing products;
   (c) Prices of competing products;
   (d) Likely reactions of competitors;
   (e) Product advantages.

(4) *Services expected by Buyers*
   (a) Technical advice;
   (b) Replacement of defective merchandise;
   (c) Guarantees;
   (d) Repair, maintenance and spare parts;
   (e) Training of operators.

(5) *Advertising and Sales Promotion*
  (a) Amount of money being spent to support competing products (including expenditure as percentage of each company's sales);
  (b) Media and techniques mainly used, and the breakdown of expenditure among them;
  (c) Timing and geographical concentration;
  (d) Sales messages emphasized in advertising of important competitors;
  (e) Breakdown of expenditures between suppliers, distributors, retailers.

# APPENDIX 3
# CITY OF LONDON
# FINANCIAL SERVICES

(1) *Services*
   (a) Money Transmission Services
   (b) Foreign Exchange Market –
       Spot and Future
   (c) Sterling Money Market
   (d) Sterling Credit Market –
       Borrowing and lending in Sterling
   (e) Currency Money Markets
   (f) Currency Credit Markets –
       Borrowing Short-Term and Medium-Term
   (g) Euro Currency Market
   (h) Export and Import Finance –
       Sterling (Bills on London),
       Foreign Currencies
   (i) Sterling Capital Market
   (j) Currency Capital Markets –
       Eurobonds

(2) *Institutions*
   (a) Banks –
       Domestic and Overseas
   (b) Merchant Banks
   (c) Licensed Deposit Takers –
       Domestic and Overseas
   (d) Discount Houses (Money Brokers)
   (e) Stock Exchange –
       Brokers and Jobbers

# APPENDIX 4
# EXPORT PRICING AUDIT

(1) *Cost Factors*
  *1. Marginal cost of manufacturing goods for export.
  *2. Research, development and other overhead allocations that should be made to export sales.
   3. Shipping and insurance costs.
   4. Tariffs and customs duties.
   5. Commercial and political risk insurance costs.

(2) *Competitive Factors*
  *1. Acceptable price thresholds to overseas customers, particularly final purchasers.
  *2. Degree of competition in the market.
   3. Prices set by the dominant supplier or price leader in the industry or product area.
  *4. Prices set to achieve specific marketing objectives.
   5. World prices for delivery to a particular market (mostly for raw materials, commodities and industrial materials).
  *6. Supply and demand situation of the overseas market.
   7. Margins necessary to ensure effective promotion overseas.

(3) *Distribution Factors*
   1. Credit and financing activities of the distributor.
   2. After-sales servicing capabilities of the distributor.
   3. Warehousing facilities of the distributor.
   4. The amount of distributor participation in advertising and promotion.
   5. Local patterns of distributor discounts for the industry or product group.
   6. Number and type of distributors in the market.
   7. Whether the distributor handles the products of competitors.
   8. Margins on other company products that are handled by the distributor.

(4) *Comparative Factors*
   1. Domestic distributor price.
   2. Price for duty valuation.
   3. Price to licensees.
   4. Price to wholly owned subsidiaries, domestic or foreign.
   5. Price to affiliates, domestic and foreign.
   6. Price to government purchasing agencies.
   7. Price to the largest bulk buyer.

(5) *Other Factors*
  1. Voluntary and government-enforced price controls.
  2. Raising prices to circumvent currency controls.
  3. Raising prices to recapture unremittable royalties.
  4. Raising prices to cover uncollectable interest charges when payments are delayed by central banks.
 *5. Non-price competition in quality, design, delivery terms, technical assistance and after sales service.
 *6. Competition in credit, interest terms and foreign currency offers.

* Key factors

# APPENDIX 5
# ORGANIZATION OF EXTERNAL TRADE RELATIONS OF THE E.E.C

| Countries | Agreement | Trade Provisions |
|---|---|---|
| (1) E.E.C. (Belgium, Denmark, France, Germany, Ireland, Italy, Luxembourg, The Netherlands, U.K.) | Treaty of Rome (1957) Treaty of Accession (1973) | Free Trade in all goods. Common external tariff on imports from third countries. |
| (2) Greece | Accession to Membership in 1981 providing for full customs union in 1984 | Duty-free access for all industrial goods, except steel and coal, and a range of agricultural goods. Volume of cotton products not restricted under MFA but limited by VER. |
| (3) E.F.T.A. (Austria, Finland, Iceland, Norway, Portugal, Sweden, Switzerland) | Free Trade Agreements (1973 for an unlimited period) | Free trade in all manufactures except paper and some metals. |
| (4) A.C.P. (59 African, Caribbean and Pacific countries) | Lome Convention (1975 for 5 years). Second E.E.C.–A.C.P. convention (1980 for five years, not yet ratified). | Duty-free access to the E.E.C. for all industrial and many agricultural goods, though one or two products subject to safeguard clauses. Some concessions for leviable agricultural products. ORs on bananas, beef, sugar and rum; all products are also covered by a general safeguard clause. |

| Countries | Agreement | Trade Provisions |
|---|---|---|
| Spain | Preferential Trade Agreement (1970) working towards customs union. Accession likely in mid 1980s. | 60% duty reductions on most industrial goods; some concessions on agricultural products. Cotton products limited by VER. |
| Portugal | Free Trade Agreement (1972) Accession likely in mid 1980s. | Duty-free access for all industrial goods (under E.F.T.A.): some concessions on agricultural products. Cotton products limited by VER. |
| (5) Maghred countries (Algeria, Morocco, Tunisia) | Preferential Trade and Co-operation Agreements (1976) for an unlimited period. | Duty-free access to the E.E.C. for most industrial goods. Tariff concessions in some agricultural goods. |
| (6) Mashreq countries (Egypt, Jordan, Lebanon, Syria) | Preferential Trade and Co-operation (for an unlimited period)[a] | Duty-free access to the E.E.C. for most industrial goods. Tariff concessions on some agricultural goods. Egypt's exports of cotton are restricted under the MFA. |
| (7) Mediterranean countries | Association Agreements providing for full customs union with the E.E.C. | |
| Turkey | (1964 for unlimited period) | Duty-free access for industrial goods except some textiles, coal, steel and petroleum products; some concession on agricultural products. Cotton products subject to VER. |

| Countries | Agreement | Trade Provisions |
|---|---|---|
| Malta | (1971 for five years)[b] | From 1978, duty-free access for industrial goods, some concession on agricultural goods. Cotton products subject to VER. |
| Cyprus | (1973 for four years)[b] | 70–100% duty reductions on most industrial goods; some concessions on agricultural goods. Cotton products subject to VER. |
| | Preferential Trade and Co-operation Agreements | |
| Israel | (1975 for an unlimited period) | Duty-free access for most industrial goods; substantial concessions on 85% of agricultural goods. |
| Yugoslavia | (1980 for five years) | Duty-free access for most industrial goods except textiles and non-ferrous metals. Some concessions on agricultural goods, notably wine, tobacco, beef. |
| (8) Other DCs (except Taiwan) | Generalized System of Preferences[c] | Duty-free access for industrial goods – for some 150 products duty-free treatment is subject to quotas or ceilings. Duty reductions on 300 agricultural goods, of which 5 are subject to quotas. |
| (9) People's Republic of China | Generalized System of Preferences[c] | Duty-free access as above but excluding certain agricultural and manufacturing products. |
| (10) Developed countries which are GATT signatories, plus Taiwan | GATT[d] | Most favoured nation treatment. |

| Countries | Agreement | Trade Provisions |
|---|---|---|
| (11) Comecon members excluding Romania and Cuba | | Least favoured nation treatment. |

a. Subject to periodic review
b. Can be extended automatically
c. This is a unilateral offer by the E.E.C. rather than a binding agreement
d. Binding subject to safeguards

MFA – Multi-Fibre Arrangement
QR – Quantity restriction
VER – Voluntary export restraint

# APPENDIX 6
# APPLICATION OF INFORMATION TECHNOLOGY (IT) TO EXPORT PROMOTION

Modern communciations, particularly microtechnology, now make it possible for export marketing staff to use and benefit from automated information processing on overseas business assignments. Remotely accessible computers now have much to offer the export manager when he travels overseas; in countries where the national telecommunications authority does not operate a monopoly over 'message switching', it is possible to communicate with a computer service, whether the firm's or a time-sharing system, at less than half the cost of the telex (even without surcharges), and through the computer with the home-based export office.

Even more useful to export marketing staff, than the simple relay home of information, is the ability of the mobile executive, equipped with a portable or locally borrowed terminal, to provide his customers or distributors overseas with on-the-spot documentation without having to send it on later. Remote access to a well-designed text-processing system such as many companies are beginning to install, can provide the export executive overseas with an appropriately edited contract draft, technical proposal or specification, amended price list in the local currency, or export documentation; all this can be available within hours of a business meeting. Access to a project control system in a remotely accessible computer can also enable a sales engineer abroad to provide his customer with a construction and delivery schedule which is completely up-to-date (and which may have changed substantially since his departure from the U.K. factory).

The link between the export executive and his home base is one where well-designed computer systems certainly have a role which is feasible, economic and relatively simple; yet little use is made of this technology to date. Clearly the link stands or falls by the quality of telecommunications available to the traveller, a quality adequate between most European countries and North America. Moreover, the company can set up the same link for its distributors, customers and agents abroad, and thereby reduce the amount of time spent abroad problem-solving, and increase the selling potential of its own staff by the time saved.

Other types of information technology have been developed recently.

'Intelpost', is operated by the British Telecom and offers an international facsimile transmission service by satellite. The first link between London and Toronto is now open and this means that facsimiles of commercial contracts, advertising copy, promotional designs and statistical analyses can be studied within hours by the company's associates overseas. With 'Prestel' and other systems, the opportunity now exists of instantaneous 'view data' showing export information by country, product or other classification on the TV screen, for the personnel use of export management. Prestel is the first system of its kind in the world; it links an adapted television set with a computer via the public telephone system, at home or at work, and now provides a wealth of information from latest share prices to airline timetables, advertisements and economic data. The user dials one of the new regional computers which store continuously updated data provided now by 130 organizations such as the Central Office of Information, Reuters and the Stock Exchange. Already over 150,000 pages of information are available from such 'information providers', though access to specialized information is restricted to closed user groups.

It is estimated that in 1985 more than 500,000 receivers will be meeting the needs of approximately one million users. For the businessman, the advantages of Prestel are visual attraction, ease of use and lower costs. Exporters can have a small black and white receiver on their desks, with an alphanumeric keypad. Users will be guided on how to extract detailed, specific information by simple instructions and 'prompts' on the screen directing them to required pages. The importance of identifying and quantifying actual and potential export markets by using information technology is self-evident. What is required is action by management to decide where best to allocate resources for product development, supply, promotion and market follow-up in those countries which offer the best prospects; international Codes can be used here. The objective is to determine growth rates, and therefore, sales potential overseas, over a period in which exports from the U.K. can be compared with the growth of total imports by country and product. As will be clearly shown, it is impossible accurately to undertake this without the use of trade intelligence.

A new approach, Sectoral Analysis for Export Planning*, has recently been developed by the International Trade Centre UNCTAD/GATT, Geneva. It has not previously been applied to the export performance of British industry; in order to illustrate how it can be used, data from both the U.K. Customs Statistical Office, and the BOTB Export Intelligence Service have been retrieved, using the SITC and CCCN product codes and U.N. Country code. The following products have been taken from the Overseas Trade Statistics (OTS) at BOTB comprising the 30 major export product categories:

(a)  Packaging Machinery;
(b)  Electrical Machinery;

* Ancel, B. *Analysing your Export Efforts*, International Trade Forum, (ITC, UNCTAD/ GATT: Geneva, 1978).

(c)  Commercial Vehicles;
(d)  Building Materials and Fabricated Components;

and 10 of the top 50 U.K. export markets have been selected. The first step is to make a statistical analysis, using the codes referred to, which shows (1) total imports by value (CIF) of these products into other countries (2) exports by value (FOB) from U.K. of these products to each country and (3) the Index over 5 years showing rates of growth or decline in (1) and (2). The statistical analysis is shown in Table A1 where

Sector 1 – High Demand/High Supply;
Sector 2 – Low Demand/High Supply;
Sector 3 – Low Demand/Low Supply;
Sector 4 – High Demand/Low Supply.

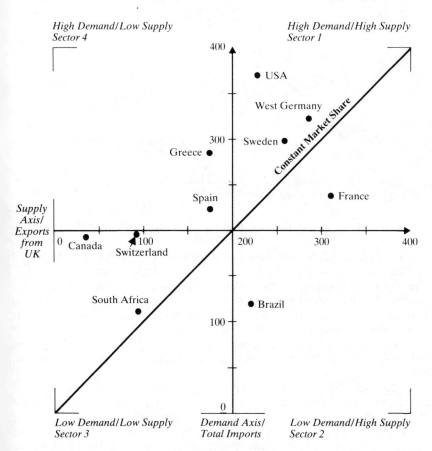

Figure A1 Sectoral Analysis of Export Markets for Packaging Machinery

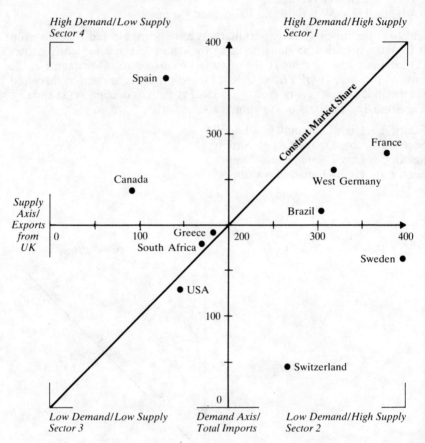

Figure A2  Sectoral Analysis of Export Markets for Electrical Machinery

The positions of these products on grids (Figures A1–A4) are plotted by reading off the Supply and Demand Index values shown in Table A1. Clearly, it follows from the positions plotted on the grid that the growth or decline in the exporting country's market share for each product is determined on each grid by its distance from the diagonal axis. This axis represents a constant market share situation, while those on the left indicate a decreasing market share. The following indicators can now be highlighted on the four products and ten overseas markets in Figures A1–A4.

U.K. market shares have remained fairly stable in those countries with rapidly rising demand (Sector 1) as follows: in Greece and South Africa for Building Materials and Fabricated Components and in Sweden and West Germany for Packaging Machinery; export of Commercial Vehicles to Greece and West Germany have also maintained market share and, in the U.S.A., have actually outpaced market growth. Demand is lower in

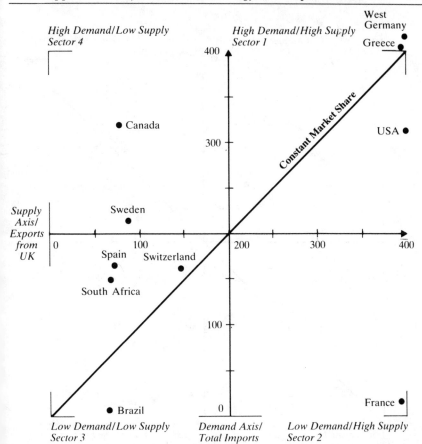

Figure A3 Sectoral Analysis of Export Markets for Commercial Vehicles

Section 3 for Electrical Machinery in South Africa and U.S.A., and for Commercial Vehicles in Switzerland. With effective promotional activities it should be possible to increase market shares in Sector 1 where demand is clearly rising faster than in Sector 3, where it is particularly low for Packaging Machinery in South Africa and Commercial Vehicles in Brazil.

U.K. market shares have increased markedly for Packaging Machinery to France, and Electrical Machinery to West Germany and Brazil, and for Commercial Vehicles to the U.S.A. (that is, markets plotted farthest to the right of the diagonal axis). High performance in these markets suggests strong competitive advantage which should be analysed and strengthened by management. This means planning a high level of promotional activity in markets where demand is already high and justifies further investment. In the case of Sector 3, a very low level of demand for packaging Machinery in Canada and Switzerland, and for Commercial Vehicles in Spain does not offer good prospects for a fast recovery and they are not products which, at present, warrant strong marketing campaigns.

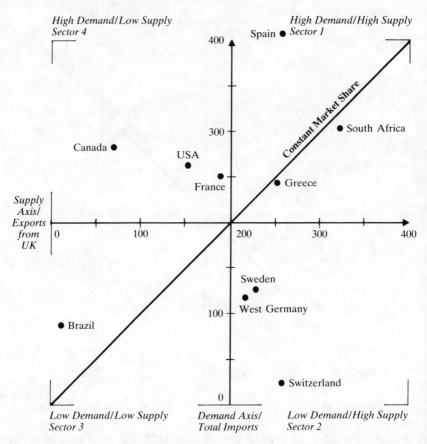

Figure A4  Sectoral Analysis of Export Markets for Building Materials and
          Fabricated Components

Most significant for U.K. export promotion strategy is the group of
overseas markets in Sector 4 for which demand is clearly high and U.K.'s
supply is currently low. For example, there is low-export performance by
U.K. industry in the supply of Packaging Machinery to Greece and Spain,
Commercial Vehicles to Canada and Sweden, Electrical Machinery to
Canada and Spain and Building Materials and Fabricated Components to
the U.S.A. and France. These indicators suggest that there are some
marketing weaknesses in U.K. exporting to countries where demand is
high, whether in product design and adaptation, in supply and delivery,
pricing or effective promotion, compared to other exporting countries
supplying these products. Sector 4 demands and indeed should repay
detailed investigation by export management of why their particular
industry has actually fallen behind in high growth markets.

In general terms, therefore, Sectoral Analysis can be applied precisely to countries and products. In fact, it offers two dimensions for analysis and planning:

1.1   The growth or decline in value of U.K. exports of one product to selected overseas markets (horizontal supply axis).
1.2   The growth or decline in value of imports of a selected product into a group of overseas markets (vertical demand axis).
2.1   The growth or decline in value of U.K. exports to one selected overseas market of a number of products (horizontal supply axis).
2.2   The growth or decline in value of imports into one selected market of a group of export products (vertical demand axis).

For example, whilst some well-established overseas markets can be clearly positioned in Sector 1 for a particular product, other overseas markets may be located in Sector 2 of the Grid perhaps because of foreign exchange problems or new local industries supplying more of the domestic demand; nevertheless, if one or two countries can be identified in Sector 4 of the Grid, High Demand/Low Supply, the export potential of that product in those markets is very high.

Each of these Sectors clearly has different implications for export marketing strategy. Products in the Sector 4 for instance warrant the most active promotional efforts because exporters have not tapped the large market that exists. Those in the other sectors offer less favourable prospects for increased trade. The products that fall into each of the 4 Sectors can, therefore, be categorized into top-, medium- and low-priority targets with this breakdown forming the basis of export marketing planning.

Of course, it is necessary to take into account in this analysis the general economic situation in both the supplying (exporting) and the overseas target markets, the particularities of the product, the local supply situation, the structure of sub-markets or market segments in each overseas (importing) country, the impact of inflation on export values and currency fluctuations.

Clearly, what is of value to management is to know in which group of products there are overseas countries with untapped demand, and which groups of countries have similar sales potential for one homeogeneous group of products. Once the sector where exports can be increased has been identified, management action in terms of overseas representation, supply capacity, finance, promotion and follow-up can be put on a planned basis. It follows that where stagnant or declining overseas markets are identified, the action to generate more demand or pull out and devote resources to markets with better potential must be taken. But this strategic appraisal using Sectoral Analysis must clearly come first; planning second. In too many companies in U.K. there is little planning, and sadly deficient strategic analysis, partly because a short-term view of business overseas is prevalent, and secondly, because such techniques as Sectoral Analysis using Trade Intelligence are not known or used.

Table A1
Sectoral Analysis of Export Markets

| | | | | | DEMAND | | SUPPLY | |
| | | | | | Total Imports of Product into Country | | Product Exports To Country From U.K. | |
| SITC | CCCN | PRODUCT | UN CC | COUNTRY | £m Value 1979 | Index 1974/1979 | £m Value 1979 | Index 1974/1979 |
|---|---|---|---|---|---|---|---|---|
| **SECTOR 1** **HIGH DEMAND/HIGH SUPPLY** | | | | | | | | |
| 745.20 | 84.19 | Packaging Machinery | 21840 | U.S.A. | 37.1 | 371 | 3.08 | 218 |
| | | | 55752 | Sweden | 3.61 | 292 | .177 | 256 |
| | | | 53280 | West Germany | 23.34 | 318 | 1.24 | 284 |
| | | | 53250 | France | 12.64 | 234 | .395 | 312 |
| 716.21 | 85.01 | Electrical Machinery | 53250 | France | 19.7 | 277 | 1.26 | 374 |
| | | | 53280 | West Germany | 80.79 | 257 | 4.44 | 314 |
| | | | 33076 | Brazil | 2.77 | 211 | .052 | 301 |
| 783.10 | 87.02 | Commercial Vehicles | 53280 | West Germany | 674 | 409 | 12.0 | 402 |
| | | | 53300 | Greece | 4.6 | 406 | .26 | 398 |
| | | | 21840 | U.S.A. | 909.5 | 311 | 2.81 | 406 |

| | | | | | | | | |
|---|---|---|---|---|---|---|---|---|
| 278.12 | 25.02 | Building Materials and | 57724 | Spain | .556 | 410 | .042 | 252 |
| | −25.10 | Fabricated Components | 11710 | South Africa | 9.03 | 300 | .484 | 320 |
| | | | 53300 | Greece | .192 | 246 | .025 | 245 |

SECTOR 2
LOW DEMAND/HIGH SUPPLY

| | | | | | | | | |
|---|---|---|---|---|---|---|---|---|
| 745.20 | 84.19 | Packaging Machinery | 33076 | Brazil | .389 | 114 | .044 | 219 |
| 716.21 | 85.01 | Electrical Machinery | 55752 | Sweden | 10.89 | 158 | 3.17 | 398 |
| | | | 55756 | Switzerland | 1.86 | 37 | .50 | 264 |
| 783.10 | 87.02 | Commercial Vehicles | 53250 | France | 168.8 | 14 | 6.17 | 400 |
| 278.12 | 25.02 | Building Materials and | 55752 | Sweden | 4.15 | 124 | 1.59 | 229 |
| | −25.10 | Frabricated Components | 53280 | West Germany | 36.63 | 116 | 5.37 | 209 |
| | | | 55756 | Switzerland | 3.52 | 23 | 72 | 260 |

SECTOR 3
LOW DEMAND/LOW SUPPLY

| | | | | | DEMAND | | SUPPLY | |
| | | | | | Total Imports of Product into Country | | Product Exports To Country From U.K. | |
| SITC | CCCN | PRODUCT | UN CC | COUNTRY | £m Value 1979 | Index 1974/1979 | £m Value 1979 | Index 1974/1979 |
|---|---|---|---|---|---|---|---|---|
| 745.20 | 84.19 | Packaging Machinery | 55756 | Switzerland | 5.66 | 199 | .199 | 98 |
| | | | 21124 | Canada | 7.62 | 190 | .069 | 35 |
| | | | 11710 | South Africa | 6.63 | 105 | .90 | 89 |
| 716.21 | 85.01 | Electrical Machinery | 53300 | Greece | .416 | 188 | .087 | 184 |
| | | | 11710 | South Africa | 37.1 | 179 | 10.5 | 171 |
| | | | 21840 | U.S.A. | 1512.0 | 126 | 40.5 | 148 |
| 783.10 | 87.02 | Commerical Vehicles | 57724 | Spain | .367 | 163 | .023 | 68 |
| | | | 55756 | Switzerland | 91.3 | 157 | 5.16 | 145 |
| | | | 11710 | South Africa | 219.2 | 146 | 1.11 | 67 |
| | | | 33076 | Brazil | .28 | 4 | .110 | 67 |
| 278.12 | 25.02–25.10 | Building Materials and Fabricated Components | 33076 | Brazil | 1.25 | 83 | .070 | 13 |

## SECTOR 4
## HIGH DEMAND/LOW SUPPLY

| | | | | | | | |
|---|---|---|---|---|---|---|---|
| 745.20 | 84.19 | Packaging Machinery | 53300 Greece | .144 | 283 | .090 | 176 |
| | | | 57724 Spain | .222 | 223 | .074 | 176 |
| 716.21 | 85.01 | Electrical Machinery | 57724 Spain | .319 | 359 | .015 | 125 |
| | | | 21124 Canada | 155.2 | 236 | 3.53 | 90 |
| 783.10 | 87.03 | Commercial Vehicles | 21124 Canada | 222.3 | 315 | .092 | 72 |
| | | | 55752 Sweden | 51.46 | 209 | .962 | 83 |
| 278.12 | 25.02 | Building Materials and | 21124 Canada | 46.2 | 281 | .35 | 64 |
| | −25.10 | Fabricated Components | 21840 U.S.A. | 1317.6 | 266 | 13.66 | 155 |
| | | | 53250 France | 17.6 | 251 | 1.3 | 191 |

*1974 Index = 100*

# APPENDIX 7
# OVERSEAS PRICING AND
# INVESTMENT – CRITICAL
# PATH ANALYSIS (CPA)

Critical Path Analysis sets out the stages of financial commitment, but recognizes that business development rests fundamentally on market potential; marketing management, in realizing this potential has much to gain in drawing on financial expertise. The analysis re-formulates the original concept of Windle and Sizer.*

There are three Critical Paths as follows:

C.P.1.   Improving financial terms with no change in marketing or in supply;

C.P.2.   Increasing marketing activities which requires change in supply;

C.P.3.   Making long-term investment overseas requiring production capital change.

Critical Paths 1 and 2 are not, of course, mutually exclusive but they do represent a planned approach to decision making. In C.P.1. and C.P.2 marginal costing should be used to evaluate the profitability of export orders. But in Critical Path 3 where a larger investment over a long period is required, not only must the costs and revenues which will follow from the investment be calculated, but the time factor must be taken into account. Discounted Cash Flow (DCF) provides a single earnings rate which can be compared with the company's rate of return. The company is concerned here with the cost of capital and the return from exporting compared with alternative uses, e.g. developing the home market. It is here also that analysis and appraisal must be on a joint basis between marketing and financial management.

This Critical Path Analysis sets out practical decision routes which require a logical appraisal of both the company's financial terms and marketing policies as a total basis for developing profitable business overseas.

*Windle, A. and Sizer, J. *Exporting is for Profit – A Guide to the Financial Evaluation of Exporting Opportunities*, (National Economic Development Office (NEDO); London, 1975) (adapted).

236

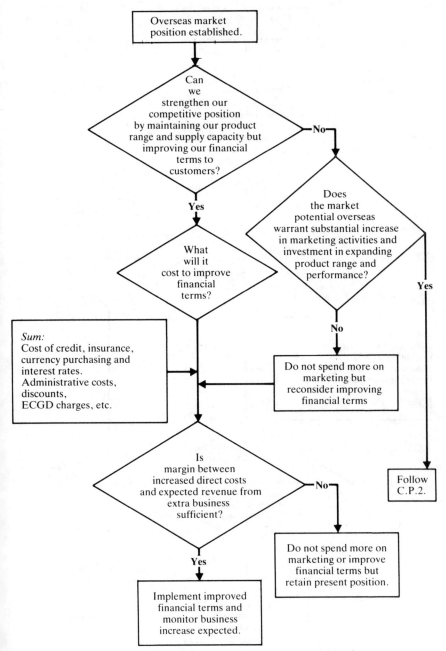

Figure A5 C.P.1. Improving Financial Terms with No Change in Marketing or Supply

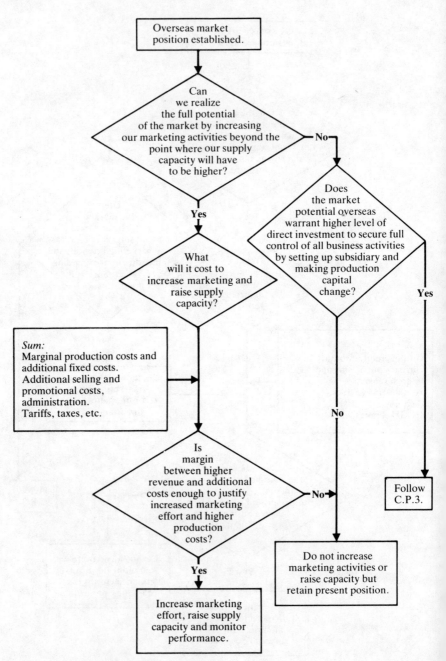

Figure A6  C.P.2. Increasing Marketing Activities which require Change in Supply

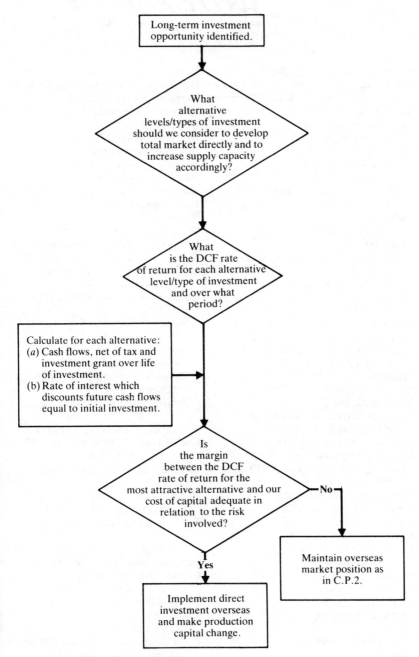

Figure A.7 C.P.3. Making Long-Term Investment Overseas requiring Production Capital Change

# *INDEX*

240